COMPLEX COMMUNITIES

Complex Communities
The Archaeology of Early Iron Age West-Central Jordan

BENJAMIN W. PORTER

THE UNIVERSITY OF
ARIZONA PRESS
TUCSON

The University of Arizona Press
www.uapress.arizona.edu

We respectfully acknowledge the University of Arizona is on the land and territories of Indigenous peoples. Today, Arizona is home to twenty-two federally recognized tribes, with Tucson being home to the O'odham and the Yaqui. The university strives to build sustainable relationships with sovereign Native Nations and Indigenous communities through education offerings, partnerships, and community service.

© 2013 The Arizona Board of Regents
All rights reserved. Published 2013
First paperback edition published 2025

ISBN-13: 978-0-8165-3032-8 (cloth)
ISBN-13: 978-0-8165-5551-2 (paper)
ISBN-13: 978-0-8165-9914-1 (ebook)

Publication of this book is made possible in part by funding from the University of California, Berkeley.

Library of Congress Cataloging-in-Publication Data
Porter, Benjamin W., 1974–
  Complex communities : the archaeology of early Iron Age West-Central Jordan / Benjamin W. Porter.
      pages cm
  Includes bibliographical references and index.
  ISBN 978-0-8165-3032-8 (cloth : alk. paper)
  1. Jordan—Antiquities. 2. Iron Age—Jordan. 3. Human settlements—Jordan—History. I. Title.
  DS153.3.P64 2013
  956.95—dc23
                                                                                          2012046519

Printed in the United States of America
♾ This paper meets the requirements of ANSI/NISO Z39.48-1992 (Permanence of Paper).

This book is dedicated to my parents, Joseph and Athna May Porter, for teaching me the resilience that I have used throughout my life.

Contents

	List of Illustrations	ix
	Acknowledgments	xi
1.	Introduction: The Persistence of Community	1
2.	Communal Complexity on the Margins	13
3.	Measuring Social Complexity in the Early Iron Age	38
4.	Producing Community	69
5.	Managing Community	104
6.	Conclusion: The Complex Community	133
	Notes	149
	References	169
	Index	197

Illustrations

Figures

1.1.	Map of the southern Levant	8
3.1.	Map of Early Iron Age settlements in west-central Jordan	50
3.2.	(A) Map of Lahun's Early Iron Age settlement (B) Aerial image of Lahun looking south	63
3.3.	(A) Map of al-'Aliya denoting buildings and other structures (B) Aerial image of al-'Aliya looking north	64
3.4.	(A) Map of al-Mu'arradja denoting various structures (B) Aerial image of al-Mu'arradja looking south	65
4.1.	Al-'Aliya Building 200	76
4.2	Al-'Aliya Building 600	77
4.3.	Fortification walls of al-'Aliya	79
4.4.	Fortification walls of al-Mu'arradja	80
4.5.	(A) Al-'Aliya tower looking east (B) Corner of al-Mu'arradja tower illustrating free-standing tower	81
4.6.	The wadi riparian zone below al-'Aliya and al-Mu'arradja	84
4.7.	Al-Mu'ammariyya citadel building	92
4.8.	Al-'Aliya Building 100	93
4.9.	Bowls, kraters, jars, cooking pots, and juglets from al-'Aliya	97

5.1.	The Balu'a stele	110
5.2.	Lahun's (A) "Scarab House" and (B) Building 100	117
5.3.	Al-'Aliya Building 500 and Room 503's kitchen	119
5.4.	Illustration and profile drawing of bowl with red pigments	123
5.5.	Two simulations of reconstructed vessels. (A) Vessels in a low-lit building interior. (B) Same vessels in a low-lit open courtyard context.	126

Table

4.1	Identification for all bones recovered at al-'Aliya	88

Acknowledgments

This book is the culmination of research conducted over the past decade on the Early Iron Age communities of the Levant. I first became intrigued by Iron Age Jordan as a graduate student at the University of Pennsylvania, and my participation on two excavation projects at Tall Madaba and Khirbat al-Mudayna al-'Aliya solidified my interests. The early Iron Age has been a period of much research and debate over the past century, and the data that are emerging from west-central Jordan promise to complicate prior understandings. Approximately 50 percent of the book is revised material from my doctoral dissertation, *The Archaeology of Community in Iron I Central Jordan*, submitted to the University of Pennsylvania's Anthropology Department in 2007.[1] The dissertation was a synthesis of unpublished as well as previously published data from multiple early Iron Age settlements in west-central Jordan. Since the submission of the dissertation, additional evidence has been gathered and analyzed that strengthens the project's principal conclusions. Additional reading and research has led me to develop the community-based framework used in the dissertation into the more substantial notion of communal complexity presented in this book.

I would like to acknowledge the generosity of my colleagues that work in west-central Jordan who were willing to share unpublished data as well as their thoughts on previously published materials. These individuals include Larry Herr and Douglas Clark, directors of the Madaba Plains Project's Tall al-'Umayri excavations; Denyse Homès-Fredericq, director of Belgian excavations at Lahun, and her assistant, Ingrid Swinnen; Bruce Routledge, director of the Khirbat al-Mudayna al-'Aliya excavations; and

Udo Worschech and Friedbert Ninow, past and present directors of the Friedensau Theologische Hochshule's excavations at Baluʻa. Carlos Cardova contributed clay samples from his geological survey of west-central Jordan. I also wish to thank the late Dr. Fawwaz al-Khraysheh, the former director of Jordan's Department of Antiquities, and various past and present staff members, Ali al-Khayyat, Reem Shqoor, Bassam al-Mahameed, and Ahmed Shammi, for their assistance in locating archived collections in Jordan. Pierre Bikai, the former director of the American Center of Oriental Research (ACOR) in ʻAmman, introduced me to many of the colleagues mentioned above. ACOR's current director, Barbara Porter, and associate director, Christopher Tuttle, have continued to offer me valuable help in this and related research projects. Michael D. Glascock, Stanley Klassen, Justin Lev-Tov, Ellen Simmons, Robert J. Speakman, Shannon White, and Andrew Wilson also provided technical assistance at various stages of my research.

I am grateful to the many agencies that provided funding for researching and writing this book: The Council of American Overseas Research Centers (CAORC), Missouri's University Research Reactor (MURR), the National Science Foundation (NSF; Dissertation Improvement Grant No. 0328347), and the Louis J. Kolb Society of Fellows at the University of Pennsylvania. I am also thankful for the opportunities to present portions of my research to public and academic audiences at Drexel University, the University of California–Los Angeles, the University of California–Berkeley, Stanford University, the Field Museum of Natural History, Purdue University, Columbia University, and the University of Pennsylvania. The feedback I received was helpful in envisioning the larger implications of my work as well as audiences working beyond the ancient Near East. Not least, I would like to thank the two anonymous reviewers of the manuscript whose comments helped improve the final version.

This book would not exist without the dedicated encouragement that I have received from Bruce Routledge, whose mentoring, friendship, and collaboration I have so valued over the years. I would also like to thank Meredith Chesson, Timothy Harrison, Øystein LaBianca, and Thomas Levy for their generous encouragement of my research. Their intellectual influences on this book will be obvious to any readers of their scholarship. I also have my cohorts from the University of Pennsylvania's departments of Anthropology and of Near Eastern Languages and Civilization to thank for their professional and personal support, including Alexander Bauer, Alexis Boutin, Larry Coben, Michael Frachetti, Pamela Geller, Charles Golden, Matthew Liebmann, Kevin McGeough, Jeremiah Peterson,

Miranda Stockett, Uzma Rizvi, Matthew Rutz, Christopher Thornton, and William Zimmerle. My colleagues in Berkeley and the Bay Area have fostered a refreshing intellectual setting for me, and for that I thank Daniel Boyarin, Aaron Brody, Meg Conkey, Robert Coote, Marian Feldman, Christine Hastorf, Ron Hendel, Rosemary Joyce, Eric Kansa, Sarah Kansa, Kent Lightfoot, Lisa Maher, Carol Redmount, Francesca Rochberg, Jun Sunseri, Nicholas Tripcevich, Niek Veldhuis, Laurie Wilkie, and many others. Current and former Berkeley graduate students, including Stephanie Brown, Antonietta Catanzariti, Melissa Cradic, Andrea Creel, Alan Farahani, Catherine Foster, Jean Li, Elizabeth Minor, Randy Souza, and Martin Weber, listened and responded to many of the ideas presented here. Thanks are also due to Allyson Carter and her staff at the University of Arizona Press for managing the production of this book. I also thank my sister, Jamie Porter, as well as my spouse, Jenny Jacobs, and her parents, Stephen and Jeannie Jacobs, for their steadfast support over the years.

COMPLEX COMMUNITIES

CHAPTER ONE

Introduction

The Persistence of Community

COMMUNITY: A dream. Sometimes we do not know that we had it until we wake up from it.
                                    WILLIAM T. VOLLMAN, *POOR PEOPLE* (2007)

Thinking clearly about the notion of "community" in today's world is difficult. Politicians, marketers, and civic groups use the term to unite people within social groups that promise intimacy and egalitarianism. The call for community evokes nostalgia for presumably utopian pasts that existed apart from impersonal state institutions, a mode of "being together" that is barely recognizable in today's cities and suburbs. Yet when it is possible to see through the ideologies that laden such commentaries, one finds that communities are, in fact, fascinatingly complex entities that form around shared resources and issues. Far from utopias, they are often rife with conflict over priorities, led by covert hierarchies, and have blurry membership rosters. Fortunately, the community's complexity has not escaped the attention of recent philosophers and social scientists,[1] who express a range of sentiments, from skepticism about the community's function, to anxiety and optimism about its future. The philosopher Jean-Luc Nancy speculates that "the thought of the community or the desire for it might well be nothing other than a belated invention that tried to respond to the harsh reality of modern experience" (Nancy 1991:10) and argues that "society was not built on the ruins of a community" (Nancy 1991:11). Yet when looking deep into the historical and archaeological record, it is difficult to agree with Nancy and others who believe the community is only a recent response to the alienating conditions of modernity. Historically remote groups have often crafted their own versions of community, resulting in an enormous diversity of the form over time. How these past communities

1

developed, sometimes in the interstices of civilizations, mattered for the subsequent rise of more complex forms of human organization. Archaeologists, with their abilities to recover physical evidence of social life in past societies, have much to contribute to this conversation.

And yet the limited research archaeologists have done on communities has not appeared in broader interdisciplinary discussions. One reason why archaeologists may not be participating is that unlike other forms of human organization such as chiefdoms and archaic states, they did not help to "discover" the community. Rather, they inherited the concept from an intellectual tradition that first identified the community as it was responding to the rise of nineteenth-century European industrial capitalism. As agricultural production was mechanized and unemployment in the countryside increased, families abandoned their rural towns in search of employment in growing industrialized urban centers. In the neighborhoods and in the workplace, individuals and families found themselves in living arrangements fundamentally different from the villages they had left. Newly arrived workers lived among strangers, working for foremen and owners rather than cooperatively for a group or individually for their own households.

Observing these changes in arrangements at the turn of the twentieth century were scholars who believed the community on the wane, and, for some writers, in need of rescue.[2] German sociologist Ferdinand Tönnies explained this transformation as a process through which individuals moved from social collectives based on a shared will (Gemeinschaft) to collectives based on the will of individuals (Gesellschaft) (Tönnies 1887). Tönnies writes at the beginning of his book, "All intimate, private, and exclusive living together . . . is understood as life in *Gemeinschaft. Gesellschaft* is public life—it is the world itself" (1887:33). For Tönnies, Gesellschaft was "transitory and artificial," "a mechanical aggregate and artifact," whereas Gemeinschaft was a "lasting and genuine form of living together" and a "living organism" (1887:35). As Europe's agricultural villages disbanded and as business and markets became organized for individual gain, Gemeinschaft unraveled and in its place the "mechanical aggregate" of Gesellschaft arose. Tönnies's dualism had a lasting effect on interpretations that followed his scholarship, such as in Émile Durkheim's *The Division of Labour in Society* (1893). Durkheim assigned his own labels, "mechanical and organic solidarity," to explain how the division of labor differed in traditional and modern societies. Interested in those features that maintain solidarity in a society, Durkheim argued that members of traditional societies "are not only individually attracted to one another because they resemble one another, but they are also linked to what is the condition for the existence of this collective type, that is, to the society that they form by coming together" (1893:60). In the process, a person's sense of self is subsumed within a community's collective consciousness.[3]

The rigid structural divisions between community and society continued to permeate twentieth-century research, especially in the budding fields of anthropology and sociology. Yet one of the principal problems with this division is that it established small-scale societies as a foil for the large urban societies that industrialism had fostered. Small-scale societies such as the community were supposed to lack complexity because social relationships based on face-to-face interactions were in some way "simple." Such a division also advanced the idea that small-scale societies were fleeting and vulnerable to change. These early writers assumed that as the twentieth century progressed, traditional face-to-face communities would give way to impersonal, industrial societies. Ostensibly, scholars had little choice but to observe and to document the passing of the community out of existence. But as the century progressed through two world wars, global economic depressions, and attempts at decolonization, the community remained a resilient way of organizing human collectives and continued to be a prominent subject of research (Arensberg 1961; Arensberg and Kimball 1940, 1965; Cohen 1985; Murdock and Wilson 1972; Redfield 1955; Wolf 1956).

This brief genealogy of the community concept reveals an opportunity for archaeologists to complicate scholarly ontologies that reduce preindustrial communities to "simple" and primordial groups. Due to the limited amount of historical and archaeological evidence available to early theorists as well as the tendency of some social scientists to downplay deep historical antecedents, archaeologists' definitions of preindustrial communities have been constructed using either the armchair musings of late nineteenth-century scholars or the ethnographic fieldwork of twentieth-century social scientists (e.g., Wolf, Redfield). The latter group enjoyed the advantages of working in living communities where subjects could be questioned and behaviors observed. Consequently, archaeology's notion of community is colored by the fact that the form has been studied during a time when modern colonialism, imperialism, industrialism, and globalization have made significant impacts on small-scale societies throughout the world. Are these ontologies of recent communities responding to a quickly changing world still useful when investigating those in the preindustrial past? This book sets out to answer this and related questions using archaeology, an alternative and complementary mode of socio-historical inquiry, to refute Nancy's accusation that the community is merely a "belated invention" of modernity.

Excavating Communities on the Margins

Of course, this book is not the first archaeological investigation of preindustrial communities, but it is one of the few to consider communities that lived under challenging circumstances. Archaeologists have often disregarded such communities, favoring those groups who lived under more ideal conditions. Sedentary settlements in such marginal zones can be admittedly fleeting and the physical evidence can be poorly preserved. Furthermore, marginal societies do not often produce texts commenting upon themselves. Instead, they are often written about—represented—by outsiders living in text-based societies with more structurally beneficial conditions. Those scholars who rely solely on written sources to write "histories" or who value an archaeological record complemented by substantial inscriptional corpora are not often drawn to such "textless" societies. This tendency to ignore the margins of society has been common in archaeology and ancient history, two fields that the academy and public alike celebrate for focusing on the elites of the world's ancient civilizations. Past societies living on the margins, however, can be just as interesting—perhaps just as thrilling—as the Mayans, the Egyptians, or the Babylonians because they were often required to develop innovative strategies to mitigate uncertainties. These strategies played a critical role in structuring the practices of everyday life as well as shaping the bonds that linked together persons and households. The distribution of resources and wealth, the organization of labor, concern for defense, and other issues were essential to organizing societies in these unstable venues. Whatever the reasons for being placed on the margins, the community was a potentially well-formulated mode of social life that could help households survive—sometimes even thrive—together under difficult circumstances.

Although the number of ways in which past communities could find themselves situated in marginal conditions are infinite, this book focuses on those groups who lived in arid and semi-arid environments where naturally available resources such as precipitation were limited, soil quality was poor, and environmental uncertainty was high.[4] The environment has been selected as a structuring condition because it presents an opportunity to examine a force that continues to preoccupy contemporary conversations about climate change and human-induced environmental degradation.

Popular examinations have often characterized communities living on the edge of sustainability as pursuing an unwise cultural logic that decimates local resources and leads to their inevitable demise (e.g., Diamond 1997, 2005). In some small manner, this book offers an alternative way to think about social life and subsistence in an environmentally marginal zone by paying equal, if not more, attention to the ways communities managed such difficult conditions rather than focusing exclusively on their collapse.

This tendency to overlook communities on the margins is embedded in a deeper reluctance of archaeologists to recognize nonnormative iterations of social life in past societies. By taking up the investigation of community, this book does not mean to construct a typology of the form as archaeologists have treated political categories such as tribes, chiefdoms, states, and empires (e.g., Adams 1966; Feinman and Marcus 1998; Service 1975). These efforts have certainly expanded an appreciation of these cultural forms, but at the expense of flattening the contingencies that explain how they were variously deployed in particular historical and cultural settings. If indeed the community is a form that characterizes a large part of preindustrial societies, as Tönnies, Durkheim, and others believed, then it is the job of the archaeologist to discover it in all of its varied manifestations.

These issues will be developed further in chapter 2, where key problems with the ways archaeologists have envisioned communities in preindustrial societies, particularly those that lived in marginal zones, are considered. An alternative way to think about small-scale societies is "communal complexity," a process through which communities shift between egalitarian and hierarchical modes. Randall McGuire and Dean Saitta (1996) first discussed the phenomenon in the American Southwest, where scholars have debated if prehispanic pueblo societies in the American Southwest were organized communally or hierarchically. McGuire and Saitta offered a dialectical solution, one in which communities could move between alternative modes of organization as their circumstances changed. This notion of communal complexity has broader potential for understanding communities in venues outside of the New World, particularly in resource-scarce environments.

One way communal complexity can be developed is by turning to recent conversations that combine historical ecology and complexity theory to understand the strategies societies use to adapt themselves to changing environmental conditions. "Resilience" has been a key concept in these discussions, that is, the capacity for a group to retain its function and form upon encountering disturbances (Walker and Salt 2006). Use of this term does not imply that the group remains unchanged following a disturbance, however. A resilient group must demonstrate enough flexibility to allow itself to adapt to new circumstances. If unable to adapt to new conditions—usually because they have organized themselves too rigidly—groups have a reduced chance of managing disturbances successfully. Communal complexity facilitated practices of resilience that small-scale societies required when living under marginal conditions.

Locating the Community in the Middle East

Compared to research on New World societies (e.g., Redfield 1955; Yaeger and Canuto 2000), scholars of the ancient and modern Middle East[5] have been reluctant to conceive of social life in terms of community, preferring alternative analytical categories such as household, tribe, state, and empire.[6] However, when the concept of community has been deployed, it has proven to be useful. Near Eastern prehistoric archaeologists have used the concept more often to envision social life than have archaeologists working in periods with historical documentation (Kuijt 2000). In the latter case, the term "community" is used in casual references to nonurban social life, although a handful of works have used the category with more sophistication (Faust 2000; Knapp 2003; Magness-Gardiner and Falconer 1994; Wilkinson et al. 2007). This gradual emergence of the community in Near Eastern archaeological scholarship may in part be explained by the growing recognition that urban modes of settlement frequently used to characterize the region's civilizations were less normative than previously believed. By ignoring the agro-pastoral settlements that lived in the shadows, archaeologists missed an essential component of ancient Near Eastern social life.

The Fertile Crescent, the arching strip of cultivatable land that begins in the Levant and extends into Mesopotamia, has been the dominant geographic metaphor in twentieth-century Near Eastern archaeology. The region presents a nexus of rich soils, sufficient precipitation, and irrigable rivers such as the Euphrates and Orontes Rivers that creates an ideal venue for irrigated and rain-fed agricultural production. Traditional demographic paradigms have understood the Fertile Crescent to be largely the domain of the sedentary farmer, with nomadic pastoralists entering during fallow periods to graze their flocks on field stubble. But when not grazing, nomadic pastoralists inhabited the arid desert environments where they exploited naturally available resources for their own and their herds' subsistence. Yet recent research has determined that this stark division between the "desert and the sown" is indeed too stark (e.g., Wilkinson et al. 2007). Rather, surveys and excavations have demonstrated that sedentary communities could also occupy the thin marginal semi-arid zones that divided the Fertile Crescent from the arid desert environments. Throughout Middle Eastern history, these marginal zones saw settlement and agricultural intensification during times when growing and grazing lands were in demand. These periods usually took place during eras of increased political complexity in the region, particularly when polities such as city-states and empires sought to intensify agricultural production in such underdeveloped zones.

The idea that the settlement of the Middle East's marginal zones was motivated by economic and political forces makes sense when one reflects on how the region's states and empires worked to maximize production in their less powerful peripheries. But how then does one explain the settlement of these marginal zones when these external political and economic pressures were absent? The presence of sedentary life during such eras defies the Fertile Crescent paradigm of the "desert and sown," leading one to ask why communities would be living under such difficult environmental conditions when more ideal conditions were located not much further away? To explain their presence in these marginal zones, one needs to search for other, perhaps internal, motivations. These could include alienation from groups living in more hospitable areas or perhaps a rare coalescence of environmental resources that made subsistence in a marginal zone possible.

Although the Middle East presents several marginal zones for such an investigation, this book focuses on those found in the Levant during a slightly more than two-century period of history called the Early Iron Age (1250–1000 BCE) (fig. 1.1).[7] Beginning in the latter half of the thirteenth century BCE, Levantine society, like its counterparts throughout the eastern Mediterranean, gradually reemerged from a political and economic upheaval whose precise and possibly multiple causes remain debated (Oren 2000; Ward and Joukowsky 1992). Where the Late Kingdom Egyptian empire had once held sway over much of the Levant's southern half during the Late Bronze Age (1550–1250 BCE), the onset of the Early Iron Age saw the demise of this imperial administration and along with it the elite Canaanite palace economies that had often benefitted from the Egyptians' presence. With the decline of this social order at the very beginning of the Early Iron Age, Levantine society became an uneven patchwork of societies that written sources describe as "Canaanite," "Philistine," "Israelite,"

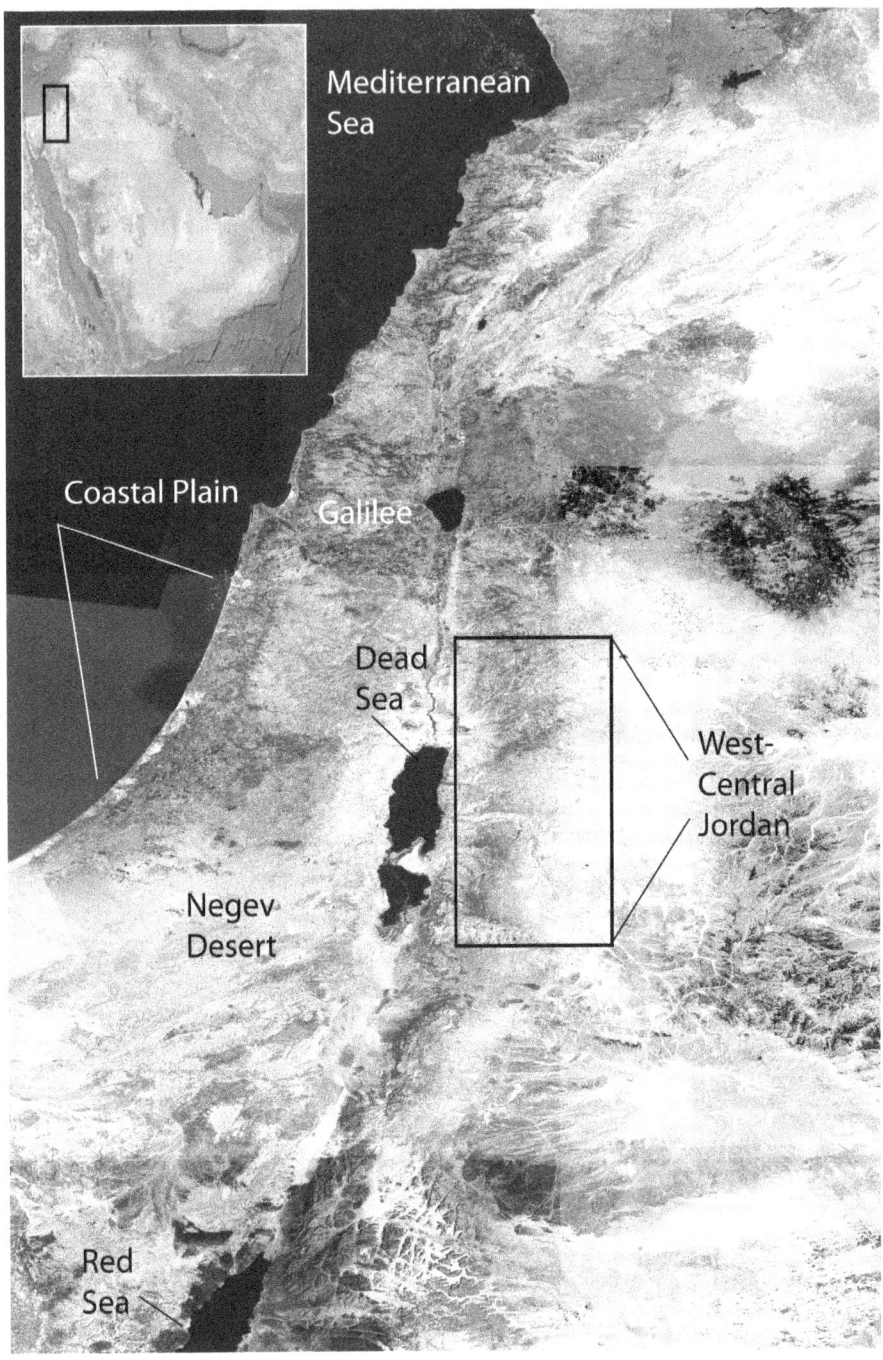

Figure 1.1. Map of the southern Levant. (*Sources*: Landsat 5; data: U.S. Geological Survey. Inset: Google Earth 2012; image: 2012; data: SIO, NOAA, U.S. Navy, NGA, GEBCO)

and "Moabite." Whatever their names, archaeological investigations reveal that these Early Iron Age societies were distinct from their Late Bronze Age urban predecessors. In the southern Levantine central highlands (Finkelstein 1988; Finkelstein and Naʻaman 1994), Lebanon's Bekaʻa Valley (Marfoe 1979), and west-central Jordan (Ibach 1987) settlements were largely based on limited agro-pastoral subsistence practices with an equally limited craft economy. Since their identification, a disproportional amount of scholarship has concentrated on this relatively narrow data set. Many of these settlements, especially in the southern Levantine central highlands, are believed to be the first settlement of what were, or were to soon become, the ancient Israelites (Albright 1939; Dever 2003; Faust 2006; Finkelstein and Naʻaman 1994; Gottwald 1979; Killebrew 2005; Mendenhall 1962). Combining the archaeological evidence with Egyptian written sources, key portions of the Hebrew Bible, and a handful of excavated epigraphic pieces, scholars have reconstructed the social organization of these settlements according to theological (e.g., Hanson 2001), subsistence (e.g., Alt 1966; Hopkins 1985; LaBianca 1990), peasant (e.g., Mendenhall 1962, 1976), kinship (e.g., Stager 1985), egalitarian (e.g., Robinson 1961, 1964), and social evolutionary frameworks (Faust 2006; Flanagan 1981; Frick 1985; Killebrew 2005; Miller 2005).[8] These attempts have resulted in frustratingly static depictions of a society that was deceptively complex and worthy of a more nuanced understanding.

In search of a fresh perspective, this book has chosen the Early Iron Age settlements of west-central Jordan, an area demarcated by the Jordan Valley on the west, the Arabian Desert on the east, the Wadi al-Zarqa on the north, and the Wadi al-Hasa on the south. West-central Jordan is an excellent and often overlooked venue in which to explore Early Iron Age societies. Following the collapse of the Late Bronze Age palace economies, a collection of settlements dependent on mixed agro-pastoral subsistence practices were founded beginning in the late thirteenth century BCE and continued for more than two centuries. These settlements are commonly characterized by the distinctive oval shape of the settlement, the pillared buildings that line the perimeter, large empty central courtyards, and substantial fortification systems. Although most settlements were abandoned after only a century of occupation, it is clear from the archaeological evidence that the people who occupied them organized their societies in ways that demonstrate a degree of emergent social complexity.

Yet this acknowledgment of complexity in Early Iron Age west-central Jordan has led to problematic attempts to characterize the region's political and economic organization. Scholars regularly defer to textual sources that were either composed outside of west-central Jordan (e.g., Egyptian texts) or written down after the Early Iron Age (e.g., the Hebrew Bible, esp. the Books of Numbers, Joshua, Judges, and Samuel) rather than west-central Jordan's archaeological record (Boling 1988; Dearman 1992; Glueck 1940; Mattingly 1992). An additional issue is scholars' use of social evolutionary paradigms. Such frameworks are applied to the Early Iron Age data set, not for the purpose of explaining cultural processes or social change (as is common in anthropological archaeology, e.g., Flannery 1972; Haas 1982; Service 1975), but as descriptive, static categories of social traits. When what is believed to be a "tribe" or "state" does not easily map onto the available evidence, frustrations ensue (Bienkowski 2009; Finkelstein and Lipschits 2011; Mattingly 1992; Miller 1992). These discussions will be considered in chapter 3 where the written and material evidence for second millennium west-central Jordan is examined.

Past treatments of the Early Iron Age have relied on regional settlement patterns and architectural arrangements, balking at data sets such as those of faunal remains and botanical evidence that would provide a deeper understanding of cultural practices at local resolutions. Therefore, chapters 4 and 5 will go deep inside the communities of west-central Jordan to demonstrate how such a fine-grained perspective can offer a new understanding of the arrangements of production, wealth, authority, and inequality. Households, given their shared concerns with subsistence, "produced" community through the creation of built space, agro-pastoralism, the sharing of storage facilities, and the crafting of ceramic vessels. Together, these activities constituted a flexible system that could be adapted to changing circumstances. This flexibility was essential as many, but not all, of the known Early Iron Age settlements subsisted in semi-arid zones that fall between 100 and 300 millimeter isohyets (el-Sherbini 1979:174, table 2), and therefore received only the minimum amount of precipitation needed to practice rain-fed agriculture. Furthermore, the yellow Mediterranean and yellow steppic soils surrounding these settlements challenged grain production. The lush riparian zones located far below the settlements in the deep canyons around the settlements offered some reprieve from these difficulties. This persistent water source fostered a microclimate of wild fauna, flora, and soils where production routines were conducted.

One intriguing result of this investigation of production strategies is the discovery of emergent inequalities within the communities. Not all households appeared to possess equal amounts of wealth, and evidence indicates that leaders emerged to manage the communities. The evidence found within the communities reveals how patrimonial and charismatic genres manifested themselves in Early Iron Age social life. Given the potential for frequent periods of scarcity and the emphasis placed on agriculture and pastoralism, food was an important basis for household wealth that could be circulated between households and between communities. When considering the food storage and preparation facilities, it is apparent that larger households had more complex facilities, suggesting that they had the potential to feed people beyond their immediate household. In turn, evidence for feasting is considered in an assemblage of decorated serving vessels that were present throughout many of the communities. Together, these materials suggest community leaders combined genres of patrimonial and charismatic authority to garner power over other households and mobilize them in projects for individual and mutual gain. These shifts between egalitarian and hierarchical modes of organization helped communities build and maintain resilience. But this authority certainly had its limits as evidence indicates that households left the community gradually over time, likely to found their own nearby or adopt alternative practices such as nomadism. The fragility of leadership and the co-presence of patrimonial and charismatic genres in the Early Iron Age communities suggest that the investigation of authority cannot easily be summarized in one or another typological category that is so common in research. In order to prepare the reader for these later discussions and conclusions, chapter 2 interrogates the frameworks that archaeologists have used in their investigations of preindustrial communities.

This evidence for subsistence and social life in the Early Iron Age communities is useful for deciphering how west-central Jordan's settlement system developed over its more than two-century history. Chapter 6 integrates archaeological evidence explored in earlier chapters within a model that considers the different pathways communities followed in their development through phases in an adaptive cycle. Inspired by discussions in resilience studies, this framework explains how the communities responded to environmental challenges by reorganizing their subsistence strategies and social organization. This framework also helps explain why communities were eventually abandoned, deliberate acts that likely made sense given the difficult conditions the final households faced in sustaining themselves. As much as this broader understanding of the communities' growth and demise reveals about the mechanics of Early Iron Age Levantine society, it also exposes archaeologists' and historians' gaps in their knowledge that can only be filled in with future research. Only with more excavation, analysis, and publication of fast-disappearing archaeological sites can the diverse ways that communities adapted to their specific historical and environmental conditions be understood. But given what is so far known about west-central Jordan's communities, these brief communal attempts to persist on the edge of sustainability offer lessons of endurance and resilience for societies facing similar challenges today.

CHAPTER TWO

Communal Complexity on the Margins

Public audiences celebrate archaeology for its investigation of "civilizations"—Mesopotamian, Roman, the Mayan and the Aztec, to name only a handful—that consistently dominate television programming and glossy magazine covers. The broad appeal of civilization persists into the new century as societies remain concerned with maintaining their existence in the face of widespread economic turbulence and global climate change. Indeed, the ancient civilization has become the default category to which the contemporary is compared in hopes that past mistakes will not be repeated. What is striking in these anachronistic valuings of the past is the way other forms of human organization are regularly overlooked despite their persistence in human history. Small-scale societies such as communities are no exception to this oversight despite their popularity in modern discourse. Equally problematic is how nineteenth- and twentieth-century social scientists gestured to the community's primordial past, despite a lack of knowledge about what these iterations looked like in material terms. These assumptions that the community is some kind of "natural" human condition are unconvincing for archaeologists who are charged with explaining cultural phenomena in the past. Still, it is difficult to ignore that the community is the form from which states and empires grew, and it is where groups often returned to once civilizations had "collapsed." What is so enticing about the community that has made it such a persistent form of social organization throughout human history?

Archaeological Ontologies of the Community

Archaeologists have not sought an answer to this question for very long, despite its recognition in earlier social scientific research. One of the earliest references to community appeared in Gordon Willey's *Prehistoric Settlement Patterns in the Virú Valley, Perú* (1953:371–395). Willey described settlements sharing assemblages as united under a "community pattern." Although he did not venture a definition of community, he did establish it as an analytical unit requiring archaeological investigation. The physical boundaries of the "site" marked the community's edges, he argued, whereas a shared assemblage between settlements defined a broader community connected through ideological or ethnic connections. Not until a 1955 seminar entitled "Functional and Evolutionary Implications of Community Patterning" was a deliberate attempt made to improve upon Willey's notion of community (Beardsley et al. 1956). The seminar's participants adopted a definition of community that found broad applicability: "the largest grouping of persons in any particular culture whose normal activities bind them together into a self-conscious, corporate unit, which is economically self-sufficient and politically independent" (Beardsley et al. 1956:133). From this definition, the seminar participants built a typology of community patterns, each a nexus of relationships between economic, social, political, and ideological structures. In all, seven patterns were identified based on a group's mobility practices, ranging from "restricted wandering" to "semi-permanent sedentary" and "supra nuclear integrated" (Beardsley et al. 1956:134). For each type, the authors defined a pattern, the dynamics that produced them, economic aspects, social organization, ethnographic and archaeological criteria and examples, and corresponding terminology in other schemes.

The 1955 seminar participants wrestled with additional questions that preoccupy any cross-cultural, transhistorical study of communities. Why did communities demonstrate so much diversity in form across time and societies? Central to their explanation was the relationship between subsistence practices, the environment, and resources (Beardsley et al. 1956:150). Community decisions based on these factors determined their form, particularly the level of group mobility. This functionalist interpretation was supported by ethnographic evidence, Beardsley and others argued. Semi-permanent sedentary groups, for example, subsisted within an environment with abundant resources that did not require management through permanent agricultural infrastructure. North American Northwest Coast communities could lead a semi-transient lifestyle, leaving for new gardens when the previous ones had been exhausted. The seminar participants also questioned why the phenomenon of the community could be identified at all levels of social complexity. Self-conscious, economic, and politically independent corporate units existed in all types of societies, from nomadic bands to large-scale nations and even empires (Beardsley et al. 1956:152–153). Furthermore, communities could progress through the seven types, from the simplest, free-wandering form of organization through each pattern, adopting greater levels of permanent residency along the way. The seminar participants described community as a social evolutionary phenomenon, which moved from one stage to the next, as its relationship with the environment grew more complicated, subsistence practices changed, and agricultural technologies grew more sophisticated. The authors were careful, however, to point out that not all societies were required to move through each stage of community pattern. Rather, communities that acquired agricultural technologies through their diffusion often bypassed several stages. Communities isolated from each other, on the other hand, were more likely to move evenly through stages if subsistence skills were acquired through independent innovation.

Early statements on the preindustrial community such as Willey's and the 1955 seminar's established a foundation on which archaeologists would build over the next several decades (e.g., Canuto and Yaeger 2000; Knapp 2003; Nelson 1994; Varien and Potter 2008; Wilk and Ashmore 1988). Yet the discipline's engagement with the idea of community has unfolded so unevenly that a linear chronological review of this research makes little sense.[1] Instead, a selective, thematic review of this research can draw out collective concerns as well as successes and shortcomings. The most-discussed theme, not surprisingly, is how to identify the community in the material record, a necessary initial step in any archaeological study. Kolb and Snead define the community as a "minimal, spatially defined locus of human activity" (1997:611) that is dependent on three characteristics: social reproduction, subsistence production, and self-identification. Although the authors do not speculate on the processual aspects of their definition—how communities may come into being based on their three criteria, for instance—they do explain how it is possible to investigate the community. The authors cite the problems of circumscribing the community in spatial terms, and pointed out how archaeologists often establish the community's terminus at the site's edge, when in fact the community often extends out into the landscape (1997:612–613). The archaeological investigation of the community, therefore, requires applying different scales, both at the site and at the regional level. Investigations at the regional scale help identify off-site practices, such as agricultural and ceramic vessel production, and also reveal how communities were embedded in their surrounding landscape and conjoined to other settlements.

Kolb and Snead also present a way to study communities through the use of analytical strategies. The different ways communities organize and manage labor projects is the first of three strategies. Labor projects may include agricultural and other subsistence-based investments, but the most readily observable in the archaeological record is architectural evidence. Both ordinary and monumental features communicate lasting and tangible messages to communities. Kolb and Snead suggest a separation between projects that are organized and managed at the household level and custodial projects that are managed by leaders who use peaceful and coercive measures to elicit participation. The second strategy requires attention to the relationships between communities. The ways communities are organized in the landscape may suggest the extent to which they shared or competed over resources, cooperated in regional endeavors, and shared a sense of regional identification. The third strategy identifies boundary-preserving measures visible in the architectural and artifactual record. The manner in which houses were constructed and artifacts decorated may suggest that communities sought to differentiate themselves from their neighbors, fostering a unique sense of social cohesion.

These analytical strategies offer a productive starting point in any investigation of preindustrial communities. But it is also necessary to consider the actors, factions, and events that structured social life within communities. Hayden and Cannon suggest that segmenting communities into corporate groups is one way to identify factions that form around environmental and economic issues (1982:135). Hayden and Cannon provide a typology of corporate groups, dividing the category into three types based on residential proximity: (1) multiple nuclear families share a single residence, (2) nuclear families live in separate, but adjacent residences, and (3) nuclear families live in separate and less conjoined residences (i.e., neighborhoods). Like Kolb and Snead, Hayden and Cannon (1982:147–149) provide analytical strategies for measuring corporate group dynamics. The settlement's architectural arrangement, and the size and complexity of individual buildings provide qualitative means to evaluate group social composition and cohesiveness. Settlements with repetitive building designs whose entrances face each other suggest a more integrated and cohesive social environment, indicative of modern ethnographic attestations of corporate groups. Like architecture, material cultural patterning provides an additional means of identifying corporate groups. Homogeneity in artifact style—an indication that members learned technologies and styles in their birthplace and then stayed in the community—suggests endogamous marriage practices, whereas heterogeneity in artifact style suggests members married outside of the corporate group. Physical evidence for social stratification may be present in corporate groups, but not overwhelmingly so. In ethnographic attestations, for example, community leaders are present and live in slightly enhanced versions of the repetitive building design.

The recognition of corporate groups is an important step toward identifying the internal dynamics of social life within preindustrial communities. It dismisses the widely held notion that preindustrial communities were necessarily egalitarian and replaces it with the possibility of identifying factions that produced social differentiation. So what caused factions to emerge in preindustrial communities? According to Hayden and Cannon, environmental and economic factors are the prime movers in generating and maintaining corporate groups (1982:135). Although the structuring roles that environmental and economic conditions have on communities are undeniable, dismissing additional, less tangible, causes in the production of corporate groups is unreasonable. Alternatively, the emergence of factions and the reorganization of social life in communities also requires examination within its historical and archaeological context.

Archaeologists studying communities have drawn on poststructural social theories (e.g., Varien and Potter 2008; Yaeger 2000), particularly the ideas of Pierre Bourdieu (1977) and Anthony Giddens (1984), to inspire perspectives that appreciate the activities and relationships shared between individuals and groups. Jason Yaeger's (2000) investigation of a Classic Mayan community, San Lorenzo, in western Belize was one attempt to understand communities from this perspective.[2] Yaeger approached the San Lorenzo community as a social entity contingent on members' daily routines and interactions. These elements were sorted into different categories of practice that shaped social relationships at San Lorenzo. Production and consumption activities, the orientation and arrangement of houses, and shared raw material sources suggest San Lorenzo residents participated in a set of everyday routines. Yaeger likened these routines to Bourdieu's notion of "habitus," those practices that are shared, often implicitly, between members of a group (Bourdieu 1977:78–87, 1990:52–65). Feasting and the construction of larger houses were also understood to be practices of affiliation that forged a more discursive sense of communal identity. Additional practices that affiliated the San Lorenzo community with the nearby political capital, Xunantunich, were identified, such as San Lorenzo's elite residences that replicated styles in the capital.

The use of habitus in this analysis of a community's social life is a productive way to envision how households experienced a communal ethos. As a broadly shared set of unconscious dispositions, the habitus is the generative source of practices, behaviors, and routines that constitute social life (Bourdieu 1977:72, 78). Although produced through a collective's shared experiences, the habitus is also the recursive glue that bonds communities together with an unspoken sense of cohesion. Yet habitus is not an irreducible, unchanging fact in a community's social life; rather, it has a mechanics all its own. Bourdieu's discussion of "doxa," and discourse, and the ways these regimes structure habitus, provides a way to understand a community as an unfolding and always shifting cultural phenomenon. Doxa is the realm of social consciousness where traditions and beliefs about the social order go unspoken and unquestioned, where social knowledge, as Bourdieu himself famously remarked, "goes without saying because it comes without saying" (1977:167). Doxa stands opposed to the realm of discourse, where social knowledge is objectified in consciousness as laws and opinions. But the realm of discourse is not so simply stated. Rather, within the realm of discourse is a tension between orthodoxy—norms, values, and laws instituted within a society—and heterodoxy, the noncodified possibilities and choices individual members have available to them.

This more nuanced sense of habitus, of conscious and social knowledge, complicates Yaeger's interpretation of San Lorenzo. These practices of affiliation—feasting, cooperative labor projects, and elite's emulation of their counterparts in the Xunantunich metropole—are, as Yaeger (2000) contends, discursively created, sanctioned events and practices that established and confirmed the social order. Community events at San Lorenzo did more than simply foster a local identity. They instilled the "natural" order of the community's consciousness. Community leaders participating in these rituals rationalized their authority within this orthodoxy, and members were reminded of their prescribed roles. But what of the everyday practices and routines that patterned San Lorenzo's archaeological record? Many of these unconscious practices remained within the realm of doxa, activities that went unquestioned as part of tradition.

It is difficult to imagine that social knowledge, whether found in the realm of doxa or of discourse, was static in the San Lorenzo community. External events such as environmental change and historical events outside the community no doubt played an important role in members' consciousness. But internally, how can the process through which shifts in a community's consciousness come about be explained? Stated more specifically in terms of San Lorenzo, how does a community leader come to demand that others build his or her house in a society where members are responsible for their own house construction? Or, how does the obligation to feed the entire community become established in a society where feeding one's own family is enough? The answer to these specific questions and to the larger question of consciousness lies in the recognition that social knowledge moves between doxa and discourse. What was once unthinkable and unspeakable is no longer part of doxa and is now debatable, a possibility, law, or fact. Conversely, what was once law or norm is forgotten and slips back into tradition, pastime, things "taken for granted." This fluidity guarantees that social knowledge will not be evenly distributed across the community. In fact, those members who perceived this flow of ideas between doxa and discourse were best suited to organize the community's worldview, accumulate power, and establish themselves as community leaders. Leaders with this social knowledge were the origin of those San Lorenzo elites, then, who transformed everyday unquestioned practices, such as building and cooking, into more established routines, such as labor projects and feasts.

This concern with leadership in communities raises the question of how hierarchical forms of social organization and authority emerge in small-scale societies. As the previous chapter observed, preindustrial communities are often imagined to have been primeval egalitarian collectives, in part thanks to classic social scientific perspectives such as those of Durkheim (1893) and Weber (1968) that present communities as pristine starting points from which stratified bureaucratic societies grow. Yet what many archaeological investigations have demonstrated over the past decade is that preindustrial communities did possess genres of authority and incipient forms of hierarchy that defy strict classification as egalitarian societies. Even more complicated is the recognition that these inequalities can sometimes be concurrent with evidence for collaboration and shared decision making. This apparent tension between two opposing modes of social life is exemplified in the American Southwest where archaeologists have debated whether to characterize prehispanic pueblo society as communal or ranked.[3] The arguments focus on differing interpretations of agricultural intensification, mortuary practices, and exchange at two fourteenth-century CE settlements in east-central Arizona: Grasshopper Pueblo and Chavez Pass. Grasshopper Pueblo was a settlement containing about thirteen blocks divided into some five hundred rooms, three enclosed plazas, and a large kiva. Researchers have argued that social life at Grasshopper was egalitarian, motivated by a mutual desire for safety.

Chavez Pass is approximately one hundred kilometers away and was a larger pueblo with nearly one thousand rooms, several large plazas, and a large kiva. Researchers at Chavez Pass have argued that their site served as a regional administrative center for elites who managed networks of agricultural settlements.

Participants in the great Grasshopper Pueblo–Chavez Pass debate have argued to a standstill the nature of pueblo society. McGuire and Saitta (1996) sought to resolve the debate by suggesting that pueblo society could be characterized dialectically, in both egalitarian and ranked conditions. In prosperous times, such societies held the means of production and wealth in common. But in periods of stress, hierarchies would develop as families fought over resources and wealth. Leaders emerged from the most successful families. As ideal conditions reappeared, these hierarchies dissolved and egalitarian practices regained popularity. These changes were, then, a product of egalitarian and ranked conditions that together motivated groups to organize themselves in increasingly complex arrangements.

The lessons learned from the Grasshopper Pueblo–Chavez Pass debate are important for envisioning other preindustrial communities. The appearance of hierarchical forms does not always result in the elimination of egalitarian ones. Several studies posit that corporate decision making and wealth distribution can occur in even the most stratified societies (Blanton 1998; Blanton et al. 1996; Feinman 2000a, 2000b, 2001; Feinman, Lightfoot, and Upham 2000). Therefore, instead of focusing on egalitarian and ranked *societies*, it is more accurate to examine convergent egalitarian and ranked practices and ideologies *within* societies no matter where they fall on the social evolutionary ladder. Whereas emergent hierarchies give rise to inequities in social life, egalitarianism strives to maintain equal distributions of wealth and power. Egalitarian social relations are not natural states of social organization but require efforts and expenditures to maintain (Flanagan 1989). Thus egalitarianism can be understood as a pushing back against hierarchy, in an effort to redistribute wealth. The potential coexistence and tension between the two forms is what could give preindustrial communities a degree of complexity.

Communal Complexity

A question that preoccupied the 1955 seminar persists today: What made communities so different from each other even when they shared a set of analytically distinctive features? At first glance, preindustrial communities seem to have shared common trajectories. Once communities were founded, they often experienced opportunities for growth as well as setbacks because of changing circumstances. If they did not suddenly collapse or experience gradual decline, some grew into organizations in which members were arranged in impersonal structures that lacked the intimacy that characterizes communal social life. But a closer look reveals that individual patterns of organizational dynamics (i.e., their "histories") unfolded in complicated ways that defy expectations and frustrate comparisons. Most instances do not appear to follow periodic rates of change, rising and falling under predictable circumstances, as earlier social scientists anticipated. Preindustrial communities, at the same time, are not necessarily chaotic entities. Each exhibits a degree of cyclical patterning and internal organizational logic, although how these circumstances unfold is impossible to predict. The organizational dynamics of most preindustrial communities fall in between periodicity and chaos, in a realm characterized by complexity.

Recent transdisciplinary research on human complexity helps make sense of the unpredictable trajectories that preindustrial communities often demonstrated. That human societies can grow in complexity has been a principal idea in political and social evolutionary frameworks for decades (Cohen and Service 1978; Fried 1967; Steward [1955] 1963, among several others). Archaeological contributions to these conversations have remained steady, despite critiques that these frameworks were based on unilineal social evolutionary assumptions (Yoffee 1993) or did not take into account the ways that power, agency, and gender can play roles in social change (Brumfiel 1992). Complexity studies persist in archaeological research, in part because it is difficult to ignore that human social systems change and adapt to the shifting circumstances in which they are embedded. In recent research, archaeologists have grown attracted to the idea that humans are entangled within, and organize themselves into, complex adaptive systems (Kohler and Gumerman 2000; Kohler and van der Leeuw 2007)[4] that are, as Yoffee (2005) describes in plain language, "network(s) of interacting parts that exhibit a dynamic, aggregate behavior" (169). Complex adaptive systems possess a number of features that are useful for thinking about preindustrial communities. In principal, they are nonlinear in their development, exhibit several (rather than merely one) organizing elements, and are self-organizing and self-managing systems usually through collective behavior or a small number of powerful agents. Complex adaptive systems do not merely operate on an internal basis, however. They interact with the larger historical and environmental contexts in which they reside. Nor are complex adaptive systems always necessarily passive victims of their contexts. They influence the world as much as they adapt to the shifting conditions around them.

Small-scale societies such as communities have important roles to play in the investigation of complex adaptive systems. Archaeologists have looked to such societies to model the different ways inequality emerged in the unique conditions they present, such as limited populations taking part in face-to-face relationships. Although not a surprising line of inquiry—archaeologists have regularly looked to small-scale societies for the origins of inequality (Vaughn, Eerkens, and Kantner 2010)—a complex adaptive systems approach is attractive because it can consider multiple variables simultaneously and project several, sometimes opposing, outcomes. Smith and Choi (2007) modeled how a patron-client scenario can follow a different path to emergent inequality in small-scale societies compared to a managerial mutualism scenario in which select individuals organize members into projects that provide benefits for the entire population. Although both simulations led to conditions of inequality, the nature of this inequality was projected to be different in its scope and intensity. This anticipation of different trajectories and outcomes generates hypotheses that can be tested using evidence from particular instances.

Research on complex adaptive systems informs the community framework that is being developed in this book. One important lesson is that the preindustrial community was embedded in different kinds of contexts. For most communities, the principal context was often a socionatural system in which human societies were engaged in recursive relationships with their environment (van der Leeuw and Redman 2002). This link was recognized in Hayden and Cannon's (1982) research, but in their framework, the environment played a unidirectional role in structuring subsistence practices. Alternatively, in this new perspective, communities can act in ways that structure their environment through interventions that seek to manage natural resources. A second type of context was historical. Communities were not immune to the local, regional, and even far-flung global events that occurred around them. A state or empire's reorganization of a region that encompassed the community could play a decisive role in altering its constitution. But in invoking historical processes, one should not underestimate a community's agentive role in shaping its own destiny. Communities were not necessarily weak entities to be preyed upon by larger organizational forces, but could resist through their own initiatives. In fact, communities could mount their own transformative initiatives to instigate historical forces.

These environmental and historical contexts in which preindustrial communities unfolded required them to be dynamic, ever-adapting entities. Communities responded to multiple forces generated from surrounding contexts, some of which was feedback from their own actions in these arenas. So if a community overexploited the natural resources around them, leading to landscape degradation, their annual yields would be reduced, causing the community to reorganize their production routines and possibly to rethink their strategies of landscape use. Or by refusing to participate in new regional political and economic organizations, communities might find themselves left behind or victims of ambitious polities seeking to expand their reach. That communities could adapt to these shifting circumstances should not be surprising; after all, the 1955 seminar participants recognized that communities followed evolutionary trajectories based on their mobility patterns. This community perspective, in emphasizing adaptation, instead recognizes that because the sources of change were potentially multiple and varied in their intensity, the configuration in which communities reorganized themselves was highly unpredictable. Therefore, a community must be investigated at multiple points in its historical development, and the reasons for these changes identified.

When invoking the language of adaptation that complex adaptive systems research employs, one must not lose sight of the fact that in preindustrial communities, face-to-face interactions were a distinguishing characteristic of members' relationships. Such intimacy between members fostered the dependent relationships that formed the basic fabric of a community's social life. The community is the outcome of all the relationships it contains; without the complex nexus of all interactions, the community ceases to exist. This community perspective therefore, like Yaeger's (2000) investigation of the San Lorenzo community, draws on many aspects of practice theory that complements the frameworks offered by complex adaptive systems thinking. Practice theory offers ways to envision relationships within a social field. Members participate in this field according to a set of conscious (discourse) and unconscious (doxa) norms and beliefs about relationships and behaviors, and are connected to each other through a web of interactions and relationships. Community solidarity is maintained through both discursive and nondiscursive social contracts expressed in language, metaphors, symbols, everyday practices, and rituals that rationalize communal life. Yet these shared sets of ideas about membership and community are potentially unstable, moving between community doxa and discourse. Actors may invent and experiment with new ways of being and belonging that challenge broadly shared understandings of membership.[5]

A second contribution of practice theory to this community perspective is the finding that various types of capital, which members and segments may use to position themselves, circulate within this social field. Following Bourdieu (1977, 1984), such capital can be divided into different kinds of spheres, such as symbolic and economic wealth. Individuals may garner and convert capital between these spheres. In preindustrial communities, economic capital would include, for instance, naturally occurring resources or surplus agricultural products that could be exchanged for services or other goods. Such a division between symbolic and economic capital, however, is limited in preindustrial economies where markets were often unregulated and where gifting and redistribution practices were normative. In preindustrial communities, intangible forms of capital such as knowledge, labor, and charisma could have played both pragmatic and symbolic roles. Members could exchange or withhold information from each other, cooperate or boycott group labor projects, join or abandon different communities, and follow or ignore individuals who established themselves in positions of authority. Because capital is an important resource in the reproduction of community relationships, the ways it is produced structure and mediate these relationships. Through production, capital is converted into usable resources on which the community depends. In ancient communities, locally available and naturally occurring resources are transformed into agricultural products, tools, and buildings. Less tangible, but equally important, forms of capital such as labor and charisma are likewise converted into tangible resources such as buildings and surplus agricultural products. How individuals, segments, and the overall community think about production and discover new ways of converting capital are located in consciousness, and like norms and beliefs about relationships, are subject to change as knowledge moves between doxa and discourse, heterodoxy and orthodoxy.

This attention to the production, distribution, and conversion of capital is useful for examining preindustrial communities from the archaeological record they have left behind. In preindustrial settings, agrarian communities dedicated a considerable amount of their time to the production of food, buildings, and tools needed for subsistence. Physical evidence for production as well as the finished products that were the result of these practices are commonplace. Attending to the distribution of capital helps recognize how and where wealth accumulates and can produce inequalities between persons or households. In other words, investigating the distribution and flow of capital within a community makes these hierarchies apparent. As this control over production becomes concentrated in individuals and institutions, positions of leadership in the community may emerge and come to control different aspects of social life.

Recognizing that social differentiation can emerge in communities pushes against the notion that the form is by definition a strictly egalitarian social nexus. Instead, capital can become concentrated in particular persons or segments, bolstering owners' authority over fellow members. Individuals who invent, control, and manage the flow of ideas about power, wealth, and production are most likely to organize the community's worldview, accumulate power, and grow to become community leaders. Successfully transforming everyday unquestioned production routines such as building and cooking into required labor projects and feasts permitted these emergent leaders to redirect wealth in their own direction. Leadership in preindustrial communities was more than simply managing the production of capital, though. Leaders could manipulate the community's consciousness about social cohesion and everyday life. They provided and supported a community's rationalizations for different relationships and unequal access to power, knowledge, and capital. In managing "consciousness," leaders walked a fine line between doxa and discourse, possessing knowledge about the community and its social organization that was not broadly shared by their constituents. But authority cannot merely be described as a feature that is present or absent in preindustrial communities. The extent to which leadership pervaded the community was not necessarily absolute, and the extent to which leaders held sway over their constituents must be investigated. Leaders' abilities to manage community practices would depend on their access to symbolic and physical capital that could be used to coerce members into participation. Just as the extent to which leaders dominated every aspect of the community's social life can be questioned, one should also suspect the regularity of their authority over time. Leaders' authority may have peaked and declined throughout the year, depending on community events such as agricultural harvests and scheduled festivals.

Careful attention to the arrangement and intensity of production activities helps determine the extent to which leaders' authority pervaded the community. Building on Hayden and Cannon's (1982) suggestions described earlier, it is possible to consider, on the one hand, those activities that required management and scheduling and, on the other hand, those activities that required cooperation between members and between members and leaders. One can ask whether it is possible to identify differences between production practices that benefit the larger community and practices that benefit certain individuals or segments in the community. In instances where the latter case is identifiable, there is the opportunity to learn how capital was accumulated through the organization of mundane activities in which the entire community participated.

This community perspective developed in the last several pages integrates elements of both complex adaptive systems thinking and practice theory into a phenomenon that will be referred to in this work as "communal complexity." Communal complexity is a condition in which communities demonstrated unpredictable transformations in their organizational structure, but still retained the features of small-scale societies. Communal complexity may be the first moment in the very long and uneven chain of organizational developments, the trials and errors of small-scale political and economic institutions that could eventually grow into larger systems that preoccupy archaeological research such as preindustrial cities (Marcus and Sabloff 2008) and archaic states (Feinman and Marcus 1998). The phenomenon of communal complexity will continue to be developed in this and later chapters, but it must be stated at the onset that not all preindustrial communities necessarily demonstrated such dynamic forms of organization. Communal complexity was in itself a strategic response to conditions that offered communities the resilience needed to maintain their existence.

Communal Resilience in Marginal Conditions

Resilience studies offers human organizational studies, including archaeology (Redman 2005), useful ways for understanding how social cohesion is maintained during periods of stress. Recent transdisciplinary research on complex adaptive systems shares a definition of resilience as "the ability of a system to absorb disturbance and still retain its function and structure" (Walker and Salt 2006:1). These studies take issue with the commonplace viewpoint that organizational optimization is a positive goal, an aim in which a system's ideal state is reached and maintained in order to maximize benefits. Although such conditions are attractive, resilience theory warns that a system in its optimal state often grows increasingly specialized, potentially losing the flexibility to adapt to unpredictable stressors that challenge the system's integrity. Therefore, the more optimization a system builds, the less resilient it becomes to change. If the system cannot adapt to new conditions—a return to more flexible practices, for instance—it may enter a period of transformation that could lead to its decline.[6]

Human societies have demonstrated tendencies to optimize their organizational capacities for millennia, only to find that the strategies they had developed could not be sustained in the face of adversity. Some challenges originate from outside society, such as climate change and increased economic competition. Other challenges may be feedback resulting from their own optimization strategies such as landscape degradation. Scholars, particularly historical ecologists, geographers, and of course archaeologists, have consistently demonstrated in their research on the human past how societies weather these changes. The popular "collapse" discourse that has persisted in Western historiography, from Edward Gibbon's classic *The History of the Decline and Fall of the Roman Empire* (1776–1789) to Jared Diamond's recent and very popular *Guns, Germs, and Steel: The Fates of Human Societies* (1997) and *Collapse: How Societies Choose to Fail or Succeed* (2005), reflects deep desires to interpret these failed attempts at optimization in moral terms—they are the result of some human shortcoming, whether it is religious belief or abuse of environmental resources. Complex adaptive systems thinking offers alternative and often more empirical frameworks for evaluating changes in human organizational dynamics, as a recent volume of studies responding to Diamond's *Collapse* demonstrates (McAnany and Yoffee 2010).

One such offering from resilience studies conceives of these changes in organizational dynamics as phases in an adaptive cycle.[7] At the beginning of the cycle, an organization can experience rapid growth (r phase) as new opportunities and resources are exploited aggressively under weakly regulated conditions. In the next, conservation phase (K phase), organizations begin to optimize their management strategies under more specialized conditions. Materials accumulate, expertise increases, and connections between actors and institutions grow more regulated. Growth may continue, but not at the rate it did in the prior stage. In the later stages of this phase, groups can approach the rigid optimization levels that make them less resilient to uncertainty. One distinguishing feature between the growth and the conservation phases is the differences in actors' behaviors that create the conditions under which each phase develops. In the growth phase, actors are opportunists who think in short time horizons and operate in dynamic environments in their accumulation of resources. Alternatively, actors who are conservative and efficient in their management strategies characterize the conservation phase. They are specialists who think and operate at larger scales. The growth and the conservation phases together contribute to a development loop that fosters the organization's generation and growth. As the adaptive cycle continues, however, organizations can enter a back loop, characterized by two other phases. In the first release phase (Omega phase), the system encounters a disturbance that surpasses its resilience. The specialized infrastructure built to optimize benefits begins to unravel, and control of resources is weakened or lost altogether. Following this is the reorganization phase (Alpha phase) in which a system reconfigures itself. New leaders and management modes can appear during this phase that will shape the system in the next growth phase in ways that are unrecognizable from its previous configuration.

These moments of transition between (and sometimes within) phases deserve a closer look. Multiple variables act on and react to a system, shaping its development over time. Resilience studies have envisioned the way this shaping unfolds using a ball-in-a-basin metaphor in which the ball is the system and the basin is a set of variables (Gunderson, Allen, and Holling 2009; Walker and Salt 2006). While the ball moves toward equilibrium—the bottom of the basin—the variables that shape the basin shift, making the equilibrium point difficult to reach and impossible to maintain. When variables change significantly, a new equilibrium is established around them, creating a new basin. This basin may be either a new phase in an adaptive cycle or a new subphase within a cycle, but in both instances, the system has crossed over a threshold in which it is difficult, if not impossible, to return. A system's resilience, then, is most tested when the ball reaches the basin's edge, the point furthest from a basin's equilibrium. In such a position, the system is absorbing the most disturbances from the variables shaping it. The potential for the system to migrate to a new basin is high if it cannot completely manage these changes while operating within its current conditions. A sustainable system, therefore, requires an awareness of these thresholds and the construction of buffers that avoid them or at least mitigate them as they are approached and crossed.[8]

Thinking about resilience in terms of adaptive phases, equilibriums, and thresholds has implications for archaeological investigations of preindustrial communities and the phenomenon of communal complexity. The organizational shifts that characterize communal complexity can be envisioned as a group's attempts to recalibrate itself for the sake of maintaining equilibrium in response to changes. Communal complexity strategies could assist groups in building buffers that helped avoid rigid organizational optimization. Resilience frameworks also offer ways to rethink a community's final moments, when it enters the back loop of an adaptive cycle, its release and reorganization phases. The reconstitution of the community under its former guise may not necessarily have been the most ideal choice under the new conditions members faced. Other alternatives may have been more viable, such as new locations, lifestyle modes (e.g., nomadism), and resource uses. Therefore, the end of the community, or any other organizational form for that matter, should not bear the retrospective judgments that are so popular in current collapse studies (e.g., Diamond 2005).

Investigations of resilience in past societies emphasize instances that emerged in contexts that were initially well suited for political, economic, and organizational complexity. But because of the human interventions needed to maintain this complexity, as well as external events beyond a society's control, these contexts grew less ideal over time. Often overlooked are those societies that established themselves in already challenging contexts. These less-than-optimal spaces and conditions that some communities came to inhabit are broadly classified in this work as marginal. Invoking the notion of marginality introduces essentializing images of spatial binaries between core and periphery—if there are margins, there must be a center, after all—that have persisted in the social sciences, as in Immanuel Wallerstein's writings on world-systems theory (1974). Archaeologists, too, have used core-periphery frameworks for characterizing those societies that fall on the edges of powerful polities such as states and empires. In several instances, these interpretations of peripheries have been skewed by twentieth-century perceptions of underdeveloped "third world" societies (Rowlands 1987; more broadly, Escobar 1995). Marginal societies are perceived to be victims who were pushed to peripheries by more powerful groups. Living in the margins, they are not capable of organizing self-sustaining practices and institutions that can match that of the core society.

But a closer consideration of peripheries reveals a far more complicated picture that cannot be explained merely by its location vis-à-vis a center. People, places, and things located on the margins are not necessarily faint shadows of more normative conditions found in dominant centers, a lesson that the postcolonial critique of core-periphery relations has revealed (Bhabha 1994). The margins can be places where innovation and creativity are born from the unique position in which societies find themselves. Entirely new ways of being and becoming can be fostered there to create unprecedented cultural practices. Until recently (e.g., Liebmann and Rizvi 2008), archaeologists struggled to identify such subaltern practices in past societies. Societies on the margins can be located in areas that are physically difficult to reach or some distance away from elite or sizable population centers, contexts that archaeological sampling strategies have traditionally favored. Marginal societies, furthermore, may not always produce the kinds of written sources that make their historical reconstruction easy. This lack of written sources could have been because of low rates of literacy or the absence of cultural industries in which scribes and artisans often played key roles in documenting group identities, beliefs, and practices. This absence of written records does not imply that societies on the margins are "without history" (sensu Wolf 1982). Rather, cultural memory and identities can be expressed through media other than texts. Nor are conditions on the margins necessarily permanent. Climates could change, dominant political powers could crumble, and shifting market demands could create new avenues to wealth. An archaeology of the margins, therefore, requires an entirely new set of sensibilities.

That communities could have persisted and even sometimes thrived in marginal spaces can be surprising to those scholars who operate under rational-choice assumptions that humans make decisions to maximize reproductive fitness, safety, and wealth. So when considering the archaeological investigation of preindustrial communities, one is faced with the question of how communities survived under difficult conditions. One might predict that a community living under marginal conditions would move through adaptive cycles faster than their counterparts in more ideal conditions because of the number of stresses marginal conditions offered. An initial growth phase could establish a community infrastructure; during a conservation phase, it could adjust this infrastructure and associated practices to the difficult conditions. Still, maintaining equilibrium would be difficult when unanticipated events destabilized the organizational practices that the community had developed. When a community grew too optimized and failed to build buffers to insulate itself from unanticipated events, it could enter a release phase in which control over resources was lost. If fortunate, the community could enter a reorganization phase in which it could recover its footing. A community would potentially increase its resilience as it moved through these adaptive cycles, learning from its missteps and instituting changes in practices during the growth phase of a new adaptive cycle.

Potentially, then, communal complexity could be both a necessary consequence of this system as well as a flexible means through which resilience was built over time. The dynamic shifts that a community faced during the course of an adaptive cycle could have, for instance, consequences for the circulation of wealth among members. Those who were more successful than others in amassing capital in tangible and intangible forms were more likely to survive the back loops of adaptive cycles. Inequality, therefore, could emerge during such periods of stress, say, when weaker households became dependent on more successful ones. Additionally, as noted earlier, the organization of leadership could shift at certain points in the cycle, depending on what kind of opportunities were available to seize authority. One might imagine that during periods of stress, strong leaders with managerial skills could appear, making decisions that either benefitted them and their immediate dependents alone or the broader community. The ability to make these shifts in a manner in which wealth circulated and decisions were made was one important element in building a resilient community.

Communal Complexity in Middle Eastern Marginal Zones

Archaeological investigations have determined that preindustrial Middle Eastern communities have persisted throughout the region's history since sedentary life began in limited form during the Epipaleolithic Period twenty millennia ago. Prehistoric communities have admittedly received more sophisticated treatment than their counterparts in historic periods. In the former, questions of social organization (Kuijt 2000), subsistence strategies (Köhler-Rollefson and Rollefson 1990), and adaptation to climate change (McCorriston and Hole 1991) are common lines of inquiry. Communities dating to historical periods, on the other hand, are studied first and foremost to determine where they fit in regional cultural-historical frameworks. Only occasionally do studies that consider the evidence in terms of larger themes like those discussed earlier appear (e.g., Faust 2006).[9] A panoramic glance at Near Eastern communities, regardless of their dates of existence, reveals that many were based on varying combinations of agriculture, pastoralism, and craft production. These production practices were primarily designed to meet local subsistence needs for daily consumption and, at times, build surplus buffers against unpredictable events (e.g., drought). Communities that resided within polities like city-states and empires often increased outputs in order to participate in market systems or meet extraction demands from governing authorities. Despite the growth and decline of these political systems, however, the Middle Eastern community persisted as a *genre de vie*, albeit in various manifestations depending on the local, regional, and global contingencies that structured them. A longitudinal panoramic perspective indicates that the agro-pastoral community was a persistent building block in preindustrial Middle Eastern societies.

The community in Mesoamerica and North America has received more acknowledgment than its counterpart in the Middle East, despite its demonstrated persistence throughout the latter region's history. This oversight is partly a result of archaeological sampling strategies. Near Eastern archaeologists and the universities, museums, and agencies that fund their research have commonly based their research on large settlements that hosted the urban societies that have come to typify Near Eastern civilizations. The introduction of landscape survey techniques in the discipline did lead to the identification of smaller settlements, although the number that have been sampled over the decades pales compared to the attention that tell settlements receive in Near Eastern archaeology. When smaller settlements are excavated, horizontal exposures of the settlement are limited to a few buildings. Instead, deep vertical investigations are favored to understand questions of diachronic change. These data collection strategies consequently impede the ability to measure the nature of relationships across a significant portion of a single settlement.

The other reason the community is underconsidered in Near Eastern archaeological research is that data have been interpreted in terms of alternative analytical units, such as the household (Schloen 2001; Stager 1985) and the tribe (LaBianca and Younker 1995; Younker 1997). Although both are perennial units in the analysis of Middle Eastern societies, past and present, one can consider the extent to which they are appropriate scales at which to examine local collectives. Household archaeology is a necessary component of a community perspective because it could be a basic denominator in organizing production and social life. Understanding how household production practices compared to each other within a single community reveals patterns that can be compared to determine relative wealth and opportunities for collaboration. The tribe, however, is problematic because it does not necessarily "fit" easily over physical evidence; it is a way of organizing people who are within a broad kin group but are not necessarily living adjacent to each other. For these reasons, community perspectives have long been a missing and undervalued element in Near Eastern archaeology. Its use can potentially bring several benefits to the analysis of small-scale societies in the region, regardless of time period and political and economic conditions.

Whether or not small-scale sedentary groups in the Near East are examined as communities, the discipline's emphasis on the geographic paradigm of the Fertile Crescent draws scholarly attention away from instances residing on the margins. First envisioned by James Henry Breasted (1906), the Fertile Crescent paradigm instructs that the arc that begins in the Levant, turns east into northern Syria and southeastern Turkey, and then travels south and east down the Zagros Mountains into Iraq and Iran was the only place where sedentary settlement was possible. Indeed, the Fertile Crescent possesses several zones of relative natural abundance, including sufficient precipitation, freshwater streams, and above-average soils that together make much of the region ideal for agricultural production. Given these conditions, it should not be surprising that archaeologists have concentrated their attention on the agro-pastoral settlements in this region. What is lacking, however, is an understanding of the sedentary communities that lived in the Middle East's marginal zones, on the edges or even outside the Fertile Crescent. These areas, although vastly different in their composition, can be broadly categorized as arid zones that are marked by limited amounts of seasonal precipitation and borderline to inadequate soil quality. Together, these two factors played significant structuring roles in the subsistence regimes of those who lived in such zones.

Not only has the Fertile Crescent paradigm drawn scholars' attention away from the Middle East's arid zones, but an associated paradigm leads them to believe that sedentary societies could not even inhabit such zones. The desert and sown paradigm has persisted in Near Eastern archaeological research for almost a century (Bell 1907; Coon 1951). According to this model, those groups that typically lived outside of the Fertile Crescent were believed to be pastoral nomads who spent the cooler months in the region's arid climates and moved into more temperate climates during the warmer months. The origin of this paradigm is based on early observations of nineteenth- and early twentieth-century Middle Eastern settlement dynamics that historians and archaeologists adopted to explain past societies. A superficial glance at the available archaeological evidence, however, indicates that the Middle East's arid zones were characterized by limited population numbers and below-average investment in settlement infrastructure. Middle Eastern countries falling outside the Fertile Crescent paradigm, where Near Eastern archaeological research has been relatively less intensive, are the best contexts in which to search for such settlement activity. Archaeological evidence from Yemen, Saudi Arabia, and other Gulf countries like Oman, Qatar, and Bahrain indicate that past societies living in these countries' arid zones had the capacity to organize sedentary populations, build sophisticated hydrological infrastructure, and manage agricultural production (e.g., Wilkinson 2006). Considering this evidence, however, is difficult because arid-zone settlements tend to be either understudied or underpublished in the available literature.

Of course, not all Middle Eastern arid zones are similar in their constitution, and each presents unique and changing circumstances. Changes in weather and climate over the millennia, as well as human interventions in the landscape such as intensified agriculture, have transformed Middle Eastern landscapes so much that current conditions may not reflect those in the past.[10] Semi-arid zones, a particular subgenre of arid zones, present an interesting venue for the investigation of preindustrial communities in the Middle East. Semi-arid zones are characterized by poor soils and limited annual precipitation (150 to 300 mm), conditions barely suitable for rain-fed agricultural production (Wallén 1967). Ethnographic and archaeological investigations demonstrate that producers working in semi-arid zones can intensify output beyond subsistence levels to produce surplus amounts of product (e.g., Barker 1996; Doolittle 1988; Larson 1996; Rosen 2007:150–171; see various authors in Barker and Gilbertson 2000), despite the long-held popular belief that such projects are impossible. Because semi-arid environments are often characterized by desiccated landscapes with uneven distributions and differences in quality of natural resources, producers in semi-arid zones can choose different strategies to maximize their use of available resources, to reduce risk, and to create subsistence buffers in anticipation of lean years. For example, agricultural producers can either invest labor and resources in agricultural technologies that can create new or preserve currently eroding soil beds (e.g., terraces) or organize production in locations with preexisting resources that require little front-end investment but may be distant from their homes or processing centers. Animal economies can also take various forms, such as adjustments in the time and amount of herd culling based on market demand or on the limited amounts of water and fodder during the late summer months or lean years. Craft producers who depend on resources such as clays, water, and fuel that can be limited in semi-arid environments can organize their industries to meet the local subsistence needs or expand to service agricultural and animal industries (e.g., the production of storage vessels).

Evidence for sedentary life in the Middle East's semi-arid zones is most abundant in the narrow regions between the Fertile Crescent and the arid zones of the Arabian Peninsula. Settlement in these zones occurs in almost every period of Middle Eastern history. Yet the most intensive settlement activity occurred during periods when states and empires sought to intensify their agrarian economies. Either at the behest of these polities, or on their own initiative in response to market demands, producers sought to develop these marginal lands to increase product output. The best-documented instances of these intensification measures are visible during the Near East's Classical Period under the Roman and Byzantine Empires. Examples include the so-called Dead Cities in northwest Syria, the Haran region in southern Syria, and the sedentary settlements in the northern Negev Desert such as Byzantine-era Subeita (Segal 1983). In Jordan's semi-arid zones, the Roman army constructed a network of forts and settlements to defend the Levant from nomadic groups who threatened the empire's agricultural investments (Parker 2006). The demands of states and empires for raw materials and the markets these polities inevitably created explain why semi-arid zones saw so much intensification. Producers, assuming a guaranteed return on whatever they grew or made, were confident enough to invest their labor and time in water- and soil-management infrastructure that made agriculture possible.

But Middle Eastern societies did not necessarily need empires and markets to convince them to create sedentary settlements in arid zones. There are instances where settlements arose on their own accord in marginal environments. For example, in the deserts of northeast Jordan, Jawa was occupied twice: once in the late fourth millennium during the Early Bronze Ib period; and again in the second millennium BCE during the MBIIA period (Betts 1991; Helms 1981). Each settlement episode existed for only a few decades, and there is no evidence that the town was designed for anything more than the immediate subsistence of the community. The Early Bronze Age settlement was over twelve hectares in overall size, and at least five hectares were used for human settlement. Helms (1981:130) estimated a maximum population of between four and five thousand people based on demographic calculations using aerial and surface survey of building architecture exposed on the site's surface. Public architecture such as gates and fortifications were also built, indicating that local populations dedicated resources and energy to their construction. Additionally, a complex hydrological storage system designed to capture and store seasonal runoff precipitation was built next to the settlement. The impressive size and sophistications of a sedentary settlement such as Jawa in an arid zone illustrate that complex social formations were possible in the Middle East's marginal zones without the guiding hand of larger political and economic regional institutions.

There are several reasons to suspect that communal complexity facilitated sedentary life in arid and semi-arid zone settlements such as Jawa and elsewhere in the Middle East. One reason is the nature of production, as subsistence under such austere conditions could yield unequal amounts of wealth. To reduce competition over resources, communities could manage production and wealth collectively. However, if household and communal production co-occurred, individual households might still accrue more wealth than their neighbors. During droughts or famine, those households that accumulated surplus wealth increased their chances for survival. Because this wealth could be shared with other households, relationships of dependency were formed. These emergent asymmetrical relationships did not necessarily bring an end to communal conditions, however. Rather, these debts and dependencies could be temporary, like gifts, since the arrangements of power had been carefully set for the whims of marginal environments. Moreover, shifting between communal and ranked conditions might ultimately be viewed as a strategy for the groups' long-term survival. Communal complexity also provided the resilience needed to adapt to new circumstances. In small-scale societies living under marginal economic conditions, subsistence and social organization are carefully arranged to maximize output and to maintain buffers to guarantee survival. On the one hand, such societies were vulnerable to shifts in environmental conditions that could lead them to reorganize their practices or their governing structures or to dismantle the community. On the other hand, the effects that small-scale societies could have on the socionatural system of which they were a part should not be underestimated. The tendency to overexploit the natural resources around them or the mismanagement of subsistence infrastructure could have dire effects on the environment.

Conclusion

Resilient communities in the preindustrial past exhibited several features that made it possible to face the uncertainties of environmental, economic, and political change. Therefore, documenting their diversity in the archaeological record is as important as doing so for any larger phenomenon such as cities and states. Because communities, like all social phenomena, are dynamic entities, they should be expected to change as the circumstances around them unfold. The archaeological investigation of communities is littered with examples in which communities reorganized themselves and even chose to abandon their circumstances altogether. Retrospectively judging these changes in moral terms makes little sense. Rather, these decisions should be interpreted with a neutral tone, as responses to changing circumstances. Such a stance is quite different from the "collapse" perspectives that often characterize the ends of societies as unfortunate (Diamond 1997, 2005). Perhaps the abandonment of the community was the best decision its members could make considering the circumstances they faced? This and related questions will be explored in later chapters when the development of west-central Jordan's Early Iron Age communities are investigated.

CHAPTER THREE

Measuring Social Complexity in the Early Iron Age

Archaeologists are rarely drawn to periods in history known for declining levels of social complexity. These eras lack the traditional trappings of civilization—urban centers, bureaucracies, written archives, and monumental architecture—for which archaeological research is most celebrated. The enormous amount of scholarly attention the Early Iron Age southern Levant has received throughout the twentieth century therefore stands as a surprising exception. When surveying the vast body of secondary literature, it is easy to surmise that the number of scholars writing on the subject could possibly exceed the number of people who lived during this two-century period of Levantine history! The reason this period has received so much attention, of course, is its relationship to the Hebrew Bible, a document that European and North American societies as well as three major world religions claim as a foundational source. The Hebrew Bible, particularly its Books of Joshua, Judges, and Samuel, describes the introduction of the narrative's key protagonist, the Israelites, and a number of their adversaries, such as the Philistines, Moabites, and the indigenous Canaanites.[1] Indeed, an entire disciplinary industry, biblical archaeology, emerged in the early twentieth century with the goal of locating physical evidence for biblical societies and the historical events described in the narrative (Moorey 1991). These efforts have continued relatively unabated up to the current day (e.g., Hoffmeier and Millard 2004; Levy 2010). Whether or not one believes that the search for an archaeological realia for the biblical narrative is a worthwhile endeavor, one must admit that these efforts have produced an enormous body of archaeological data from which Early Iron Age

Levantine societies can be studied using historical and social scientific research methods. Landscape surveys, settlement excavations, and artifact analyses have produced data that help reconstruct the period's political and economic organization, subsistence strategies, ethnic identities, and religious practices. Collectively, this evidence indicates that the southern Levant during the Early Iron Age was a period of widespread deflated social complexity compared to the centuries before and after it. The once great urban city-states of the Bronze Age Canaanites were almost completely abandoned during this period. Aside from the commercial entrepots lining the Mediterranean coastal plain, much of the region experienced a widespread ruralization in which political and economic organization was managed at local levels—a perfect setting for the investigation of complex communities.

Crisis and Recovery in the Late Second Millennium BCE

The extent to which regional social complexity deflated in the Early Iron Age Levant is evident when one compares this period to the centuries leading up to and following it. The Early Iron Age was framed by two periods of region-wide political and economic complexity: the Bronze Age city-states that dominated the region for most of the second millennium BCE, and the territorial polities that developed during the first half of the first millennium such as Ammon, Israel, Judah, and Moab. The Middle Bronze Age (2000–1550 BCE) had witnessed the florescence of a society organized into city-states that shared similar linguistic and cultural practices that scholars collectively describe as "Canaanite."[2] Written sources as well as archaeological evidence attest to the degree of social complexity Middle Bronze Age societies experienced during the almost five-century period. Urban centers along the Mediterranean coast as well as inland were positioned along commercial routes linking the region with the rest of the Mediterranean Basin (e.g., Greece and Egypt) and the Near East (e.g., Mesopotamia and Anatolia). Many settlements such as Hazor, Shechem, and Megiddo boasted urban centers with complex fortification systems that required a significant contribution of human labor (Burke 2008). The material culture of this period indicates sophisticated craft industries, especially bronze, ivory, and decorated ceramic vessels. By the eighteenth century, Canaanite society was powerful enough to fill the vacuum left behind by the demise of Egypt's Middle Kingdom. Soon after, Canaanites described in Egyptian textual sources as "Hyksos" appeared throughout the Nile Delta, founding a capital at Avaris, modern Tell el-Daba'a.

Canaanite society's development was curtailed in the Late Bronze Age (1550–1200 BCE) when Egypt's Eighteenth Dynasty under its founder, Pharaoh Ahmose, began efforts to reconsolidate Egyptian rule. Almost a century later, Thutmose III campaigned through the southern Levant, weakening or destroying a number of Canaanite city-states, a feat described in the Amun temple at Karnak in Thebes. Thus, from this point on until approximately 1200 BCE, New Kingdom Egypt managed southern Levantine society, albeit at varying levels of intensity (Higginbotham 2000; Leonard 1989; Redford 1992:192–213; Weinstein 1982). Egyptian interest in the southern Levant was strategic, concerned most with controlling the region's commercial routes leading to lucrative markets in Syria and Mesopotamia (Redford 1992:192–213). In order to monitor these roads, military garrisons were stationed along commercial routes and adjacent agricultural lands that supplied rations for officials and soldiers. Although historical sources describe the tribute they collected from the region, Egypt seems to have had little interest in developing the southern Levant's agricultural output beyond that of preexisting levels (Ahituv 1978; Redford 1992:213).

Despite the limited interest New Kingdom Egypt held for the southern Levant, local Canaanite elites were influenced by Egyptian society. The type and number of objects bearing Egyptian qualities that were discovered in the palaces and tombs of the region suggest that local Canaanite leaders emulated the practices and the styles of their Egyptian overlords (Higginbotham 2000). Living apart from the Egyptian garrisons, these elites resided in the capitals of the former Middle Bronze Age city-states. Imported Egyptian, as well as Mycenaean and Cypriot, artifacts have been discovered in these residences as well as in mortuary contexts, signaling the relative wealth of elites and their access to international markets. The relationship between Egypt and Canaan is partially revealed in the correspondence between the pharaohs of the Eighteenth Dynasty and Levantine elites in an archive of fourteenth-century letters from Amarna, an Egyptian capital (Moran 1992). These letters describe a world in which royal elites appealed to the pharaoh for protection, while in return, they promised to perform the Egyptians' bidding whenever asked. The Amarna correspondence as well as archives found at Ugarit on the Syrian coast provide some glimpse into the structure of Canaanite society during the Late Bronze Age. Beneath the king who ruled a political territory akin to a city-state from his palace were *maryannu*, estate-owning nobles who managed the *hupshu*, or farmers, who carried out agricultural production in the countryside. Artisans were often attached to the palace and valued for the products they crafted, many of which circulated around the Near East and Eastern Mediterranean.[3] Beyond the palace's control were the *'apiru* and *shasu*, groups that the Canaanite kings frequently complained about for the problems they caused their administration and the region's safety.

In the second half of the thirteenth century, the Levant, along with the rest of the eastern Mediterranean, experienced a series of events that unsettled the region's political, economic, and social organization. The reasons for the destabilization are multiple, ranging from climate change to population movements. Although the sequence of these events and the roles they played in the region's collapse are still uncertain (Oren 2000; Ward and Joukowsky 1992), their effects are identifiable in both the written and archaeological record. These disturbances were severe enough to bring an end to the Hittite Empire and seriously curtail the eastern Mediterranean's palace economies and commercial networks. Written sources describe in a tone of peril the looming attack of marauding seafaring groups. The destruction of towns such as Ugarit along the Mediterranean coast suggests that these warnings were not mere false alarms. Scholars have described these groups collectively as the "Sea Peoples," a body of loosely united migrating groups that likely originated from the Aegean Sea and Cyprus (Yasur-Landau 2010). Ramses III described on the walls of his mortuary temple at Medinet Habu in Thebes how he fought and subdued these attackers in land and sea battles near the mouth of the Nile River. Following their defeat, the Egyptians settled what was left of these groups along the Levantine coast. One group, the Philistines mentioned in the Hebrew Bible, would go on to prosper through the Early Iron Age on the southern coastal plain between contemporary Gaza and Tel Aviv.

Beginning around 1200 BCE, southern Levantine society, like its counterparts throughout the eastern Mediterranean, began a slow recovery and once again became visible in archaeological and written evidence. The onset of the time period saw the demise of whatever was left of Egyptian imperial administration, and the Canaanite palace economies that had served as its vassals. Whatever happened during the Early Iron Age would eventually give way to a resurgence in political and social complexity across the region beginning in the tenth century and accelerating even more in the ninth century BCE (Herr 1997; Holladay 1995; Joffe 2002; Porter 2004; Routledge 2000). Most societies took the form of polities defined by royal elites who ruled a territory and agricultural hinterland from an urban capital. The most common sources used to reconstruct the history of polities such as ancient Israel, Judah, Moab, Edom, Phoenicia, Ammon, and Philistia are a number of epigraphic sources discovered in excavations (e.g., the Mesha Inscription, the Tel Dan Stele) and the Hebrew Bible, particularly the Books of Kings, Chronicles, and some of the prophetic books (e.g., the Books of Isaiah and Jeremiah). Most scholars agree that at least some portions of these biblical sources were written concurrently to the events they describe or at least used sources now lost to compose a narrative of events. By now, archaeologists and historians have collected enough data to determine that although these polities shared many features in common, they each developed a distinctive society based on local responses to their geographical and historical contexts. Each met a unique demise as well. Beginning in the ninth century BCE, each polity faced challenges from the empires that began in Mesopotamia—first the Assyrian Empire, and later, in the sixth century, the Babylonian Empire. By the time the Achaemenid Empire took administrative control of the southern Levant in the late sixth century, these polities were but mere shadows of their former selves.[4]

Beyond Ethnicity and History in the Early Iron Age

Given the emergence of these complex polities beginning in the tenth century BCE, one is left to wonder what developments occurred during the two centuries of the Early Iron Age that laid the groundwork for such changes? This question is not easily answered because of the paucity of reliable written sources and the partial nature of the published Early Iron Age archaeological record.[5] One cannot write the history of the Early Iron Age southern Levant in the same way that Bronze Age and later Iron Age histories are assembled. Epigraphic sources are limited to a handful of excavated inscriptions (e.g., the 'Izbet Sartah Inscription) that provide valuable paleographic insight into the continuity of writing traditions and scribal activity (Byrne 2007) but do not supply the kinds of information needed to piece together a broader regional history. Twelfth- and eleventh-century Egyptian sources do not add much more information about the southern Levant, unfortunately. This period saw the decline of the New Kingdom empire and a period of economic and political instability during the Twentieth Dynasty and the beginning of the Third Intermediate Period, a time of decentralization of the Egyptian state. Unlike the Late Bronze Age Amarna archives, there is no correspondence between Levantine rulers and the pharaohs to piece together a detailed Early Iron Age history of the relationship between the regions.

Scholars have found the brief mention of a group named "Israel" on a victory stele commemorating Pharaoh Merneptah's campaign through the Levant around 1207 BCE to be convincing enough proof for ancient Israel's existence at the start of the Early Iron Age (Hasel 1994). This brief citation has also justified the use of the Hebrew Bible, particularly the Books of Joshua, Judges, and Samuel, as a source for Early Iron Age historical events as well as mise-en-scène descriptions of daily life.[6] These books describe how the ancient Israelites settled Canaan following their migration from Egypt through Sinai and Jordan, displacing the Canaanites and clashing with the Philistines, a group who had also recently arrived in the Levant and settled on the southern coastal plain. The Israelites eventually established themselves throughout the southern Levant in what are described as rural agro-pastoral villages grouped into tribal territories. The Hebrew Bible defines early ancient Israel's political organization as a relatively decentralized tribal confederacy that united under a common cause when threatened by adversaries. The Book of Judges records that following Joshua's death, twelve successive charismatic leaders led the Israelites in war and adjudicated legal disputes. The Israelites eventually requested that a king be appointed to lead them (1 Samuel 8). The administration of their first king, Saul, was disastrous, but David eventually ascended the throne and established Jerusalem as a capital for the ancient Israelite polity, an event that historians date to around 1000 BCE.

Despite this early mention of ancient Israel in Merneptah's stele, the extent to which the biblical narrative is a reliable source for reconstructing Early Iron Age history is debated. Early twentieth-century archaeologists understood the narratives to be accounts that were orally transmitted over time before being written down in texts that would eventually be collated into the text's current form (e.g., Albright 1949:219–237, esp. 224–226). The chore for these early archaeologists therefore was to verify these descriptions through archaeological research. Assisted by the fact that many ancient site names had been preserved over the millennia in indigenous toponyms, these early projects gave priority to settlements featured in the narrative of the Israelites' conquest and settlement of Canaan, such as Jericho and Hazor. This research was instrumental in defining Early Iron Age settlement patterns and assemblages, although their primary goal was to link this evidence to the biblical narrative. Although interest in the archaeology of the Early Iron Age has never waned, its investigation from the latter half of the twentieth century until the current day has been structured by contemporary Middle Eastern geopolitical history. After the end of the British Mandate in Palestine and Transjordan, and the establishment of the State of Israel and the Hashemite Kingdom of Jordan in the late 1940s, archaeologists had less access to sites in militarized zones. Research continued in the Jordanian-controlled West Bank and the Israeli-controlled Galilee and coastal plain. After Israel occupied the West Bank and the Gaza Strip in 1967, Israeli archaeologists conducted surveys and excavations in these areas, greatly adding to the Early Iron Age data set (e.g., Dothan 2008; Finkelstein 1988; Finkelstein and Na'aman 1994; Zertal 2004). In Jordan, the number of excavation projects increased as well, focusing on west-central Jordan, particularly around 'Amman, the capital, and the Madaba Plains region to the south (e.g., Merling and Geraty 1993). As landscape survey became an essential part of project research design in the 1970s and 1980s, more regions were surveyed, settlements documented, and excavations conducted (e.g., Ibach 1987; Miller 1991). Currently, the Early Iron Age remains one of the Levant's most heavily researched time periods, although regional coverage across the Levant is uneven. Most excavations are concentrated in the southern coastal plain, west-central Jordan, and the Galilee.[7]

Collectively, this research demonstrates that settlement activity continued throughout much of the southern Levant during the Early Iron Age, although it was different from the previous Late Bronze Age. The limited occupational activity at the urban centers that administered the Levant's city-states indicates that palace-based elites lost control of the surrounding territory and their grip on agricultural producers. Instead, new settlement patterns emerged throughout the region that were diverse in character. Most syntheses focus on two contrasting regions in particular, the central highlands and the southern coastal plain, because it is in these regions that the biblical societies of early ancient Israel and Philistia are believed to have germinated (Albright 1939; Dever 2003; Finkelstein and Na'aman 1994; Gottwald 1979; Mendenhall 1962; Yasur-Landau 2010). Several small villages practicing agriculture and pastoralism to meet local subsistence needs occupied the central highlands according to landscape surveys and archaeological investigations. Many of these villages exhibit a distinct blueprint in which building walls are joined together to create an interior circular courtyard. Excavations have identified cisterns and storage bins associated with these structures that provided facilities for grain and water storage. Conversely, on the southern coastal plain, more densely populated settlements have been identified on the Mediterranean coast (e.g., Ashkelon, Gaza) and slightly inland along the river corridors that drained westward into the sea (e.g., Ekron, Gath). The organization of these settlements was more complex than those in the central highlands.

Not only did they participate in Mediterranean commercial activities but they also constructed towns with monumental architecture and organized grain, viticulture, and animal economies at levels beyond mere subsistence production.

When surveying the evidence for the Early Iron Age Levant, the marked differences between regions are striking. Although small agro-pastoralist settlements littered the landscape—even in the more environmentally marginal zones—larger populated settlements with more specialized and intensified economies lined the Mediterranean coast and the fertile river valley inland. An even closer examination of evidence within each region reveals some diversity in settlement planning, architectural design, artifact assemblages, and subsistence practices. These differences across space suggest that groups responded differently to historical events depending on local contingencies, such as availability of natural resources and access to markets, rather than region-wide political and economic forces. Consequently, any investigation of Early Iron Age society requires a careful consideration of evidence at the site-specific level to account for this diversity in social organization and practice. Although such local examination is often de rigueur for global archaeological research, the investigation of the Early Iron Age evidence has tended to remain at regional resolutions that miss the nuances of local diversity. Instead, scholars have practiced what can be described as ethnicizing and historicizing techniques that, by flattening diversity, create homogenized culture groups that can be emplaced in the biblical narrative, particularly those located in the Books of Joshua, Judges, and Samuel.

Ethnicizing and historicizing techniques have been practiced since evidence from the period was first discovered (Albright 1939). As Early Iron Age evidence emerged, ethnopolitical "zones" were designed using parameters typical of culture-historical archaeological research in the first half of the twentieth century (Willey and Sabloff 1993). Using the territorial boundaries described in the biblical narrative, archaeologists assigned ethnic labels to architectural and artifact assemblages found within these zones. Consequently, particular building designs and artifact types acquired labels such as "Israelite," "Moabite," and "Philistine." Scholars have also insisted on historicizing the Early Iron Age assemblage, that is, interpreting archaeological data in terms of the historical events that are reported to have taken place during the time period. Like ethnicizing, historicizing archaeological evidence was a common hermeneutical practice in early twentieth-century scholarship. Archaeological evidence was used to "fill in" periods lacking written sources or to corroborate events described in the sources. Although it was believed that history could be written using archaeological evidence alone, scholars often remained reluctant to point out instances that countered or complicated the written sources. If archaeological data did not fit the written sources, the evidence was classified as anomalous and set aside in favor of evidence that complemented the biblical evidence. Beginning in the early twentieth century, the growing Early Iron Age assemblage—everything from settlement and building design to ceramic vessel forms and faunal evidence—was studied with the intent of piecing together a history of Early Iron Age societies. The destruction of Late Bronze Age settlements and the appearance of an assemblage classified as "Israelite," for instance, was said to corroborate the conquest and settlement narrative described in the Books of Joshua and Judges.

Despite refinements and challenges, these ethnicizing and historicizing practices persisted through the twentieth century and continue to dominate the lenses that are used to interpret the Early Iron Age archaeological record (Bloch-Smith and Nakhai 1999; Dever 2003; Faust 2006; Killebrew 2005; Miller 2005; Stager 1995). To be fair, these frameworks do hold some practical utility as they provide a common nomenclature for scholars to share and discuss evidence. They are also categories that resonate with public audiences who are eager to see physical evidence for a text that is central to their faith or that strengthens nationalist and ethnic sentiments. More so, there are striking visible differences between regional assemblages that are impossible to deny, such as the contrast between the crude, plain cooking pots and storage jars of the "Israelite" central highlands with the well-decorated and highly fired vessels of the "Philistine" coastal plain. Yet just how homogenous are these ethnic assemblages when analyzed at the closest resolution possible? Their internal diversity raises the twin suspicion that ethnic groups were more permeable in antiquity than previously believed, and that one's membership in an ethnic group did not necessarily motivate the production and use of similar cultural forms within defined geographic areas.

This book is not the first, of course, to raise concerns with the reception of the Early Iron Age written and archaeological evidence. A handful of scholars have attempted to write social histories of the period using only excavated written sources, the archaeological evidence, and insights from the social sciences, particularly anthropology and geography (Coote 1990; Coote and Whitelam 1987; Lemche 1998; Thompson 1992; Whitelam 1996). Although different in their treatment of the evidence, these attempts have collectively played a critical role in highlighting problems with the evidence used to reconstruct the time period. A key concern for these scholars—and for those evaluating the utility of ethnicizing and historicizing practices—is with the treatment of the biblical narratives that inspired the ontology used to classify the Early Iron Age assemblage. Although the Books of Joshua, Judges, and Samuel describe events that purportedly took place in the Early Iron Age, most scholars agree that these episodes were not inscribed in written form until the early first millennium BCE, that is, a few centuries after they are assumed to have taken place. Accounts likely began as compositions that were transmitted from generation to generation in oral, not written, forms.[8] However early their date of composition, these texts were subjected to subsequent editing in the following centuries by scribes that scholars have labeled collectively as the Deuteronomistic School (Knoppers and McConville 2000). The school's scribes redacted the texts first in the eighth and seventh centuries in Jerusalem and again during the sixth-century exile in Babylon (Noth 1981). The Deuteronomistic School, loyal to the Davidic royal lineage and the cult of the Israelite's patrion deity, Yahweh, structured the Books of Joshua, Judges, Samuel, and others as a foil for later periods when ancient Israel was united under one king and a single cult. In the scribes' imagining of the Early Iron Age, anarchy and confusion predominate, and they report retrospectively, "In those days, there was no king in Israel; all the people did what was right in their own eyes" (Judges 21:25). Only after the Israelites request a king and Saul fails to successfully administer the office does David ascend the throne, unite the Israelite tribes, and establish the cult of Yahweh in Jerusalem, ushering in what the Deuteronomistic School believed to be a golden age in ancient Israel's history. Having undergone several editions, then, the Books of Joshua, Judges, and Samuel are not eyewitness accounts of Early Iron Age communities, but are in fact an assortment of stories, epic narratives, and songs subjected to a series of scribal additions and rearrangements that were made to present a specific proto-history of ancient Israel.

Perspective and authorship are also concerns for evaluating the use of the biblical narrative. Although irregular in its intensity and organization, Iron Age rural life—compared to that of urban environments—demonstrated more continuity in form and practice over time. As recent research on later Iron Age rural communities demonstrates (Faust 2000), the major difference between the Early Iron Age and later Iron Age was the urban, not the rural, social settings. It was scribes, not rural villagers, who participated in new bureaucratic and urban societies. With its focus on agricultural production in tiny settlement enclaves, Early Iron Age social life must have appeared quite different to the Deuteronomistic School, a group of trained specialists living in the urban, centralized polities that were the kingdoms of Israel and Judah. Some scribes may have lacked, or had limited, firsthand knowledge of manual labor, agricultural production, and village social organization that would have helped them accurately depict rural life. In order to present these oral and written compositions with some logical order, scribes may have looked to rural life in the later Iron Age period to create an analog for a more historically remote Early Iron Age rural setting.

This debate over whether or not the biblical narrative is an appropriate source for reconstructing Early Iron Age societies appears irresolvable and, indeed, an air of unsatisfying stalemate hangs over the conversation at this point. One's answer depends on one's intellectual position regarding how written sources are to be used in constructing histories as well as on how one is to harmonize archaeological data with written sources. All written sources, regardless of age or genre, contain their own internal problems of authorship, perspective, and translation that require contextualization and source criticism before they can be used to write a history. Yet, the complete rejection of the biblical narrative as a historical source is too extreme a position. This source contains several irresolvable complications such as those just described, of course, but it is also a rare, albeit dimly lit, window into Early Iron Age societies. For archaeologists, then, the most cautionary use of the Hebrew Bible is one in which the narrative is used to generate hypotheses that can be subsequently tested using data external to the text (e.g., archaeological evidence, visual culture, and excavated, provenanced epigraphic sources). In other words, the Hebrew Bible can neither confirm nor deny scholarly interpretations of the Early Iron Age archaeological record, but it can be a good source "to think with" (as will be done in this and later chapters), so long as the reader is aware of the source's limitations.

This admittedly conservative position on the use of the biblical narrative resists the urge to follow the scholarly conventions of ethnicizing and historicizing the Early Iron Age assemblage.[9] This position is taken in order to avoid two consequences these techniques have had on disciplinary inquiry. The first effect is that in the rush to place data in presupposed ethnic and chronological schema, subtle differences in features and patterning tend to be ignored or downplayed in order to arrive at "normative" presentations of social life. Instead, emphasis is placed on the presence or absence of key components (e.g., collared-rim jars, "four-room" houses) that fall within the defined ethnicized assemblage. In fact, these practices have often not encouraged archaeologists to recover the kinds of data that would permit higher-resolution analyses of Early Iron Age settlements such as paleobotanical remains, microartifacts, and architectural plans. It is possible that if less emphasis was placed on the ethnic identities of these Early Iron Age societies, it would open up other avenues of inquiry that would consider the internal diversity of recovered data. A community framework would permit an understanding of how each group organized themselves in light of the local contingencies that they faced rather than viewing communities and their actors as automatons who organized themselves according to an ethnic blueprint.

A second consequence of these ethnocizing and historicizing practices is that they have produced panoramas of Early Iron Age social life based on data from mainly two regions, the central highlands and the southern coastal plain, whereas they downplayed or ignored data in other Levantine regions. Consequently, scholarly reconstructions of Early Iron Age history present narratives that echo that of the biblical narrative: disparately organized highland agro-pastoralists ("Israelites") are contrasted with more organized coastal plain societies ("Philistines"). It is well past time to consider what other regions of the southern Levant can offer the investigation of Early Iron Age societies.

Measuring Social Complexity in West Central Jordan

One such productive but underconsidered region where Early Iron Age settlements are abundant is west-central Jordan, delimited by the Wadi al-Zarqa on the north, the Wadi al-Hasa on the south, and the Jordan Valley and the Arabian Desert on the west and east, respectively (fig. 3.1).[10] Archaeological investigations in the region have revealed a number of patterns that both compare and contrast with archaeological data from other Levantine regions, particularly the central highlands. Until the archaeological investigation of west-central Jordan began in the early twentieth century, scholars depended on the Hebrew Bible's description of the region's political organization during the second millennium BCE (e.g., Hope 1897). The Hebrew Bible reports that when the Israelites entered the region in the final decades of the Late Bronze Age, they encountered a political entity organized according to territory and ethnicity. The Arnon River—the modern Wadi al-Mujib—divided the territories of the Ammonites and the Moabites on the north and south, respectively (Numbers 21:26). In each territory were established kings such as Sihon of Heshbon

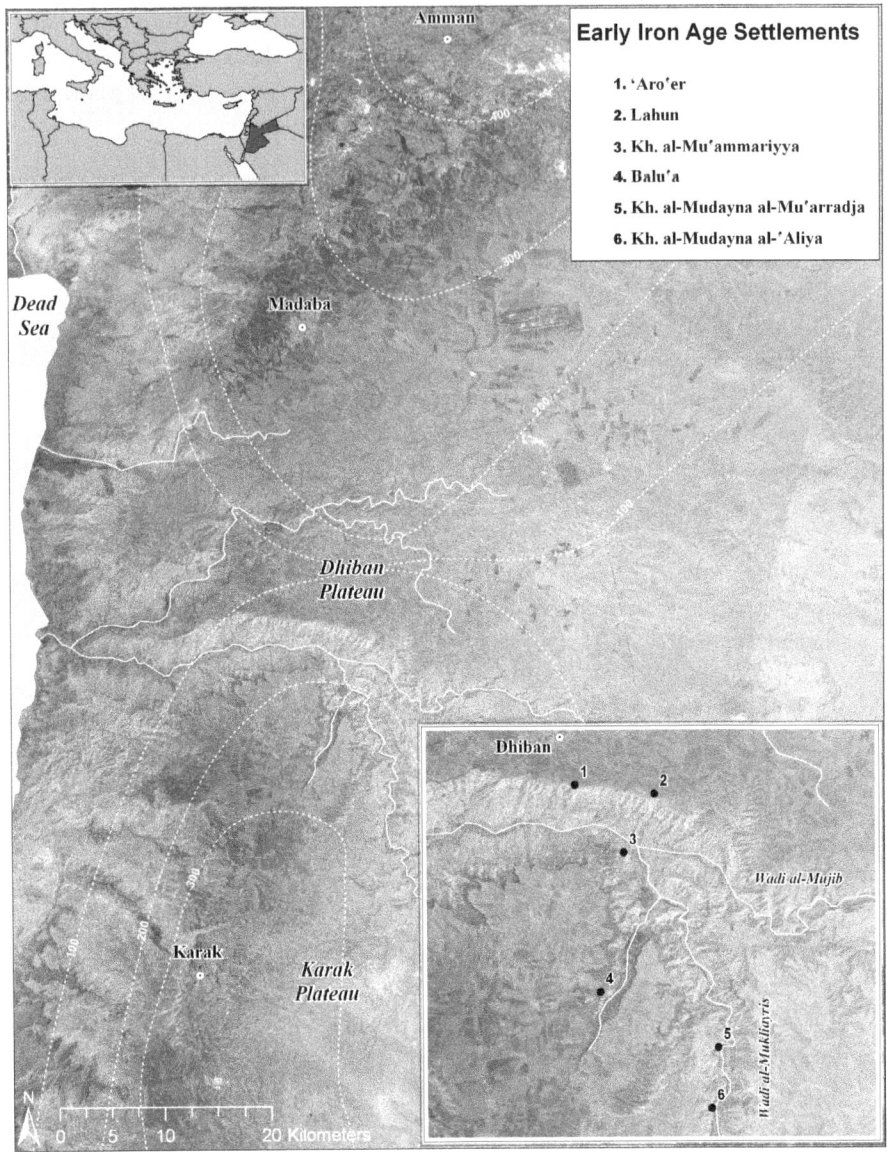

Figure 3.1. Map of Early Iron Age settlements in west-central Jordan concentrated on either side of the Wadi al-Mujib. Precipitation isohyets are represented as dashed lines. (*Source*: Image modified from SPOT; © Equinox Publishing Ltd. 2011)

(Numbers 21:26) and Balak of Moab (Numbers 22–23). Following the Israelites' military campaigns against these kings, the Israelite tribes of Reuben, Gad, and half of Manasseh reportedly settled the territory as far south as the Arnon (Joshua 22). The weakened Ammonites were pushed east and north, confined to the vicinity of modern 'Amman, while the Moabites remained south of the Arnon. Throughout the Early Iron Age, the Ammonites, Israelites, and Moabites remained adversaries. Stories of their conflicts are memorialized in the Book of Judges, most notably Ehud's assassination of Moab's King Eglon in Judges 3:12–30.

The biblical descriptions of political territories often describe the kings who administered them. The Hebrew Bible mentions four kings in Early Iron Age west-central Jordan: Sihon (Numbers 21:21–30), an anonymous Moabite king (Numbers 21: 26), Balak (Numbers 22–24), and Eglon (Judges 3:12–30). Before fighting with the Israelites and losing territory to them, Sihon is said to have battled with the anonymous Moabite king, the former winning territory from the latter as far as the Arnon River. Soon after, during the Israelites' encampment in the Plains of Moab (likely located in the Jordan Valley slightly northeast of the Dead Sea), Balak hires Bala'am to curse the Israelites. In a fourth instance, occurring much later in the biblical narrative during the period of the Judges, the biblical narrative reports how the Moabite king Eglon controlled the Israelites for eighteen years before Ehud assassinated him in his palace. Altogether, the Hebrew Bible's descriptions of west-central Jordan's elites suggest that kings were already established in the region by the end of the Late Bronze Age.

The biblical description of west-central Jordan's political organization would support the conclusion that the region was organized into kingdoms if it were not for the problematic date of this historical evidence. Commentators have concurred that Numbers 21–36, where many of these descriptions are located, was the work of multiple authors and editors, some of whom wrote several centuries after the events they purported to describe (Levine 2000:37–59; Milgrom 1992:1148; Noth 1968:4–11). The analysis of language and narrative suggests that Numbers 21–36 contains several early pericopae (e.g., the Heshbon Ballad, the Balaam narrative, and the Baal Peor episode) that could date to the Early Iron Age or slightly later. These extracts, epic and legendary in nature, likely occurred first in an oral form and were not written down until centuries after the events they describe. Later editors organized the earlier texts and made their own additions for the purpose of writing a theological narrative of the Israelites' experiences in Jordan.

The circumstances through which these descriptions of west-central Jordan's political complexity were transmitted into what is today regarded as Numbers 21–36 suggest that this written evidence deserves careful consideration before it can be accepted as historically accurate. The details of these accounts likely changed over the centuries as they circulated in oral form and made their way into the texts that were a product of the dynamic scribal practices of the later Iron Age. Furthermore, the biblical descriptions of Late Bronze and Early Iron Age west-central Jordan make for problematic historical data because of the motivations of those who wrote and edited the evidence. As discussed earlier, the biblical writers composed their stories not for the purpose of writing history as factual events, but to demonstrate that their history was the result of the Israelites' unique relationship with their deity, Yahweh. One result of this authorial intention was that the Israelites' encounters with their adversaries were often embellished to highlight the Israelites' theological and cultural superiority as well as to justify their territorial claims in the area east of the Jordan Valley.[11]

Despite problems with the date and the motives of these descriptions of the region's political organization, this evidence was all that was available to scholars prior to archaeological investigation. It was widely believed that the kingdoms of Moab and Ammon had been established by the Late Bronze Age and that the Israelites' campaign and settlement in the northern half of west-central Jordan had displaced the Ammonites. Not until Nelson Glueck's (1934, 1935, 1939, 1951) comprehensive survey of the region and his culture-historical synthesis (1940) would evidence become available that both complemented and contradicted the biblical descriptions of the region's political organization. Between 1932 and 1947, Glueck surveyed more than one thousand sites in Transjordan, for which he made detailed recordings and assigned dates using his knowledge of the regional ceramic vessel sequence. Glueck noted a gap in sedentary occupation during most of the Middle and Late Bronze Ages, between the twentieth and thirteenth centuries BCE (Glueck 1934, 1939, 1940:28).[12] Glueck argued that this absence was proof that pastoral nomadic communities inhabited west-central Jordan prior to the Iron Age. Such nomadic communities were assumed to have left behind little physical evidence from their settlement activities. In the Early Iron Age, however, Glueck noted a different settlement pattern, one that he characterized as a "highly developed and well organized . . . agricultural civilization" (Glueck 1934:82). For Glueck, the most convincing evidence for this political complexity was the settlements lining Moab's perimeter that he interpreted as military installations designed to defend the supposed polity (Glueck 1939:121–122, cf. 1940:167–172). Glueck and scholars who followed him, such as van Zyl, explained the appearance of these seemingly complex political entities using a Middle Eastern subsistence model that was based on observations of twentieth-century nomadic groups (van Zyl 1960). These authors argued that nomadic communities living in and around the region gradually adopted sedentary subsistence practices, ultimately developing political institutions such as kingship. Writing the first synthesis of Moabite history and archaeology, van Zyl (1960:111–112) went so far as to date the appearance of the first settlement to the fourteenth century and the kingdom's coalescence to the thirteenth century BCE. Glueck's conclusions—the absence of a Late Bronze Age sedentary community and the full development of an Early Iron Age kingdom—and van Zyl's reconstruction only partly square with the Hebrew Bible's characterization of west-central Jordan. Although the biblical narrative describes complex political entities administered by Ammonite and Moabite kings as early as the Late Bronze Age, Glueck's synthesis instead found no evidence for such polities until a century or two later, during the Early Iron Age period.[13]

Glueck's synthesis remained the dominant paradigm from which to construct west-central Jordan's cultural history for several decades. During and slightly following Glueck's explorations, only a handful of excavations such as Adir (Albright 1934; Cleveland 1954–1956), 'Aro'er (Olàvarri 1965, 1969), Balu'a (Crowfoot 1934), and Dhiban (Morton 1989; Tushingham 1972; Winnett and Reed 1964) took place in the region. These projects encountered difficulties in dating archaeological strata because they suffered from the lack of both a clear understanding of west-central Jordan's ceramic vessel sequence and current radiometric dating techniques. Glueck's culture-historical synthesis would not be revised until the 1970s (Dornemann 1983; Sauer 1986), when more systematic surveys and excavation projects were carried out (e.g., McGovern 1986; Ray 2001) and a more reliable vessel sequence was established (e.g., Hendrix, Drey, and Storfjell 1997).

These later excavation and survey projects revealed several problems in Glueck's and van Zyl's assessments of Bronze and Iron Age west-central Jordan. Recent archaeological research has demonstrated that sedentary life in the region was more common in the Middle and Late Bronze Ages than Glueck originally believed, but not so common as to support the biblical description of kingdoms. Additional excavations and surveys have discovered little evidence for the Early Iron Age kingdoms that Glueck claimed to have discovered in his survey. Instead, several settlements that Glueck (1940:169) dated to the Early Iron Age were not founded until the later Iron Age, some as late as the seventh century BCE (e.g., Qasr al-Al, Qasr Abu al-Kharaqa). Additionally, Glueck's interpretation of some settlements as defensive in nature was challenged when excavations revealed extensive evidence for domestic subsistence practices (Parker 1987; Routledge 2000). Despite these subsequent findings, Glueck was not wrong on all counts,[14] but the redating of several key settlements reduced his Early Iron Age "kingdom" to only a handful of settlements.

Given the problematic issues of the biblical evidence and the need to revisit Glueck's original synthesis, scholars have been at an impasse regarding how best to characterize the political organization of west-central Jordan during the second half of the second millennium BCE. Udo Worschech (Worschech 1990:94–102, 131) and Stefan Timm (Timm 1989:14–33) continue to support the Hebrew Bible's description of kingship. According to Worschech, the Egyptians sponsored a region-wide program of sedentarization, elevating community leaders to the rank of king so long as they produced an agricultural surplus for their Egyptian authorities. Worschech's argument is weakened by the fact that little evidence exists to prove that the Egyptians held a political or economic interest in west-central Jordan's Early Iron Age communities.[15] Although the Egyptians were active in the Levant during the Late Bronze Age and the beginning of the Iron Age, the likelihood they undertook such broad initiatives in west-central Jordan is, in fact, low.

Most scholars, however, disagree with historical reconstructions such as Worschech's and Timm's and instead suggest that the label "kingdom" be discarded and the region's political complexity be reassessed (Boling 1988; Dearman 1992:73; Knauf 1992:48; Miller 1992; Routledge 2004:87–113).[16] Yet they remain unsure as to how to characterize the political organization of west-central Jordan during the second millennium. Gerald Mattingly (1992:61–62), in attempting to chart a course out of this impasse, suggests turning to social evolutionary classifications (e.g., tribes, chiefdoms, pristine and secondary states) and theories to understand the region's culture history. Granted, he only mentions a handful of theories, many of them alternative definitions of archaic states such as conscription and secondary-state models to be considered in future research. Still, Mattingly's suggestion that scholars not throw out social evolutionary categories altogether is an intriguing suggestion. West-central Jordan's Early Iron Age societies, Mattingly contends, may not have developed the complexity of a classic archaic state, but instead may have slid between evolutionary categories less complex than the state, such as tribe and chiefdom.

At first glance, the category of tribe might appear useful for characterizing the region's political organization.[17] Scholars who have recently considered the evidence in these terms have argued that tribalism, as a flexible system of collective identification, resource allocation, and conflict resolution, has operated as a structural constant throughout Jordan's history (Bienkowski 2009; LaBianca 1990, 1999; Labianca and Younker 1995; van der Steen 2004; Worschech 2009). Other forms of political association are seen as being imposed on, or constructed from, an underlying bedrock of kinship and tribalism. Linking this claim to the Iron Age is the biblical narrative's persistent suggestion that kinship was an important organizing principle throughout the Iron Age, and much space is dedicated to discussions of how such relations were structured. Scholars have therefore used this evidence to reconstruct kinship practices in ancient Israel and its neighbors (Andersen 1969; Faust 2000; Halpern 1996; LaBianca 1990; Meyers 1988; Prewitt 1981; Stager 1985). On the specific category of tribe, selections from the biblical narrative (e.g., Joshua 13–19, Judges 5) describe the ideal type as impermeable kin groups who were territorially demarcated, self-aware of their standing in the region and their historical legacies, and contained constituent kin groupings, namely the family and the clan (Bendor 1996:87–93).

This written evidence provides a partial motivation for recent reconstructions of tribal political structure in west-central Jordan's Early Iron Age history. Such scholars would see the Shasu nomads described in New Kingdom Egyptian texts (discussed later in this chapter) as presumably tribally organized pastoralists who founded sedentary villages in the wake of Egypt's withdrawal from the Levant at the end of the second millennium. Following this logic, these groups would have eventually coalesced sometime in the ninth century BCE into unified "supra-tribal" kingdoms in response to external military threats, especially the Assyrian Empire (Bienkowski 2009; LaBianca 1999). Although a seemingly plausible hypothesis for Iron Age political and social development, this use of the tribe paradigm in the Early Iron Age has yet to give detailed attention to the actual sequence of historical developments attested in the archaeological record. In part, this lack of attention is a product of the evidential weaknesses described previously. When the evidence is interpreted, the presumed ubiquity, continuity, and structural flexibility of tribalism reduces the significance of historically specific evidence. That is, what is not indicative of a centralized state becomes further evidence for tribal organization, with change occurring primarily as a collective reaction to external events. In addition to encouraging a static view of historical change, current approaches remain focused at a regional level, where evidence is primarily available in the form of settlement patterns lacking in chronological precision and site-specific detail. Explanations of social and historical changes inevitably gravitate toward collective actors such as "Moabites," "Ammonites," or just generic "tribes."

The category's utility can be somewhat salvaged by observing a constituent feature of its kinship system, segmentary lineages. By comparing modern Middle Eastern kinship systems with the biblical narrative, scholars have observed that Israelite kinship was constructed according to a segmentary lineage system (Andersen 1969; Prewitt 1981), a way of differentiating a society into a descending series of agnatic groups, each organized through a founding member by descent (Evans-Pritchard 1940, 1949). As time distanced each successive generation away from the primary founder, groups further segmented into increasingly smaller groups. Despite this distance, a segmented group could still trace its lineage upward to the primary founder and, when finding it necessary, could form alliances with other segments through locating their common affiliations within the lineage. Under this political system, two or more segments combined to defend threatened territories and participate in feuds, separating again when alliances were no longer necessary. Soon after, these formerly aligned tribes could find themselves opposed to each other over feuds or territory, now aligning themselves with new segments to which they were previously opposed.[18]

The flexible yet messy strategies that segmentary lineage systems afforded their users accord with the biblical narrative's descriptions of how kinship *actually* played out in practice. The written sources commonly describe instances where kin groups did not form according to the idealized definitions the texts describe.[19] In other words, while such kin terms likely persisted in the minds of the biblical authors as well as broader Iron Age Levantine society, ideal kinship types were not necessarily manifested in practice. Because kinship played both prescriptive and descriptive roles, it is not surprising that mapping organizational types onto the physical evidence presents difficulties. Reconstructing kinship without a nuanced sense of the mechanics of segmentary lineage systems, therefore, results in a representation of Early Iron Age Levantine societies as unable to change and therefore participate in the shifting circumstances that surrounded them. A shift toward a poststructural understanding is therefore necessary, a perspective that does not understand kinship as a set of rules to which individuals and societies conform, but instead as a set of strategies and situated practical acts that individuals depend on consciously and unconsciously to achieve a desired end (Bourdieu 1977:30–71). Unrelated individuals and groups sharing political and economic circumstances likely found in kinship a vocabulary and set of strategies from which to forge alliances, express affinities, and navigate social hierarchies.

On the Margins: The Second Millennium BCE in West-Central Jordan

When comparing the history of west-central Jordan's second millennium society to that of the rest of the southern Levant, one is struck by how the region experienced the time period differently from neighboring regions. West-central Jordan saw many of the same elements as those in other Levantine regions—fortified urban centers and Egyptian imperial intervention, for example—but not at the scale and intensity that was seen along the Mediterranean coast and slightly inland (e.g., the Shephelah and Galilee). However, the evidence does not suggest that west-central Jordan was some cultural "backwater" of Levantine society, as some scholars have implicitly maintained. Rather, the region developed in ways that were different from neighboring ones, partly because of its position between the Jordan Valley and the Arabian Desert, the uneven availability of natural resources such as water and soils, and other unique issues. Given these structuring factors, the region deserves to be investigated on its own terms rather than as a foil for other Levantine regions.

The earliest historical sources describing west-central Jordan's communities and their political organization appear during the Middle Bronze IIA period (2000–1800 BCE), when settlement throughout the southern Levant was recovering from wide-scale urban abandonment in the previous Early Bronze IV/Middle Bronze I period (Cohen 2002; Gerstenblith 1983). Twelfth-Dynasty Egyptian execration texts dating to the nineteenth century BCE refer to the region as a foreign land, entitled Shutu, appearing in the Mirgissa (Koenig 1990), Berlin (Sethe 1926), and Brussels (Posener 1940) archives; additionally, the toponym is mentioned in a Beni Hassan tomb (Newberry, Griffith, and Fraser 1893).[20] Seven different local rulers are mentioned in these instances: Saripu(m), Abisharru, Ayyabum, Koshar, Zabilunu, Shumu-abu, and Yakmis-'ammu. The Berlin archive mentions that three of these rulers were contemporaries, suggesting that the region was divided between multiple rulers and was not integrated under any one centralized authority. In fact, the Brussels texts designate Shumu-abu to an upper Shutu and Yakmis-'ammu to a lower Shutu, leading scholars to question where the district was bisected (e.g., Albright 1941).[21] Archaeological surveys and excavations in west-central Jordan unfortunately demonstrate little Middle Bronze IIA archaeological evidence to which these rulers could be assigned. Middle Bronze IIA ceramic evidence was identified in later architectural contexts on the 'Amman Citadel (Dornemann 1983:15) and at 'Iraq al-Amir (Lapp 1965:88–89).

Evidence for west-central Jordan's Middle Bronze Age communities grows slightly more abundant a few centuries later, during the Middle Bronze IIB (1800–1650 BCE) and IIC (1650–1500 BCE) periods, although survey data suggest this settlement was limited. In the Hesban vicinity, surveyors discovered only fourteen settlements with Middle Bronze Age evidence in an area approximately 513 kilometers square; an abundance of ceramic evidence was found in only three sites (Ibach 1987:155–157, fig. 3.2, table 3.5). Further south on the Karak Plateau, surveyors recorded fifty-five settlements with Middle Bronze Age ceramic evidence in an area of approximately 875 square kilometers between the Wadi al-Mujib and the Wadi al-Hasa; of the fifty-five, only fifteen had five or more sherds (Miller 1991:308).[22] Although the survey evidence suggests a limited and low-intensity settlement pattern, excavations have revealed that some settlements were well fortified with large walls and sloping glacis. Examples include the 'Amman Citadel (Dornemann 1983:18, fig. 8; Greene and 'Amr 1992; Zayadine et al. 1987), Sahab (Ibrahim 1987:76), and al-'Umayri (Herr et al. 1991:159, 166). The lone exception is Abu Snesleh, a small Middle Bronze IIB and IIC settlement where domestic buildings were excavated (Lamprichs 1998). In addition to settlements, Middle Bronze IIB and IIC tombs containing scarabs, alabaster vessels, and jewelry were discovered in 'Amman (Najjar 1991; Piccirillo 1978) and at Sahab (Ibrahim 1972). Although these fortified towns and artifact-rich tombs postdate the Middle Kingdom sources describing Shutu's rulers by a few centuries, the physical and historical evidence together suggest that west-central Jordan, especially its northern half, had a limited sedentary occupation. The dearth of evidence, however, unfortunately makes it impossible to determine the complexity of west-central Jordan's Middle Bronze Age political organization. At the very most, the meager evidence suggests low-intensity urbanism existed in the northern half of the region and that local leaders were prominent enough to be recognized by their Egyptian adversaries.

The ability to discern the nature of west-central Jordan's political organization improves somewhat when moving later in time to the Late Bronze Age (1550–1250 BCE). Again, Glueck's synthesis of the period is to be discarded as more recent archaeological and survey evidence has demonstrated that the period was anything but devoid of sedentary occupation. Rather, the mild intensity of the Middle Bronze Age settlement pattern continues into the Late Bronze Age. Physical evidence for palace-based elites exists in Late Bronze Age Jordan and is most prevalent in northern Jordan and the Jordan Valley. At Irbid, Pella, Tall Abu Kharaz, and Tall al-Fukhar, monumental palaces and temples have been discovered in excavation (Strange 2001). In the northern half of west-central Jordan, the evidence is less abundant, although still revealing of the region's political organization. Monumental buildings have been identified at Sahab, Area E (Ibrahim 1972; 1974:60, pl. 22; 1975:78–80, fig. 5, pl. 27), al-'Umayri (Bramlett 2004), and possibly Safut (Wimmer 1987:162, 165–166). Tomb groups with combinations of Egyptian, Mycenaean, and Cypriot imported objects are present at the 'Amman Airport (Hennessy 1966; Herr 1983), the Baq'ah Valley Cave A2 and B3 (McGovern 1986:32–52), and Madaba (Harding 1953:27–50). Altogether the evidence suggests these elites, like their counterparts to the west, possessed enough economic and symbolic capital to have access to imported prestige goods and surplus labor.

Two well-published surveys offer a glimpse of the settlement patterns around these Late Bronze Age palaces. In the vicinity of Hesban, seven sites with surface artifacts dating to the Late Bronze Age were identified (Ibach 1987:157–158). In only four instances—Hesban, Iktanu, Jalul, and al-'Umayri—was a significant amount of evidence recovered, suggesting that Late Bronze Age society was concentrated in these mid-size settlements. In three smaller settlements—Nos. 54, 128, and 132—the Late Bronze materials recovered in survey were either questionable in date or insignificant in amount. Settlement in Hesban's vicinity was limited in its intensity and appears concentrated in a handful of settlements with only a few satellite communities in each settlement's hinterland. If elites attempted to organize the hinterland surrounding their communities, they did so with little success. Populations and wealth appear to have been concentrated within and near the palace.

Evidence for Late Bronze Age palace-based political organization is even more limited in the southern half of west-central Jordan, where settlements with monumental architecture are absent and settlement patterns are even more diffuse. However, the region was not abandoned. On the Karak Plateau, 109 settlements with Late Bronze Age materials, 30 of which had five or more Late Bronze artifacts, were surveyed (Miller 1991:308–309). Two settlement clusters in the vicinity of Karak and Dubab in the southwest corner of the survey area contain six and five settlements each, respectively (Routledge 2004:78–82, fig. 4.3). These two clusters, combined with the remaining diffusely arranged Late Bronze settlements, indicate that settlements in the region were uneven across the landscape, at times concentrated and at other times dispersed (Routledge 2004:81). These conclusions, however, must be accepted with a note of caution as the continuity in ceramic vessel forms between the Late Bronze Age and the Iron Age creates difficulties in assigning settlements to a single time period. Likewise, the excavation of surveyed Early Iron Age sites has been limited, and until more data are collected, it is impossible to discern the region's rank-size hierarchy.

Although the extent to which these palaces dominated the broader region was limited, their existence did not escape the Egyptian Empire's attention. Although not mentioning the toponym "Moab" directly, a topographical list dating to the reign of Thutmose III presents a list of towns through which the pharaoh campaigned. Redford reconstructed Nos. 92 through 101 as a list of ten towns running the length of the region, including al-'Umayri (No. 96: *kurmin*), Dhiban (No. 98: *tipun*), and Karak (No. 101: *harkur*) (Redford 1982). Other thirteenth-century New Kingdom sources do identify the region as "Moab" and as a geographical entity bearing at least a handful of settled communities. One inscription, again a topographical list, located on a statue of Ramses II at the Luxor temple, suggests Egyptian campaigning in west-central Jordan continued (Simons 1937). Although the name "Moab" appears, the list is brief and not well preserved. Another inscription, again located at the Luxor temple, on the east wall of the Court of Ramses II, reports that the Pharaoh campaigned "in the land of Moab," against *b(w)trt, yn(?)d* . . . in the mountain of *mrrn*, and *tbniw*, the last of which Kitchen reconstructs as Dhiban (Kitchen 1964).[23]

The fact that the Egyptians found west-central Jordan important enough to campaign through and detail the settlements they found there could lead one to overestimate the political organization of west-central Jordan if it were not for the diffuse settlement pattern found in the survey evidence. Like that for the Middle Bronze Age, the evidence for Late Bronze Age political organization is meager and contradictory. On the one hand, the archaeological evidence and historical sources suggest that the southern half of west-central Jordan possessed a sedentary, although in places, limited settlement pattern; on the other hand, Egyptian royal correspondence reports that tent-dwelling nomadic pastoralists were living in the region and often coming into conflict with their sedentary neighbors (Ward 1972).

Whatever the regional political organization of west-central Jordan at the end of the Late Bronze Age and the beginning of the Iron Age, the entire Levant witnessed an upheaval that dramatically reconfigured southern Levantine society in the thirteenth century BCE (Gitin, Mazar, and Stern 1998; Ward and Joukowsky 1992). West-central Jordan was not excluded from these regional changes. This breakdown in the palace economies is visible in the overall abandonment of Late Bronze Age monumental architecture at Safut, Sahab, and al-'Umayri. This upheaval in the region did not result in the region's abandonment, however. Rather, sedentary life resumed and overall, the number of settlements, although reduced in size, increased in the twelfth and eleventh centuries BCE, the Early Iron Age. Survey projects, most notably the work of Miller (1991) and Worschech (1985, 1990) on the Karak Plateau, Parker (1987) on the eastern desert fringe, Ji (Ji and 'Attiyat 1997; Ji and Lee 1998, 2000) on the Dhiban Plateau, Ibach (1987) in the Hesban region, Jacobs (1983) in the Wadi 'Isal, and Clark and colleagues (1992, 1994) on the northern edge of the Wadi al-Hasa have illuminated the region's early Iron Age settlement patterns. Considering all seven surveys together (summarized in Routledge 2004, table 4.2), the number of settlements increased slightly from a total of 126 in the Late Bronze Age to 144 in the Early Iron Age period. This overall increase grows complicated, however, when examining the survey data by region. In the Hesban vicinity, the number of settlements increased from 6 to 30 settlements in the early Iron Age, the settlement's rank-size hierarchy ranging from very small ($n=7$), small ($n=9$), medium ($n=6$), large ($n=3$), and major ($n=5$), suggesting that at least a two-tier settlement system was in place at that time (Ibach 1987:160–163). But yet paradoxically, on the Karak Plateau, the number of settlements fell from 109 to 72 and were distributed throughout the region in areas where rainfall and soil conditions are poor (Miller 1991:309).[24] Again, like observations of Late Bronze Age settlement patterns, some caution must be exercised when accepting these conclusions, since the continuity in ceramic vessel forms between the Late Bronze Age and the Iron Age creates difficulties in assigning settlements to one time period or another.

This region-by-region examination of the survey evidence reveals that settlement intensity varied across west-central Jordan during the Early Iron Age. Indeed, the settlement hierarchy in Hesban's vicinity suggests a greater degree of political organization compared to the Karak Plateau. How should this variation in settlement intensity across the region be explained? Commenting on the breakdown of Late Bronze Age society in the Baq'ah Valley, McGovern (1986, 1988) notes that the collapse of the period's cosmopolitan palace economies led to a less-wealthy and relatively isolated society in the Early Iron Age. Constituents who were once attached and dependent on the palaces found themselves unsponsored, leading them to scatter throughout the countryside in search of new resources. Such movements, McGovern argues, occurred slowly and required producers to reorganize production strategies under the new economic conditions. Such changes help explain the dispersed settlement patterns that appear in the Early Iron Age survey data.

Although McGovern's hypothesis is satisfying in light of the survey data, what remains to be understood is the political organization of the resulting Early Iron Age society. Fortunately, unlike that of the Middle and Late Bronze Ages, excavated evidence of the Early Iron Age is sufficient for evaluating its political organization.[25] The best understood evidence comes from several key settlements including 'Aro'er,[26] Balu'a,[27] Lahun (fig. 3.2),[28] Khirbat al-Mudayna al-'Aliya (al-'Aliya hereafter) (fig. 3.3),[29] Khirbat al-Mudayna al-Mu'arradja (al-Mu'arradja hereafter) (fig. 3.4),[30] and Khirbat al-Mu'ammariyya (al-Mu'ammariyya hereafter),[31] all located adjacent to the Wadi al-Mujib canyon. Also helpful are two additional settlements, Sahab[32] and Tall al-'Umayri (al-'Umayri hereafter),[33] located further north in the vicinity of Hesban.[34]

The best-known Early Iron Age settlements demonstrate a noticeable degree of parity in wealth and design and thus partly frustrate any attempt to understand the political organization of the time period in west-central Jordan. When examining settlements collectively, a glance at the settlement maps reveals a repeated architectural pattern at al-'Aliya, Lahun, al-Mu'arradja, al-'Umayri, and possibly Sahab: a series of pillared buildings sharing adjacent walls form an oval or elliptical ring around a central courtyard that contains additional buildings (e.g., Lahun and al-Mu'arradja) or is left empty (e.g., al-'Aliya). Settlements are relatively similar in size also: al-'Aliya, Lahun, and al-Mu'arradja, whose Early Iron Age remains are exposed at or near the surface, range in size at 2.2, 1.6, and 1.0 hectares, respectively. Although the full extent of 'Aro'er, Balu'a, Sahab, and al-'Umayri is difficult to measure as Early Iron Age remains have only been explored in limited horizontal exposures, a reasonable estimate for each settlement would not exceed three hectares overall. These similarities in size and design indicate a single-tiered hierarchy of settlements lacking a central administrative metropole from which one settlement could dominate the others.

Another observation that frustrates attempts to understand this political organization is that these eight settlements were founded intermittently

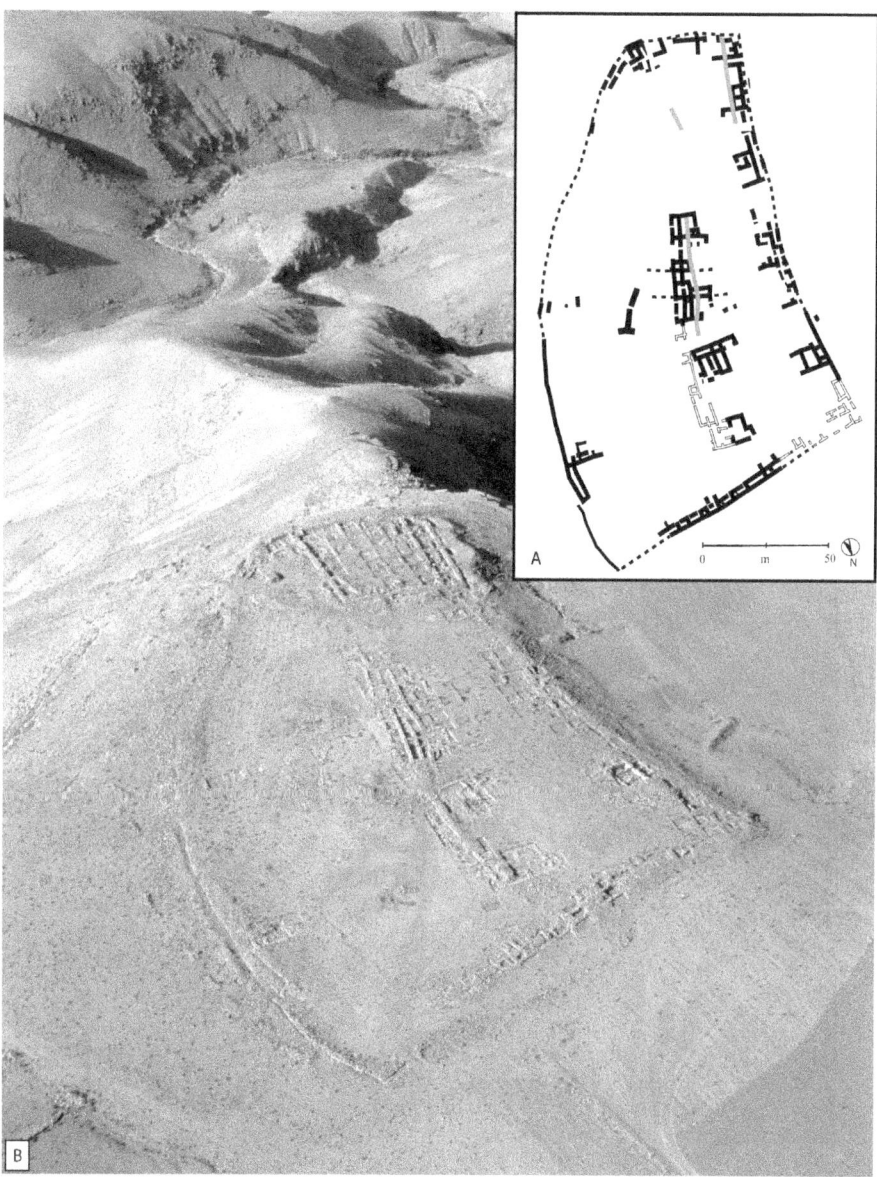

Figure 3.2. (A) Map of Lahun's Early Iron Age settlement. (B) Aerial image of Lahun looking south. (*Sources*: A: Homès-Fredericq 1997, fig. 41; © Equinox Publishing Ltd. 2011. B: Image: Lehun © Aerial Photographic Archive for Archaeology in the Middle East. APAAME_19980520_DLK-0035. Photograph: David L. Kennedy)

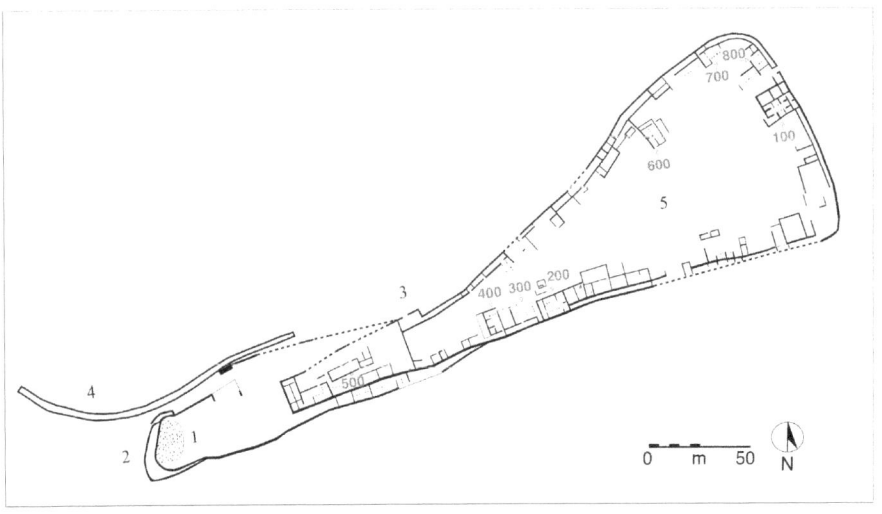

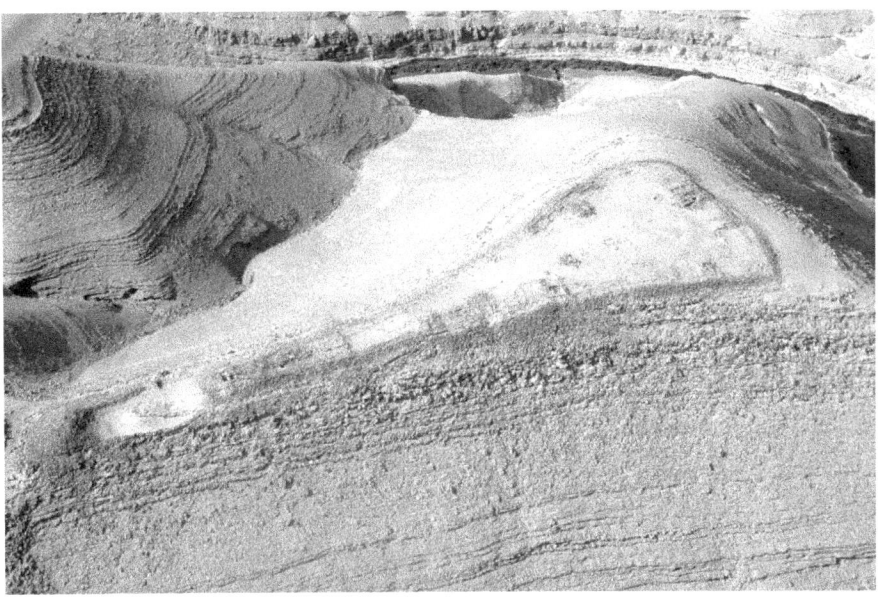

Figure 3.3. (A) Map of al-'Aliya denoting Buildings 100 through 800, tower (1), moat (2), a possible gated entrance (3), paved pathway (4), and courtyard (5). (B) Aerial image of al-'Aliya looking north. (*Sources*: A: © Equinox Publishing Ltd. 2011. B: Image: Kh. Mdeinet Aliya (Miller, no. 143) © Aerial Photographic Archive for Archaeology in the Middle East. APAAME_20011005_DLK-0021. Photograph: David L. Kennedy)

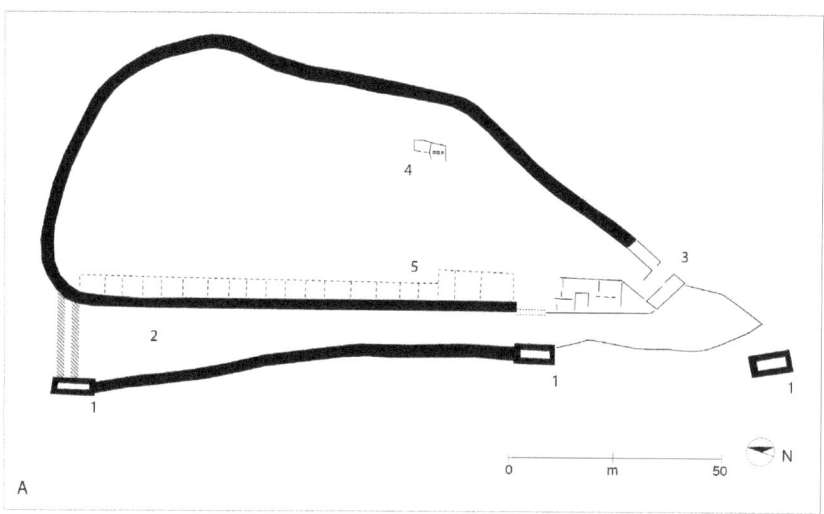

Figure 3.4. (A) Map of al-Mu'arradja denoting towers (1), moat (2), gate (3), fortified walls (4), excavated buildings (5), and hypothesized buildings. (B) Aerial image of al-Mu'arradja looking south. (*Sources*: A: Modified from Olavarri 1983, fig. 3. B: Image: Kh. Mdeinet el-Mu'arrajeh © Aerial Photographic Archive for Archaeology in the Middle East. APAAME_20081005_RHB-0226. Photograph: Robert Bewley)

over time. Excavated evidence suggests that of the eight settlements, Lahun and al-'Umayri were founded first, in the thirteenth century, during the transition between the Late Bronze Age and Early Iron Age periods. Based on ceramic parallels from the central highlands, Herr (2000:175) observes that al-'Umayri's ceramic evidence is contemporary with Mount Ebal and Giloh and precedes that of most other Early Iron Age sites such as 'Ai, Shiloh, and 'Izbet Sartah, suggesting that this settlement was destroyed around 1200 BCE. At Lahun, ceramic evidence dating to the Late Bronze/Early Iron Age transition was sealed beneath an Early Iron Age fortification wall, suggesting a late thirteenth-century date for the settlement's foundation (Homès-Fredericq 1992, 1997). Moving forward into the twelfth century, excavated evidence suggests that the Lahun settlement continues, the al-'Umayri settlement is refounded, and the Sahab community is established. The discovery at Lahun of a scarab bearing iconography of the Nineteenth and Twentieth Egyptian Dynasties suggests the settlement persisted sometime between 1186 and 1070 BCE (Homès-Fredericq 1992:189–190).[35] At al-'Umayri, settlement is evident in a storeroom constructed on top of the formerly destroyed site. Ceramic vessels excavated in this storeroom date to twelfth-century settlements in the central highlands such as 'Ai, Shiloh, and 'Izbet Sartah. At Sahab, limited excavations revealed an Early Iron Age building constructed on top of the destroyed Late Bronze settlement (Ibrahim 1974). Based on personal conversations and examination of unpublished evidence, Herr (2000:176) claims that Sahab's destruction dates to 1100 BCE, almost a century after al-'Umayri's destruction. Moving forward into the eleventh century, several settlements emerge on either side of the Wadi al-Mujib canyon. The settlement at Lahun may have continued while 'Aro'er and Balu'a were refounded, and al-'Aliya, al-Mu'arradja, and al-Mu'ammariyya were settled anew. Aside from one exception (al-'Aliya),[36] chronometric dating of these settlements has yet to be performed. For now, a relative date for these settlements can be determined by the ceramic vessel assemblage that has parallels in eleventh- and early tenth-century settlements in and west of the Jordan Valley.[37] At some point during the first half of the tenth century BCE, these settlements were abandoned (see chapter 5).

This episodic founding and abandonment of west-central Jordan's Early Iron Age communities suggests that these settlements were not the planned ventures of some bureaucratic political organization, but were instead the outcome of contingent decisions of individual communities. Despite the relative independence of each community, the similarities in the settlements' design coupled with their periodic abandonment suggest something more intriguing about the political relationship between settlements. As Routledge (2004:112–113) has suggested, this staggered settlement of communities may have been the product of disenfranchised segments abandoning one settlement and in turn founding a new one. If true, then such circumstances would explain similarities in size and design across settlements. Such a scenario would suggest that communities remained closely related to each other—possibly exchanging surplus and creating alliances through marriage—but retained a relative degree of political autonomy from each other.

Conclusion: Toward an Archaeology of Community

The historical and archaeological evidence of second millennium west-central Jordan reveals several reasons why the application of social evolutionary categories is a step in the wrong direction. During this time, the region exhibits a steady, albeit low, intensity settlement pattern. Nowhere is a diachronic increase in settlement hierarchy found that would point to increasing or decreasing social complexity. The settlement pattern also demonstrates unevenness across the landscape, bearing many of the hallmarks of an emergent complex adaptive system. Population appears to be more densely concentrated in the northern half of the region than in the southern half. This nonlinear pattern suggests sedentary communities were not organized into a regional political hierarchy but rather maintained relative autonomy from each other. Yet how can one explain how sedentary life remained resilient, flexible, and transferable without the guiding hand of an integrated regional polity? This question cannot be answered by simply scaling down the social evolutionary ladder to assumedly less complex categories. Any attempt to answer this and related questions would seek answers at the most local resolution possible, the community itself.

Despite a community perspective's suitability for examining west-central Jordan during the second millennium BCE, several unfortunate limitations hamper any such study at the current time. As should be apparent from the evidence described in this chapter, areas where communities were most abundant, such as in the northern half of west-central Jordan, have not been extensively sampled enough to permit a suitable analysis. Broad horizontal exposures of architectural units that would permit intra-site analysis of households are so far absent. Where sampling has been sufficiently broad, evidence is not always available for analysis in published excavation reports. The lone exception is the region's Early Iron Age settlements. Preservation, sampling, and exposure in these places have been sufficient, and in many instances, the evidence has been published. The remainder of this book will therefore concentrate on these Early Iron Age settlements in order to understand how they developed the resilience needed to sustain their communities. The interpretation of those communities that preceded the Early Iron Age will have to wait until the day when more evidence is available for analysis.

CHAPTER FOUR

Producing Community

Many preindustrial societies organized their relationships around the production of materials needed to sustain themselves and their immediate dependents. This observation partly explains why small-scale human organizations form in the very first instance. Production does more than make things and structure relationships, however. Ideologies are recursively generated that promote these arrangements, creating the cultural sentiment of "belonging" that is necessary for cohesion. But for these cultural ideas to take hold in a social setting such as a community, the basic material conditions for life must be present. Hence, communities in resource-scarce marginal zones face an added challenge beyond subsistence. They are required to subscribe to ideologies that justify the persistence of social attachments in the face of looming scarcity and risk. Households and the persons that constitute them must believe they benefit more from participation in the community than from facing the same difficult conditions on their own or elsewhere.[1]

These conditions present an opportunity to ask how resilience can be understood as something more than merely practice, that is, what people do to sustain themselves in the face of adversity. Resilience can potentially become a cultural ethic bundled with broader ideological visions of communal life. But in making such a claim, one must remember that resilience is not a naturally occurring attribute. It must be cultivated and maintained through expenditures of, for instance, human effort and resources. Strategies to build resilience can be discursively present in language, discussed and debated among members, or tacitly practiced as locally constituted "common sense." Resilience can be a quality entangled with cultural ethics about production and household collaboration in a particular setting. However such sentiments are expressed, the quest for resilience can bring a sense of cohesion to those who seek sustainable conditions in the face of adversity. Therefore, archaeologists must observe how such principles were expressed through actors' practices to create the material world in which they resided.

From Subsistence to Production

Scholars of Early Iron Age Levantine societies have made extensive use of the two common Middle Eastern ethnographic subsistence categories of nomadic pastoralism and sedentary agriculture. The region's nomadic pastoralists depend on herding and management of animals—usually sheep, goats, and camels—and rotate their herds seasonally between pastures and water resources (Barth 1962; Dyson-Hudson and Dyson-Hudson 1980; Lancaster and Lancaster 1995; Spooner 1973). The migratory and animal-dependent nature of this practice plays an important role in structuring nomadic pastoralist societies. Sedentary agriculturalists, the other category, depend on a combination of agriculture and pastoralism to meet their subsistence needs (Antoun 1972; Glavanis and Glavanis 1990). Throughout the region's history, a majority of the Middle East's population has resided in sedentary agricultural communities. In the past as today, they depended on cultivatable soils and sufficient precipitation or access to irrigation to produce food. The emphasis that Early Iron Age scholarship has placed on these subsistence genres is striking when compared to other moments in Levantine history. These Middle Eastern categories are substantiated in written sources throughout the ancient Near East, of course (e.g., Eyre 1995; Matthews 1978). Yet why has there been so much specific interest in the habits of Early Iron Age Levantine nomads and farmers? Like so much scholarship on these groups, the Hebrew Bible plays an inspiring role. The biblical narratives made particular use of these ethnographic tropes: the biblical patriarchs—Abraham, Isaac, and Jacob—are characterized as leaders of nomadic societies moving their herds between Mesopotamia, the Levant, and Egypt (McCarter 2011). The descriptions of ancient Israelite migration from Egypt to Canaan suggest that they exchanged nomadic pastoralism for sedentary agriculture in the Early Iron Age.

Scholars have also looked to these subsistence categories to illuminate biblical societies' *genres de vie*. Albrecht Alt (1966) was one of the first scholars to point out this connection. Based on ethnographic accounts of modern nomadic pastoralist communities, Alt argued that the Israelites were not a wandering band of refugees from Egypt, but a collection of nomadic pastoralists who adopted sedentary subsistence practices in the central highlands at the beginning of the Iron Age. Although not favorably received at the time of its publication (e.g., Albright 1939), Alt's argument for ancient Israel's nomadic pastoralist origins would later receive some validation. Landscape surveys in the late twentieth century (e.g., Finkelstein and Na'aman 1994; LaBianca 1990; Marfoe 1979) demonstrated that many regions in the southern Levant—particularly agriculturally marginal areas—experienced periods of sedentary activity followed by interludes of abatement throughout the Bronze and Iron Ages. During the Late Bronze Age, by way of an example, sedentary communities were confined to areas rich in soils and rainfall, and agriculturally marginal areas were largely devoid of settlement. But starting in the Early Iron Age, these marginal areas were slowly populated with small villages. This gradual change in settlement patterns suggests nomadic groups made a transition to sedentary lifestyles in these marginal zones, growing more reliant on agricultural practices than on pastoralism.[2]

Ethnographic subsistence categories have shown themselves to be useful when interpreting broad shifts in Bronze Age and Iron Age regional settlement patterns. But there are limits to their utility when one wishes to investigate how communities organized their subsistence practices in specific local contexts. The subsistence categories of pastoral nomad and sedentary agriculturalist are based on ideal representations assembled from ethnographic studies. Mapping these composite categories on to real instances can skew the fine details of practices and strategies. Subsistence categories are helpful when multiple communities are described in general terms, but an individual community's economy can combine elements (e.g., semi-nomadic agro-pastoralism) that defy presupposed categories. Additionally, these categories often fail to recognize how settlements adopted subsistence strategies based on local environmental possibilities and constraints. Subsistence categories can promote the idea that pastoralists and farmers chose to limit herd size, build terraces, and construct cisterns as if some ethnographic category had programmed them to do so. Finally, subsistence categories often depend on changes in external phenomena in political and economic organization or environmental conditions to explain why societies abandon old and adopt new subsistence practices. Altogether, Middle Eastern subsistence categories might help scholars imagine how Early Iron Age settlements organized their economies, but at the same time they lack the ability to characterize how individual settlements selected specific subsistence strategies and adapted them to local conditions.

Alternatively, a more detailed understanding of Early Iron Age local economies can be gained by focusing attention on the ways production practices were organized in specific settlements.[3] Such an analysis offers a more precise way to analyze Early Iron Age communities because its characterization does not set out practices such as pastoralism and agriculture, nomadic and sedentary, in opposition to each other, as classic Middle Eastern descriptions have done in the past (Bell 1907; Coon 1951). The useful frameworks for investigating production in past societies are initially helpful in this regard (e.g., Brumfiel and Earle 1987; Costin 1991:2; D'Altroy and Earle 1985; Rice 1981:219; Tosi 1984).[4] Collectively, this research emphasizes the ways production is embedded within a society's prevailing political, social, and economic conditions. In their investigation of production, archaeologists have developed multivariable frameworks for identifying and measuring production practices. These encourage archaeologists to investigate the concentration (distribution of workshops), scale (size of workshop and nature of labor recruitment), and intensity (full- or part-time specialization) of production practices while paying attention to diachronic changes in each criterion.

Costin (1991) characterizes the organization of production according to a spectrum of increasing levels of specialization, measured by the scale and intensity of production activities across space and over time. At one end of this spectrum is the domestic, or household, mode of production (Sahlins 1972:78–79), where practices are restricted to the immediate kin group. Household producers are primarily concerned with satisfying the subsistence needs of their immediate kin. But when household production surpasses basic subsistence needs and is successful in producing a surplus, production conditions are described as a cottage industry (Carrier 1995:41). The small amount of surplus produced within cottage industries allows producers to take part in local exchange networks and maintain a surplus during periods of drought and famine. The transition from domestic to cottage industries often signals increasing specialization in production practices as well as emergent relationships between producers and consumers located outside immediate kin groups. Domestic and cottage industries appear relatively underdeveloped, however, compared to the more extreme versions of specialized production taking place under workshop and industrial conditions (Brumfiel and Earle 1987:5; Rice 1981:220). The development of such specialized conditions is often linked to new or intensified commercial demands from consumers or institutions (Peregrine 1991). Where they previously produced enough to satisfy household and local demands, producers working under specialized conditions engage in their craft full-time and can become attached to larger institutions through patronage. During these changes, craftspersons are required to alter their production strategies, maximize product quantity, and control product quality. These changes are often observable in the archaeological record (Costin 1991). The size and location of workshops can increase and be reorganized to meet new output demands. Additionally, the products themselves can reveal diachronic changes in the selection of raw materials. This common description of a scalar model for production is not as rigid as it appears at first. Rather, the arrangements of production need to be investigated in each instance using all available material evidence, from faunal and botanical remains to ceramic vessels and architectural data, in their proper spatial and temporal contexts.

The historical and archaeological evidence of west-central Jordan's Early Iron Age settlements described in chapter 3 points to an emergent pattern of self-organizing small-scale societies. There is no substantial evidence that they were attached to larger bureaucratic institutions, or that they supplied international commercial markets like those that collapsed at the end of the Late Bronze Age. Based on this evidence, one would hypothesize prior to examining evidence for production strategies that practices were organized to meet local subsistence needs. But even when examining the evidence at a local resolution, it may be possible to differentiate these production practices even further, between those practices managed by households and those managed by the broader community. This differentiation is important for several reasons. As a cultural and social act that transforms raw materials into consumable and meaningful objects (Costin 1991:3), production plays a central role in the social life of households and communities. Production required members to dedicate themselves to learning and teaching practices and strategies for each new generation. An examination of production practices, then, can reveal the ways such cultural knowledge was distributed across the community.

Another reason why differentiating between household and community production practices is necessary is that it can reveal the relationships *between* households. Responsible for family subsistence, heads of households organized dependents to assist in agricultural production and the construction of the family home. But as it will be shown, some activities such as the construction of fortifications and certain aspects of agricultural production required cooperation between households or even the entire community. Although an awareness of production practices provides insight into intra- and inter-household relationships, it also helps detect practices of governance in the community—a third reason why this differentiation between household and community practices is important. Was management of inter-household production practices distributed evenly across the community, suggesting that they were governed according to communal political practices? Or did certain households play a leading role in organizing and administering community production practices? These questions can be answered by observing how wealth circulated and accumulated in physically identifiable stations.

Building the Stage: The Production of Built Space

Building was not just a means to a pragmatic end in the Early Iron Age Levant. The construction of a new residence or the repairing of roofs or agricultural installations were meaningful activities that played an important role in structuring and replicating social life. Through large-scale labor projects, seasonal repairs, and impromptu rearrangements, members created and managed the physical spaces in which interactions between individuals, families, and groups occurred. Building activities organized space into discursive as well as unconscious categories that prescribed appropriate behaviors; permitted differential access to individuals based on gender, kinship, and status; and provided members the opportunity to monitor each other's activities. The dual nature of building as a pragmatic, yet meaningful, activity produced, in part, the social field in which community members performed their daily lives.

The well-preserved architectural evidence visible on the surface of multiple settlements, particularly al-'Aliya, Lahun, al-Mu'ammariyya, and al-Mu'arradja, permits an unusually comprehensive view of Early Iron Age production techniques and routines. A suite of architectural forms was replicated across the communities, including domestic residences, gates, walls, towers, and large open courtyards. The most common form is the pillared building, a central feature whose design is conspicuously repeated throughout Early Iron Age southern Levantine settlements with limited diversity (Braemer 1982; Ji 1997; Shiloh 1970, 1973, 1987). At Lahun, a total of eighty buildings have been recorded (fig. 3.2A; Homès-Fredericq 1994, 1995, 1997; Swinnen 2009), whereas at al-'Aliya, thirty-five to forty-five buildings (fig. 3.3A; Routledge 2000:49). In limited excavations at al-Mu'arradja, two, possibly three, pillared buildings were identified.

The settlement contained space for up to thirty-five similarly designed buildings (fig. 3.4A; Olàvarri 1977–1978:138; 1983, fig. 4). Excavations at al-'Umayri have revealed two well-preserved pillared buildings (A and B) in limited soundings (Herr 2000, fig. 8). These buildings typically lined the communities' perimeters and were often attached to the inside of fortification walls.

The construction of these pillared buildings involved a considerable expenditure of time, labor, and resources, and the extent to which they were a practical and symbolic investment should not be underestimated. Buildings consisted of a combination of organic and inorganic materials, including stone, clay, wood, and plant fibers (Clark 2003; Holladay 1992; Routledge 2009; Stager 1985). Small and medium-size unworked stones, usually no more than one meter thick, were set on low stone foundations to build walls. A mud-chaff blend sometimes mixed with lime was often used as wall mortar between stones or as wall plaster. Narrower than their exterior counterparts, interior walls divided up the building into smaller rooms with beaten earth and flagstone floors. These walls, along with stone or wood pillars placed in the central room, supported a ceiling consisting of plant materials secured to wood or stone beams and rafters with mud and plaster. In some instances, a second floor was added to the primary floor for additional space. Entrances depended on each building's orientation and relationship with surrounding buildings.

Although variations on the pillared building appear throughout the Early Iron Age southern Levant, two designs dominated the west-central Jordan examples (Routledge 2000:50–53; 2009). The first design consists of a narrow and elongated central room that joins a broad rear room at a perpendicular angle; opposite the central room are smaller rooms (e.g., al-'Aliya Buildings 400–700) (fig. 4.1). The second design consists of a square central room with smaller chambers and a broad chamber located at either end (e.g., al-'Aliya: Buildings 200–300 [fig. 4.2] and al-'Umayri's Building B [Herr 2000, fig. 8]). Considering these two designs together at al-'Aliya, where these building types are best documented, the total area of the buildings including walls ranges from 71.5 to 239 square meters (Routledge 2000, table 3; Routledge and Porter 2007). The size and floor plan suggest a limited number of members, likely a multigenerational nuclear family of four to six members, occupied the buildings.[5] Excavated evidence including ceramic vessels, ovens, and faunal evidence indicates that the activities that took place in these buildings concentrated on craft production, short- and long-term grain and livestock storage, and food preparation. Food preparation and part-time production of craft goods were likely the principal activities that took place in the central room, whereas the smaller rooms were used for grain storage and occasional animal stabling. The second floor, when present, was primarily a domestic space for sleeping and socializing during cold and wet weather, and when needed, an additional space for small-scale craft production. During warmer periods, many of the activities performed in the first floor's central room or on the second floor were moved outside to the roof and the building's vicinity. Altogether, these buildings possessed a flexible design that could be rearranged as household wealth and membership fluctuated or as harvest or animal reproduction demanded additional space.[6]

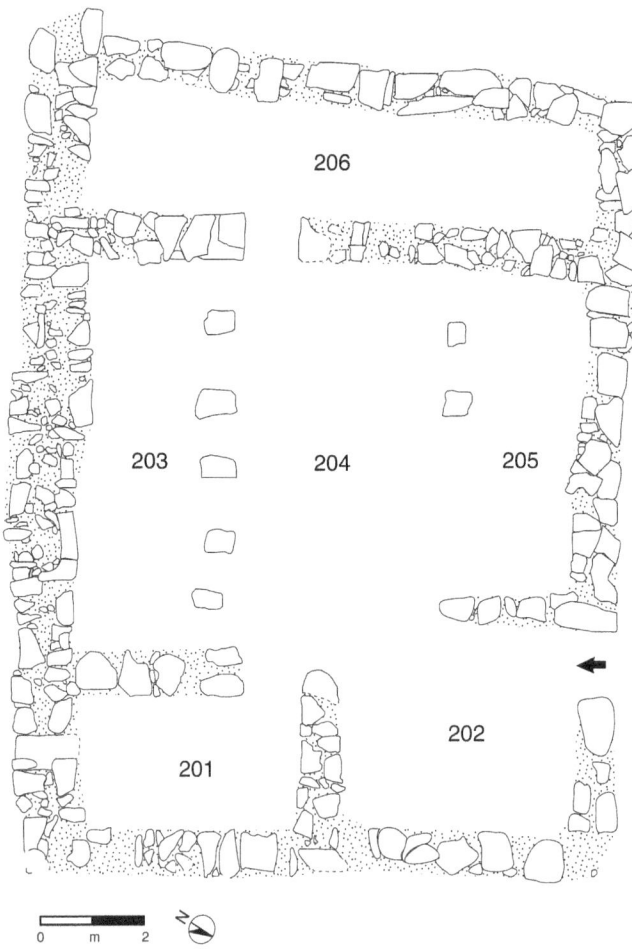

Figure 4.1. Al-'Aliya Building 200.

Producing Community · 77

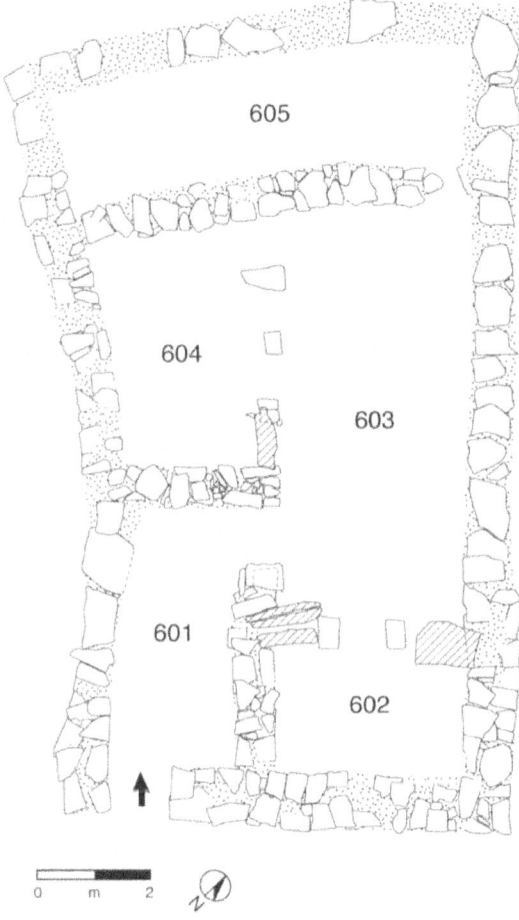

Figure 4.2. Al-'Aliya Building 600.

When examining the pillared buildings in the Early Iron Age settlements of al-'Aliya, Lahun, and al-'Umayri, the replication in building design and construction techniques within settlements is striking. The physical evidence suggests residence designs were not merely structural accidents or impromptu acts based on individual initiative. The buildings' replication indicates their construction was embedded in communal traditions and entangled with social relationships. Younger generations likely learned how buildings were designed and built through direct participation in their construction as youths. When the time came for erecting a new building, usually when a new family was founded, builders had gained the necessary knowledge required to replicate the form. Clark (2003), who based his investigation on the best-preserved Early Iron Age pillared building so far excavated, al-'Umayri's Building B, has demonstrated the substantial amount of resources and labor necessary to construct a building. The construction of the floor, both exterior and interior walls, ceilings, and the second story using mud brick, stone, wood, reeds, and lime was a labor-intensive activity that Clark (2003:42–43) estimates would have required two thousand kilocalories per day to sustain such arduous activities. This estimate requires some adjustment, however. It is likely that buildings were constructed over a longer period of time and reserved for periods when the weather was mild and agricultural responsibilities reduced. Yet this recognition of the amount of labor needed for construction projects suggests building was a collective exercise that extended beyond the efforts of one household. The building's owner faced the challenge of soliciting fellow community members to assist in a project in which only the owner's immediate family stood to benefit. For the owner, constructing a building was more than simply having the wealth and time to initiate the project. Members had to be in good standing with the community and seen as capable and willing to exchange the favor when neighbors called for their help.

Defensive systems were another important feature in the production of built space. These systems consisted of interlinked defensive features such as large walls, casemate rooms, towers, gates, and moats that were replicated throughout the settlements. Dry-laid fortification walls were present at all seven settlements. At al-'Aliya, Lahun, al-Mu'ammariyya, al-Mu'arradja and possibly Balu'a, fortifications consisted of two thick walls running parallel to each other with casemate rooms between them. At al-'Aliya, the wall system is between 4 and 4.6 meters thick with outer walls ranging in thickness between 1.1 and 1.2 meters, interior walls between 0.8 and 1 meters, and casemate rooms between 2 and 2.4 meters wide (fig. 4.3; Routledge 2000:48). At al-Mu'ammariyya, the walls extend nearly 300 meters and are almost 5 meters wide with periodic casemates (Ninow 2004:257, 2006:149). At Lahun and al-Mu'arradja, similar systems are reported, albeit somewhat smaller than al-'Aliya, ranging between 3.2 and 3.8 meters wide overall at Lahun (Homès-Fredericq 1992:188, fig. 16.11), and between 3.7 and 4 meters overall at al-Mu'arradja (fig. 4.4) (Olàvarri 1983:168). At Balu'a, a casemate wall system was excavated in Area CIII and D containing a mix of early and late Iron Age ceramic vessels, suggesting that the walls were originally constructed in the early Iron Age and reused centuries later (Worschech and Ninow 1994:199, 202, fig. 6; 1999:172).[7]

Figure 4.3. Fortification walls of al-'Aliya.

Additional features strengthened these walls and played an important role in the overall fortification system. Towers are one such example as they were strategically placed in areas where the settlement was weakest. At al-Mu'arradja, three towers were constructed on the south and west sides of the settlement, where it was most vulnerable to attack (figs. 3.4, 4.5B) (Olàvarri 1983:170). Two additional towers were located adjacent to a gate that protected the village's entrance. Individually, each tower at al-Mu'arradja measured approximately ten meters long by five meters wide. A one-meter thick wall framed each tower's structure and its interior was filled with large stones and dirt. A similar construction style was used in the single tower constructed at al-'Aliya, although on a much larger scale (fig. 4.5A). A tower approximately ten meters in height and thirty-two meters in diameter was

Figure 4.4. Fortification walls of al-Mu'arradja.

constructed on the settlement's vulnerable western edge (Routledge 2000:48–49). Excavations here revealed a three-tier structure where framing walls were filled in with stone and dirt. Finally, at al-Mu'ammariyya, a large tower 5.5 meters in diameter with adjacent support walls was constructed on a spur connected with the main settlement (Ninow 2006:148; fig. 3). At both al-'Aliya and al-Mu'arradja, these towers created platforms that people could stand on or hide behind when defending the settlements, or observe the movements of others at far distances.

Moats and gates were two additional features that strengthened these settlements' overall fortification systems. At al-'Aliya, a moat was constructed beneath the tower on the western side measuring 35 meters long by 18.75 meters wide by 5 meters deep. The moat was created by the quarrying of stones for constructing the tower and other buildings (Routledge 2000:48–49). At al-'Umayri, the moat from the Middle Bronze fortifications

Figure 4.5. (A) Al-'Aliya tower looking east. Two platforms are visible in the center trench. (B) Corner of al-Mu'arradja tower illustrating free-standing tower.

was cleaned out during the Iron Age and played an important role in the settlement's defense. Surprisingly, excavations at the seven settlements have only revealed gates at al-Mu'ammariyya and al-Mu'arradja.[8] At al-Mu'arradja, two rectilinear towers guard a 1.2-meter-wide entrance that extends nearly 10 meters before turning right into the open plaza (Olàvarri 1983:170, 173, fig. 4). Additional gates will likely be identified as excavations continue at settlements such as al-'Aliya and al-'Umayri.

The construction of fortification walls was in part connected to the construction of domestic residences. In several instances, at least one wall of the building served as a fortification wall. If the community came under attack, the secondary interior walls could provide additional support, creating sealed casemate rooms. Where residences were absent, the community built fortification walls to enclose the rest of the settlement. While this link between residence and fortification walls suggests impromptu construction, other fortified architectural features indicate a greater degree of planning. The fortified gates found at al-Mu'arradja suggest communities were concerned with access to the settlement's interior. A designated entrance that could be sealed off from outsiders would protect members and the community's wealth. Perhaps the best evidence for planned fortifications were the large defensive towers found at al-'Aliya and al-Mu'arradja. These towers were placed at the community's most vulnerable points of access and were likely locations from which settlements could come under attack.

The construction of these fortification systems was a labor-intensive activity that required the coordination of multiple households. Collectively, the outcome would have broad benefits for everyone living in the settlement. Fortifications protected communities from neighboring settlements that may attack in an effort to gain access to agricultural surplus during famines or drought. Fortifications also played another, more symbolic role, by creating a physical boundary that contained the community, designated insiders from outsiders, and established a marker of membership. Banishment from the community meant residing beyond the protection of the settlement's walls. Despite the obvious collective advantages, fortifications also benefited those who had the most to lose in terms of wealth. The possibility that such households had the capacity to motivate and manage other households in such projects will be considered in chapter 5.

Writing the Script: Agro-pastoralism

If building practices created the stage on which the communities' social life was performed, then agro-pastoralism offered a script for their survival. In particular, the analytical division of sedentary agriculture and nomadic pastoralism that Levantine archaeologists use to describe Early Iron Age societies is too rigid. Archaeological evidence recovered from many of the region's settlements indicates that the communities depended on a combination of agricultural production and pastoralism that was carefully balanced to create a buffer against scarcity and to distribute risk across the agricultural cycle. If successful, these practices created the material wealth on which households could not just sustain themselves but also use to create bonds across households.

It is impossible to generalize about agro-pastoralism in west-central Jordan, or indeed the entire Levant, because of the region's microclimatic diversity. Agro-pastoralism in west-central Jordan is partly structured by the Levant's Mediterranean climate, with its short but intense rainy seasons in the winter, offset by hot, dry summers that challenge the region's communities to manage and conserve winter precipitation for the long periods of summer drought (Ferguson and Hudson 1986; Horowitz 1979:20–22).[9] Precipitation—predominately rain, but also dew, fog, snow, sleet, and hail—is not uniformly distributed across west-central Jordan, but is instead a patchwork of temperate, semi-arid, and arid Mediterranean bioclimatic zones (Cordova 2007:38–47, figs. 2.9–2.10). Generally, precipitation is greatest (300–600 mm/year) where elevation is greatest along the plateau's western edge and decreases (100–200 mm/year) in lower elevations (e.g., the Jordan Valley) and when moving eastward toward the Arabian Desert. The uneven distribution of precipitation across the region explains the likewise uneven distribution of Early Iron Age settlements. Settlement clusters, such as those near Hesban, Karak, and Dubab, appear in areas where precipitation exceeds three hundred millimeters per year. Larger amounts of rainfall not only fed cisterns and watered crops, but also fostered soils more suitable for agricultural production. Yet interestingly, Early Iron Age settlements appear in regions where rainfall was below three hundred millimeters per year and soils were less suitable for planting.

In order to compensate for the lack of moisture in these agriculturally marginal areas, settlements were founded adjacent to wadi canyon systems that dissect the plateaus and contain either perennial or seasonal rivers that drain toward the Jordan Valley. The largest systems—the al-Zarqa, the al-Mujib, and the al-Hasa—are broad and deep natural features that are not easily crossed (fig. 3.1). Smaller, yet still impressive, canyon systems such as the al-Thamad, the al-Wala, and the al-Zarqa Ma'in also cut deeply into the plateaus and create notable topographic boundaries between regions. Producers living in settlements next to these canyons could organize their agricultural routines in the narrow riparian zones at the bottom (fig. 4.6). In these zones, perennial aquifers fed streams that create moist habitats for wild flora and fauna. Herds could be watered throughout the year, and grains could be grown, although at relatively limited levels. The colluvial benches on the canyon sides also created spaces where grains and fruits could be grown using the soil beds that had formed from eroded materials.

Central Jordan's soils also posed a challenge to Early Iron Age agropastoralist practices. The extreme temperature and humidity differences between winter and summer play a structuring role in the generation of soils in the region, as they do throughout the Mediterranean Basin (Lacelle 1986a; Yaalon 1997). This pedogenic process determines soil productivity and, therefore, determines where agricultural production is possible in

Figure 4.6. The wadi riparian zone below al-'Aliya and al-Mu'arradja. (A) Example of a pool from which crabs, fish, and other aquatic species could be collected. (B) Low-intensity floodwater farming is possible in open areas.

west-central Jordan (Cordova 2007:56–61). There are three types of calcareous soils in the region, from best to worst in agricultural productivity: red Mediterranean soils (RMS), yellow Mediterranean soils (YMS), and yellow steppic soils (YSS) (Moormann 1959). Although mature soil profiles are rare because of extensive alluvial, colluvial, and aeolian erosion over the millennia, pedogenesis is most fully developed in the clay-rich RMS that exist in areas where rainfall exceeds three hundred millimeters. Not as fertile are the YMS located in areas where precipitation exists between one hundred and three hundred millimeters and in more shallow beds, making agricultural production possible, but less efficient. YSS are the least productive of the three soil types, appearing in areas where precipitation is less than one hundred millimeters.[10]

The seasonal disparities in precipitation and the geographic unevenness of soil quality together made agro-pastoralism a difficult and tenuous endeavor for the region's producers, especially those settlements in the semi-arid zones. Precipitation and soil quality determined the local nature of specific agricultural practices, as Hopkins (1985) discovered in his examination of Early Iron Age agriculture in the neighboring central highlands. In modern west-central Jordan, rain-fed agricultural activity is most intensive on the western half where rainfall and RMS are suitable for more intensive production. On the eastern half, where precipitation is lower and YMS are less rich, agricultural yields are reduced. Observations based on modern low-intensity agricultural practices suggest production is suitable in three ecological zones (Christopherson and Guertin 1995). Most prevalent are dry-farmed, cultivated fields where deep, clay-rich soils were ideal for crop production. Dry, barren hillsides where shallow stone soils are located on eroded hills above wadi canyons were less frequent and less ideal for production. The riparian areas found at the bottom of deep wadi canyons were another and possibly the most important ecological zone available to Early Iron Age producers (fig. 4.6). The moist wadi floors held seasonal or perennial streams that could be used for low-intensive floodwater farming, watering herds, hunting wild animals, and harvesting naturally available reeds, cattails, galingale, and mint.

Knowledge of local rainfall patterns, soil quality, and landscape management was used to organize production around a seasonal calendar. Descriptions of agricultural practices in the Hebrew Bible (Borowski 1987), a tenth-century BCE paleo-Hebrew inscription called the Gezer Calendar (Albright 1943), and observations from modern nonmechanized agricultural practices in northern Jordan (Palmer 1998) permit a reconstruction of the annual agricultural cycle based on a mixed Mediterranean economy of grains, legumes, fruits, and animals. Starting in July, four months were dedicated to plowing and sowing fields prior to the beginning of the wet season in November. This work lasted into the winter, a strategy likely used to prevent the risk of crop failure caused by drought. Plowing was an essential and time-consuming endeavor as it was necessary to break up dried soil to release captured precipitation and to permit the absorption of new moisture; plowing also created furrows for seed planting. Plowing was done by hand, or cattle (usually ox) or donkeys pulled wood plows with a bronze or iron plowshare attached to the bottom that penetrated the soil, breaking and mixing it while leaving seed furrows for sowing. Once fields were plowed and weeded, cultivators distributed seed through broadcast sowing and then lightly plowed the field in order to protect the seed from predators. Barley and wheat were two overwhelmingly popular cereals sown in the winter months, the former requiring at least 250 millimeters of precipitation per year and the latter, at least 300 millimeters. Once planted, crops required so little maintenance that agriculturalists were not required to visit their fields until harvest season in the late spring and early summer when the Gezer Calendar allots one month to harvest barley, followed by one more month to harvest wheat. Grain was reaped either with a hand sickle or through route hand picking and brought to the threshing floor where reapings were dried and threshed to loosen the spikelets and remove the hulls. Further winnowing and sieving separated the chaff from the grain before storing.

Paleobotanical analyses of plant remains recovered from buildings inside the Early Iron Age communities confirm that grains were the principal crop in a producer's regiment (Clark 1997:64, 2000:78; Gilliland and Fisk 1986, esp. fig. 7.1, table 7.2; Simmons 2000).[11] At al-'Aliya, several types of wheat and barley were identified in both grain and chaff form in a storage context in Building 100 (Simmons 2000, fig. 15). The presence of chaff in these samples indicates that grain was not only grown for human consumption, but also for fodder to feed herds during the lean months after field stubble had been consumed. The paleobotanical samples' composition also potentially reveals where grains were grown. A limited number of wetland weed species mixed with cereals, barley in particular, were identified, suggesting that cereals were harvested near water sources (Simmons 2000:44–46, fig. 23). At al-'Aliya, the closest location matching this description is in the nearby riparian zones, where a perennial water source is located, making an ideal location for low-intensive floodwater farming (fig. 4.6).[12]

Still, agricultural production was a tedious and risky endeavor no matter where settlements were positioned in the region. Producers were never guaranteed to reap what they had sowed. Above all else, drought posed the greatest challenge to agricultural production, especially to settlements living in regions already receiving less than three hundred millimeters of annual precipitation. Pests such as locusts and rodents, crop and animal disease, late frosts, and weed infestations could also destroy agricultural produce, leaving communities in a precarious position. Although ultimately they were at the mercy of the elements, cultivators could use different risk-reducing strategies to manage the natural resources they had available to them as efficiently as possible. Crop diversification was one such strategy. Because they differed from each other in their sowing and harvesting schedules, a diversified assemblage of crops helped to distribute risk in years when precipitation was reduced or arrived late in the growing season. Diversification also eased labor burdens so that harvesting was staggered across the agricultural calendar. Pulses such as beans, peas, lentils, chickpeas, and bitter vetch are one such important crop category that diversified a predominately barley and wheat regime. Lentils, legumes, and peas were identified in al-'Aliya's paleobotanical remains (Simmons 2000, fig. 15). Most pulses were likely planted in late spring and harvested in mid- to late summer, having the advantage of a short growing season that did not conflict with barley and wheat's sowing and reaping periods. Although most require at least 350 millimeters of annual precipitation, pulses also depend on soil-stored moisture to resist drought. Pulses also benefit soils, humans, and animals, as they are nitrogen rich, aiding in soil regeneration, and contain two to three times more protein than cereals. Pulses like bitter vetch are also ideal for animal fodder. Vegetables such as onions, melons, cucumbers, and garlic were harvested in gardens, although the lack of irrigation agriculture confined these gardens to fields in close proximity to water sources such as those in canyon riparian zones.

The harvesting of grapes and olives as well as fruit and nut husbandry were other ways to diversify crop assemblage without conflicting with grain harvesting. Figs and grapes were identified in al-'Aliya's paleobotanical evidence (Simmons 2000, fig. 15).[13] The Gezer Calendar indicates that two months of grape cutting followed by a month of fruit collection and another two months of olive harvesting were completed in the warmer months between grain harvesting and sowing. At least three hundred millimeters of annual precipitation was required for successful viticultural and fruit harvesting. The presence of anthropogenic flora in pollen cores indicates the possibility and popularity of such agricultural practices in the Late Bronze and Iron Ages (Baruch 1990:284).[14]

Gathering naturally occurring flora and hunting wild animals were other ways that early Iron Age communities could overcome the risks of agricultural production. Surprisingly, wild or noncultivated specimens are not abundant in the paleobotanical data set, although the possibility that they were collected on occasion should not be dismissed.[15] Crawford (1986) has catalogued a number of wild flora in Hesban's vicinity that were likely available to communities. What evidence there is in the paleobotanical record from Hesban (Gilliland and Fisk 1986, fig. 7.1) and al-'Aliya (Simmons 2000, table 9.1) indicates that wild cultivars suitable for animal consumption, but not human consumption, supplemented animal fodder.[16] Like plants, a diversity of wild animal species living in the Early Iron Age communities' vicinities was available for consumption. Examined faunal evidence from excavated refuse from residences at al-'Aliya and al-'Umayri suggest a variety of species were hunted and consumed (Lev-Tov, Porter, and Routledge 2010, table 1; Peters, Pöllath, and von den Driesch 2002).[17] The analysis of a refuse pit associated with al-'Umayri Buildings A and B demonstrates how diverse this wild faunal population was. Gazelles and deer ($n = 9$), wild boars ($n = 4$), aurochs ($n = 2$), a lion ($n = 1$), and a wild cat ($n = 1$) were identified. Bird ($n = 15$) remains included ostrich, partridge, doves, pigeons, and buzzards, while fish and reptiles included tortoises and Nile perch (Peters, Pöllath, and von den Driesch 2002:311–313, fig. 14.6). Although the al-'Umayri data may suggest that an abundance of species were available across the region, it is more likely that the consumption of wild animals depended on their availability in the local environment. Case in point is the al-'Aliya settlement, located further south than al-'Umayri and adjacent to a perennial water source. At this site, zooarchaeological analysis has identified freshwater crabs, fish, red deer, and large birds such as storks in the faunal evidence (table 4.1).

Table 4.1. Identification for all bones recovered at Khirbat al-Mudayna al-'Aliya

Scientific Name	Common Name	NISP	Percent	MNI
Ardeidae/Ciconiidae	Heron or stork	1	+	1
Aves	Unidentifiable birds	10	2	—
Bos taurus	Domestic cattle	11	3	1
Camelus sp.	Camel	1	+	1
Canis familiaris	Domestic dog	3	1	2
Capra hircus	Domestic goat	10	2	3
Cervus elaphus	Red deer	1	+	1
Equus asinus	Ass or onager	8	2	1
Equus caballus	Horse	12	3	2
Equus sp.	Horse, ass, or onager	16	4	3
cf. Erinaceidae	Possible hedgehog	1	+	1
Osteichthyes	Bony fish	1	+	1
Ovis aries	Domestic sheep	8	2	2
Ovis/Capra	Sheep or goat	229	53	7
Passeriformes	Perching bird	1	+	1
Potamon potamios	Freshwater crab	100	23	27
Rodentia	Rodent	12	3	2
Sus scrofa	Pig	6	1	1
Unidentifiable bones		1798	—	—
Total Identifiable		431		29
Grand Total		2229		

+ amount fell below one percent
NISP = Number of identified species
MNI = minimum number of individuals

The Early Iron Age communities depended most on domesticated livestock. Animal husbandry diversified agricultural practices and risk-reducing strategy across the agricultural cycle (Borowski 1998). Analysis of faunal remains from al-'Aliya (Lev-Tov, Porter, and Routledge 2010, table 4.1, this volume), Hesban (von den Driesch and Boessneck 1995), and al-'Umayri (Peters, Pöllath, and von den Driesch 2002) demonstrate the extent to which the communities depended on a variety of domesticated species.[18] Sheep and goats dominated all three assemblages. Based on the total number of identified species (NISP),[19] sheep and goats comprised 81.8 percent of al-'Umayri's (3,219 sheep/goats, 205 sheep, and 101 goats) (Peters, Pöllath, and von den Driesch 2002, fig. 14.6), 70.5 percent of Hesban's (393 sheep/goats, 38 sheep, and 29 goats) (von den Driesch and Boessneck 1995, table 5.9), and 57 percent of al-'Aliya's (229 sheep/goats, 8 sheep, and 10 goats) domestic mammal population (table 4.1, this volume). Producers would have depended on these flocks for both primary (e.g., meat) and secondary (e.g., wool, milk) products. Herds grazed on green plants during the moist winter months. In the summer, they grazed on field stubble, and after this was depleted, their diets were supplemented with hay and grain until winter vegetation once again returned to the landscape. The age and sex ratios of the herds reflected the communities' needs. At al-'Umayri, where the faunal collection is sufficient enough to draw conclusions, 61.8 percent of sheep and goats were culled before the age of two, suggesting the community depended on their herds for meat (Peters, Pöllath, and von den Driesch 2002, fig. 14.8). Interestingly, however, 35.3 percent of the sheep and goat sample were culled after the age of two, suggesting that part of the herd was reserved for wool production as well (Peters, Pöllath, and von den Driesch 2002:319). The al-'Aliya community, however, appears to have managed their herds differently. Goats were slightly more common than sheep, suggesting that the community depended on goats for both meat and secondary products, whereas sheep were probably kept only for secondary products, likely wool.[20] These differences in herd management strategies between al-'Aliya and al-'Umayri may be in part due to differences in terrain and climate, as goats were more suitable than sheep for the rocky terrain in al-'Aliya's vicinity.

Although sheep and goats were by far the most popular choices in animal husbandry practices, they were by no means the only choices. Cattle were also used, supplying milk, meat, and occasionally participating in plowing and transportation. Cattle remains were present in 22.2 percent ($n=145$) of Hesban's (von den Driesch and Boessneck 1995, table 5.9), 14 percent ($n=605$) of al-'Umayri's (Peters, Pöllath, and von den Driesch 2002, fig. 14.4), and 3 percent ($n=11$) of al-'Aliya's collection (Lev-Tov,

Porter, and Routledge 2010, table 4.1, this volume). At al-'Umayri, an unusually high number of juveniles (65 percent; $n=9$) were slaughtered before the age of 2.5 years, suggesting that the community depended on cattle for meat over dairy and other uses (von den Driesch and Boessneck 1995:317, fig. 14.8).[21] Pigs, too, were an important component of diets, supplying meat for the community, and were present in 2.5 percent ($n=109$) of al-'Umayri's (Peters, et al. 2002, fig. 14.4), 4.75 percent (n = 31) of Hesban's (von den Driesch and Boessneck 1995, table 5.9), and 1 percent ($n=6$) of al-'Aliya's assemblage (Lev-Tov, Porter, and Routledge 2010, table 4.1, this volume).[22]

Agriculture and pastoralism generated the materials for food, one of the principal forms of wealth in the communities. Frustratingly, from the faunal and paleoethnobotanical evidence just presented, it is impossible to discern whether or not individual households or the larger community organized agricultural and pastoralist production. It is possible to imagine different, plausible scenarios, however. Because herding does not require a large labor force, agro-pastoral societies often practice cooperative herding strategies of household-owned animals in order to free up individuals for labor projects requiring a greater number of people. Households may also cooperate with each other during certain labor-intensive periods of the agricultural cycle. Although it may be difficult to decide with confidence on the arrangement of production strategies, it is possible to observe how organic materials were eventually distributed across the community by observing storage strategies and techniques.

Storage Strategies and Techniques

The successful storage of food surplus, whether for human or animal consumption, was the Early Iron Age communities' most important strategy for building a resilient sedentary lifestyle. A properly managed surplus was households' and communities' greatest bulwark against unpredictable drought- and famine-induced scarcity. The communities had multiple options for storage, the most obvious one being literally "on the hoof." That is, herds of domestic animals could be carefully managed to adjust for producers' current needs and future expectations. In lean years, husbandry strategies could be reorganized so that shortfalls in wheat and barley could be substituted with animal meat. Furthermore, older cattle, sheep, and goats usually reserved for the production of secondary products could be culled. The older sheep and goat specimens present in the al-'Aliya and al-'Umayri faunal assemblages, discussed in the previous section, suggest this strategy would have been a viable option for the communities. Once periods of scarcity had receded, herds could be replenished to normal operating levels.

The settlements' architectural arrangements indicate how important herds were to Early Iron Age animal economies. The large open courtyards at al-'Aliya, Lahun, al-Mu'arradja, and possibly at al-Mu'ammariyya and al-'Umayri created a protected space for herds to be fed and penned at night and during periods of poor weather and conflict. A small number of especially milk-producing and wool-bearing animals could be penned inside residences, if so desired. Regardless of where they were stabled in the settlement, animals were conveniently located close to daily food and textile production sites. Both the al-'Aliya and al-'Umayri faunal assemblages strongly suggest that herds were slaughtered and consumed inside the settlement. All body parts of animal carcasses are represented evenly in both collections (von den Driesch and Boessneck 1995:316, table 14.7; Lev-Tov, Porter, and Routledge 2010).

A second storage strategy was the production of an agricultural surplus that could be drawn on during drought and famine. Successfully maintaining a surplus had its own challenges. Communities were required to build storage facilities safe from moisture, insects, and rodents. Several such storage facilities have been excavated in the settlements. Select buildings appear to have been dedicated to agricultural storage in the communities. At the highest point of al-Mu'ammariyya, a 429-square-meter multichambered building (the "citadel") was excavated (fig. 4.7; Ninow 2004). At the building's center was a courtyard, surrounded on all sides by small chambers. Several features of this building suggest that its primary function was for storage purposes. The building's narrow entrance (B2) is marked by a double bent-axis, suggesting that access to the building's interior was restricted. Furthermore, the arrangement of certain small interior rooms (e.g., R2, R3, and R11) in the building and the small .5-meter entrances that led into them required visitors to turn several corners before arriving at their destination. Both features suggest their contents were valuable to their owners.[23] Such isolation also produced a relatively cool and confined microclimate suitable for stored agricultural goods. In the excavation of one of these rooms, R2, flat stones were discovered on the floor's surface that elevated stored goods off the ground, protecting them from moisture and rodents (Ninow 2004:261).

Another building that appears to have served as storage space is al-'Aliya's Building 100 (fig. 4.8). The building is located on the eastern

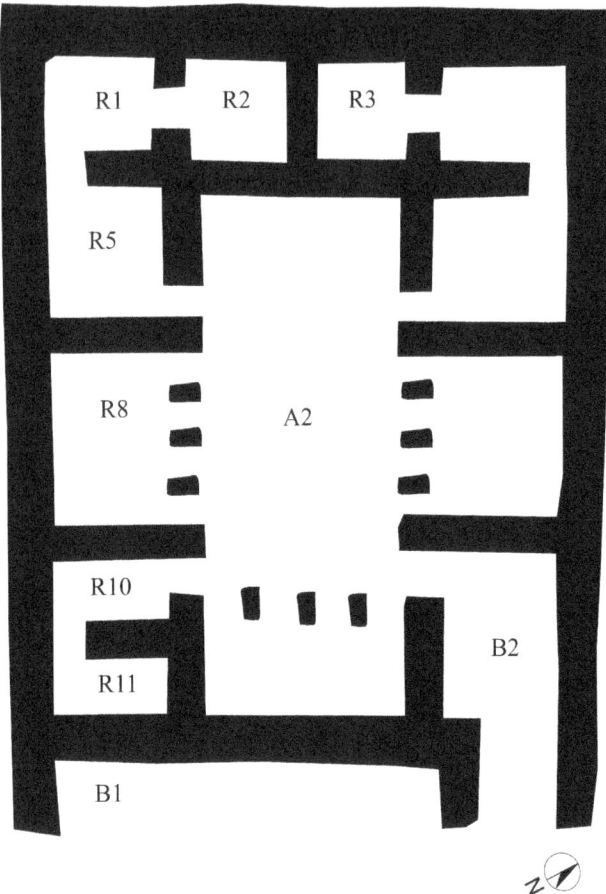

Figure 4.7. Al-Muʻammariyya citadel building, measuring between seventeen and eighteen meters wide and between twenty-four and twenty-five meters long. (*Source*: Adapted from Ninow 2004, fig. 4)

perimeter of the settlement, close to a postern gate, cisterns, and the perennial wadi springs below. Building 100 is a 178-square-meter multichambered building similar in design to, albeit smaller than, the al-Muʻammariyya citadel.[24] Courtyard 105 sits at the building's center and is surrounded on all sides by eight small chambers. Like al-Muʻammariyya's citadel building, some features suggest that this building was used for bulk storage of agricultural products. A double bent-axis entrance (Room 103) marks Building 100's entrance, suggesting that access to the building's interior was

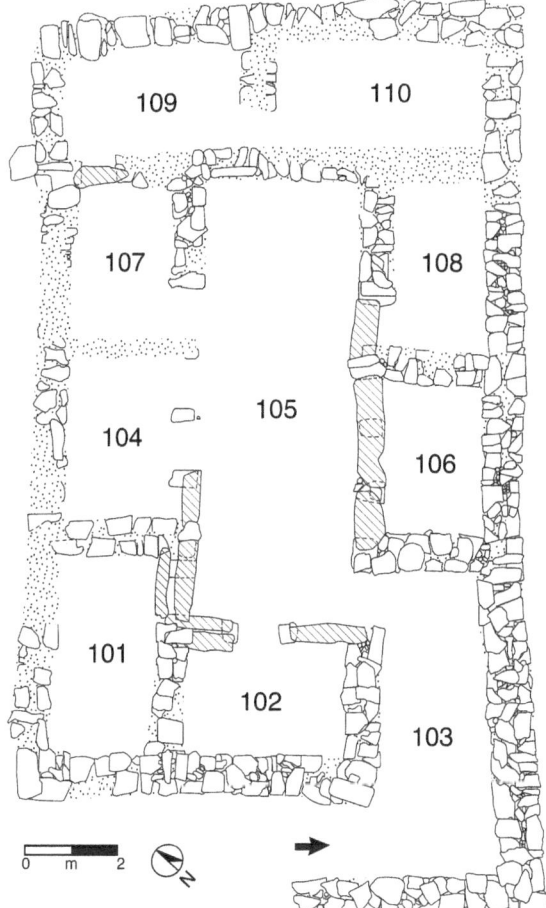

Figure 4.8. Al-'Aliya Building 100. (*Source*: Adapted from Ninow 2004, fig. 4)

sheltered from the elements. Also, the excavation of two rooms exposed features and artifacts that strongly suggest their use as storage installations. Room 102 (2.6 × 2.8 m) is framed by three solid walls on its north, west, and south sides, and by two pillars with in situ lintels on the east. A small entrance permits access from the east side. Two bins were installed on either side of the east wall that were possibly mangers used for the feeding of herds and grain storage. In a similar chamber, Room 106 (2.2 × 3.12 m), the structure was again framed by three solid walls, the northern wall remaining open to Courtyard 105.

Like the architectural evidence from al-Muʻammariyya's citadel building, that of al-ʻAliya's Rooms 102 and 106 suggests that builders were concerned with protecting produce from moisture and rodents. A section cut through one interior wall shows that these slab walls retain a layer of soil filled with small stones that runs under the exterior walls of Room 102 (Walls 2, 5, and 25). After the principal load-bearing exterior walls of Room 102 were built, the marly subsoil in the central portion of the room was cut down to bedrock. After this, the low slab walls were inserted to support the soil beneath the outer walls, and the bedrock was leveled with a surface. The construction of this central space below the foundation level of the room's exterior walls was a protective measure against the burrowing of vermin.

From these facilities, animal diets could be supplemented with fodder, especially during periods of drought and in the late summer, when field stubble had been completely grazed. Paleobotanical analysis of evidence from Room 106 found that the large number of weeds mixed with cereals, as well as the fact that cereals had not been completely processed before storing, supports the possibility that fodder was stored in Building 100 (Simmons 2000:51). So far, there is no evidence, unfortunately, that would help determine whether or not agricultural products fit for human consumption were stored in this building alongside animal fodder. However, evidence of human cultivars such as grapes and lentils found mixed with animal fodder suggests that both were stored in Building 100. Additional analysis of paleobotanical evidence from the building could determine if additional types of agricultural surplus were stored in this building.

The role these storage facilities at al-ʻAliya and al-Muʻammariyya played in agricultural production strategies suggests both may have served communal storage purposes. This interpretation is admittedly hindered by the fact that both buildings need additional excavation. Still, the available evidence supports interpreting the principal function of these buildings as storage facilities rather than as domestic residences. The layout of both buildings is distinct from that of the domestic residences examined earlier (e.g., figs. 4.1, 4.2). The multiple small chambers that line the interior of each building also suggests that these rooms were used for storage purposes. Additionally, al-ʻAliya's Building 100 has yet to yield evidence that would suggest domestic use. The same observation may be true of the al-Muʻammariyya citadel, although not enough artifactual evidence has been published. Comparing another large building, al-ʻAliya's Building 500 (fig. 5.3), where artifacts associated with food production and consumption (e.g., cooking vessels) have been found in abundance, the apparent lack of objects associated with such practices is conspicuous. Likewise, food production facilities such as that found in al-'Aliya Building 500 (discussed in chapter 5) have not yet been discovered in either building. Additional excavation in both al-'Aliya Building 100 and the al-Mu'ammariyya citadel would strengthen this interpretation of the buildings' role in surplus storage.

The presence of communal storage facilities suggests additional acts of coordination and cooperation took place. The construction of these large structures required members to participate in communal building activities and contribute their labor, resources, and time. Additionally, such communal storage practices required the community to arrive at a consensus regarding how and when to distribute this surplus and in what amounts. Replenishing the granary required further consensus among members. Either a certain portion of each household's produce was collected for storage or certain fields were set aside for communal production. In the latter instance, households would have donated their time and labor to manage these communal lands. In light of the cooperative projects examined earlier, such as the construction of residences and fortifications, it should be anticipated that households also cooperated in collective storage practices that benefitted the entire community. Although it is tempting to interpret these practices as indicative of harmonious social arrangements, it is more likely that collective storage was a complex process. One might imagine conflicts between households over how to schedule and maintain such a valuable resource that was essential to the community's survival.

One suggestion that not all agricultural materials were communally managed is that individual households still found it necessary to maintain storage facilities in each residency. Architectural evidence at both al-'Aliya and al-'Umayri indicates that storage facilities were also built in pillared buildings. The best-preserved instances are found in al-'Umayri's Buildings A and B, Room A3, 2.75 meters wide by 5 meters long (Herr et al. 1997:63–64), and Room B3, 2.3 meters wide by 5.8 meters long (Herr and Platt 2002:97–99). Several features and artifacts strongly support the interpretation that these rooms' primary function was the storage of agricultural goods. These rooms' locations at the building's rear provided the necessary dry and protected conditions needed to store agricultural goods. At least 1.80 meters squared of Room B3's floor was covered with flagstones that would have elevated stored goods off the ground, protecting them from moisture and rodents;[25] and large ceramic jars were excavated at al-'Aliya (fig. 4.9: 8–10, this volume) and in al-'Umayri Rooms A3 and B3 (Herr et al. 1997, figs. 4.14–4.21; Herr and Platt 2002, figs. 4.17–4.27). These jars protected dry goods from moisture and rodents, and liquids such as oils, wine, and water from evaporation and spoilage. The most convincing evidence that these rooms were reserved for grain storage is the finding of a wide variety of seeds. The excavators tentatively identified wheat, barley, broad bean, chickpea, grape, poppy, corn cockle, sweet helbe, lentil, vetch, green bean, and flax (Herr et al. 1997:64).

Although al-'Umayri's Rooms A3 and B3 are the best-preserved examples of residential storage units, storage facilities were constructed in the rear rooms of pillared buildings at other settlements. At Lahun, three chambers, Rooms II.1, II.2, and III, were identified at the rear of House 1 (Homès-Fredericq 2000, figs. 3, 13; Porter 2010, fig. 3b; Swinnen 2009, fig. 4). Room III conspicuously lacks an obvious entrance, suggesting its contents could be accessed through the roof. The room's floor is constructed of irregularly shaped flagstones, a characteristic feature of storage installations (Homès-Fredericq 2000:190). Moreover, the blueprints of Buildings 200, 300, 400, 600, 700, and 800 at al-'Aliya offer additional examples of rooms placed at the rear of each building where storage facilities were constructed (e.g., Rooms 206, 303, 405, 605, 701, 703, 804, and 805) (Routledge 2000, figs. 11–13, 15–17). In one instance, Building 200's Room 206 (10 m × 2.5 m; fig. 4.1), although not containing the rich deposits seen in al-'Umayri's Buildings A and B, excavations did reveal a low bench attached to a wall that may have served to elevate stored goods off the ground.[26] Additionally, postoccupational events likely destroyed a plastered floor found in other parts of the building that would have helped to preserve organic materials.

Altogether, the Early Iron Age communities employed two distinct storage strategies. On the one hand, the communal facilities at al-Mu'ammariyya and Building 100 at al-'Aliya stored animal fodder and perhaps other products for human consumption. On the other hand, each household maintained its own storage facilities in individual buildings. This pattern can be observed across specific buildings and suggests households retained portions of their yield for their own use. A household's ability to store a food surplus increased its capacity to subsist during periods of scarcity and contributed to its overall resilience. But these segmented storage facilities are also symptomatic of households' anxieties over the community's self-efficacy in the face of potential scarcity.

Crafting Resilience: Ceramic Vessel Production

The production of ceramic vessels was another important practice in the Early Iron Age communities that contributed to household and community resilience. The vessel assemblage from the Early Iron Age settlements consisted of a typical Near Eastern agro-pastoralist repertoire (figs 4.9, 5.4).[27] Although the assemblage has some diversity in form, generally it consists of hemispherical and sometimes carinated bowls of various depths, open kraters likely used for food preparation, cooking pots, sometimes bearing handles, tall two-handled ovoid jars with narrow openings for liquid and grain storage, smaller one-handled jars and juglets for serving liquids, and simple lamps.[28] Most vessels were undecorated, except for an occasional thin white slip or self-slip and a limited number of bowls decorated with a red pigment in vertical streaks on the side (fig. 5.4). Except for al-'Umayri and some vessels from Lahun, which are dated to the twelfth century, the Early Iron Age settlements clustered around the Wadi al-Mujib are fairly similar in form, a clue that production techniques were shared across the region and that some exchange of vessels—and cultural knowledge about production techniques—took place between communities.

Figure 4.9. Bowls (nos. 1–3), kraters (nos. 4–7), jars (8–14), cooking pots (15–16), and juglets (nos. 17–18) from al-'Aliya.

Vessels were essential tools in their own way for accomplishing everyday tasks such as cooking, but they also played a supporting role in other production routines. The excavation of large jars and of smaller jugs in storage contexts as the rear rooms of al-'Umayri's Buildings A and B and in the rear storage facilities of al-'Aliya's Building 500 indicate that the communities used them to protect cereals, water, olive oil, and wine from the elements. Communities depended on ceramic cooking pots, kraters, and bowls for preparing and serving food in daily meals and feasts. No matter how essential to the communities' livelihood, vessels were unfortunately not readily available items in the landscape compared to, for instance, stones for architectural production or wild animals for hunting. Vessels had to be made from scratch, and their production required proper clay, tempers, fuel, and water, all of which were naturally available to varying degrees in the landscape but still required procurement. Vessel production, if not a specialized, full-time activity, also had to be scheduled into the agricultural cycle without robbing from labor needs and resources needed elsewhere. The amount of labor and time expended on vessel production suggests that these items were relatively valuable objects in the communities. Also, as wealth in the early Iron Age communities appears to have been based partly on agricultural surplus, access to vessels was necessary for successful storage technologies. Given vessels' importance to a community's subsistence, one is led to wonder whether or not their production was managed by individual households or was a communal endeavor.

Investigation of other Early Iron Age ceramic vessel industries elsewhere in the southern Levant can provide some insight into production practices in west-central Jordan. Some workshops are so well preserved that production techniques can be reconstructed from the wheels (both single and double), kilns (horizontal and vertical, the latter being more popular), basins, hand tools, and wasters found in them.[29] Yet in west-central Jordan, no workshops or kilns have been excavated so far that would allow a direct investigation of vessel preparation and firing techniques. One possible explanation for this absence may be the likelihood that production activities occurred in informal areas outside settlements that were closer to clay, fuel, and water procurement zones. This location would have been especially appropriate for producers that used open- or pit-firing methods, an inexpensive, albeit less sufficient, firing method. Vessels to be fired were placed on top of a slow-burning fire either above ground or in a pit. More fuel was piled on the vessels, which, upon burning, insulated them, creating an oven. Both open- and pit-firing methods required more fuel than enclosed kilns, and firing temperature and oxidization levels could not be controlled as easily. Consequently, vessels were often poorly fired compared to those made in kilns. Given their impromptu nature, open- and pit-firing installations are difficult to locate in the archaeological record, and evidence for their use in antiquity can only be deduced from the vessel itself and analogical observations of contemporary potters working in preindustrial settings.

Several studies have discovered that the organization and sophistication of ancient Jordan's ceramic industries devolved during the Early Iron Age (Clark and London 2000; Franken 1969; Franken and London 1995; Glanzman and Fleming 1986). In west-central Jordan, Early Iron Age vessels exhibit low-fired, gray cores, suggesting that kiln temperatures were generally lower compared to their Late Bronze Age counterparts. Mold, coiling, and turning practices grew to become the standard practice, almost, but not completely, replacing throwing on a potter's wheel. Paste recipes changed at the same time as forming methods, from plastic to more lean textures containing larger amounts of nonplastic inclusions.[30] Alongside changes in paste recipes and forming techniques, producers reduced the amount and quality of the slips and painted decoration that made Middle and Late Bronze Age pottery so distinct.[31] These changes in ceramic production techniques and organization are not surprising given that they coincide with the relative decrease in political, economic, and social complexity during the Early Iron Age. With the decline of Egypt's dominance in the region and the subsequent collapse of the military garrisons and palace-based elites who likely sponsored specialized production activities, demand for vessel production was not as abundant. Consequently, full-time producers could no longer find the support required to sustain output levels. Despite the end of specialized industries, communities retained the knowledge of ceramic production technology, passing down this technical information of forms and materials to subsequent generations. As communities were founded, this knowledge was retained, although in modified forms adapted to current needs and local production conditions. As plausible as this reconstruction may be, it does little to explain how Early Iron Age vessel production was organized in the specific communities of west-central Jordan that are under investigation in this work, especially those settlements located in semi-arid zones where fuel, water, and clay-rich soils were often limited.

In the absence of direct evidence, materials scientific analyses of the Early Iron Age ceramic vessel assemblage can characterize the organization of its production. Instrumental neutron activation analysis (INAA hereafter) analyzes the elemental composition of individual vessels and uses multivariate statistics to measure the probability that they were crafted from similar raw materials.[32] INAA was carried out on fifty-one samples from al-'Aliya as part of a larger study on Iron Age vessel production in west-central Jordan (Porter 2007:216–317). A smaller number of samples from Balu'a ($n = 7$) and Lahun ($n = 9$) were included for regional comparative purposes. These samples sorted into two compositional groups (Porter 2007, table 5.5–5.6). Whereas Group One ($n = 53$) consisted of a variety of different vessel types from different settlements, Group Two ($n = 4$) consisted entirely of cooking vessels from al-'Aliya. Another ten samples could not be classified within either group or their own group, an indication that other compositional groups might be identified with further sampling. The results suggest that, in general, producers from different settlements used similar clay sources for all vessel types except for those designated for cooking. To obtain a more refined understanding of vessel production, particularly tempering practices, thin sections of fifty-one vessels from al-'Aliya were analyzed using petrographic techniques to measure vessels' mineral composition (Routledge, Klassen, and Porter, forthcoming). The petrographic samples sorted into five groups that reflected only a limited amount of diversity in production technologies and regional provenance. In summary, both INAA and petrographic analyses characterized vessel production as a routine that was relatively unspecialized in its technology and organization. Except for cooking vessels, neither the INAA nor the petrographic samples sorted according to a particular vessel form (e.g., bowl, jar), an indication that specific clays and tempering techniques were not selected to make a particular vessel. Nor did groups sort according to a particular household or settlement. Rather, it appears that production was a communal affair. Both petrographic and INAA results indicate that raw materials were procured locally and that no vessels seem to have been imported from outside the region.

The decentralized character of vessel production is somewhat surprising. Given jars' importance in storage and water transportation, it is reasonable to suspect that these vessels were produced under specialized conditions. Yet the compositional distribution of jars suggests the opposite. Clay pastes for jar production were similar to bowls and kraters, vessels used most commonly in food consumption. Cooking pots, however, do provide limited evidence that at least some vessels were produced under specialized conditions. The evidence for specialized cooking pot production is found in Group Two. In this group, cooking pots from al-'Aliya made up the entire group. Group Two's distinct chemical composition may be due to the addition of temper to the ceramic paste (Routledge, Klassen, and Porter, forthcoming).

These analyses also indicate that ceramic production was organized at the community rather than at the household level. At al-'Aliya, ceramic vessels from four sampled buildings dominated Group Two, whereas a handful fell into Group Three and Group Five. The same situation was identified at Lahun, where six buildings shared one group. Sampled vessels from Balu'a show more variability, however.[33] Vessels sampled from individual households shared similar compositional groups, which suggests that ceramic production was a community practice in which members from different households participated in production. It also suggests technological information such as resource procurement and levigation techniques were distributed across households.

INAA and the distribution of vessels across the settlement suggest that all households, regardless of wealth, had access to similar vessels. This similarity in composition is most readily observed when comparing the distribution of ceramic vessels according to the residence in which they were found. Ceramic vessels from al-'Aliya's Building 500, the large residence most likely occupied by the wealthiest family in the community, are located in the same compositional groups as Building 200 and Building 700, two regular-size residences. All samples ($n = 12$) from Building 200 were located in Group One. A majority of Building 700's samples were located in Group One ($n = 27$), whereas two samples were unassigned, likely belonging to compositional groups yet to be identified. Only Building 500 suggests some variability in production source, samples being divided between Group One ($n = 2$) and unassigned samples ($n = 2$). The lack of unique and concentrated production groups in Building 500 strongly suggests the al-'Aliya community managed ceramic production collectively.

The sharing of similar vessel production resources in communities that were adjacent to the Wadi al-Mujib canyon indicates that these communities found their resources in the wadi's riparian zone where clays, water, and kiln fuel were immediately available. This interpretation of Group Two requires some caution, however. The colluvial and alluvial conditions in the Mujib make it difficult to identify individual clay deposits that may have been used in antiquity (Cordova 2007). Producers likely quarried clays from the sediments that had been carried downstream and deposited on the stream banks, where clay deposits are observable still today (fig. 4.6).

The abundant samples in Group Two indicate at the very least that the wadi riparian zone was an important source for ceramic vessel production that—like production routines linked to pastoralism, hunting, and farming—provided raw materials.[34]

Conclusion

This investigation of the communities' production strategies partly answers the question presented earlier: How did Early Iron Age sedentary life in the region remain resilient, flexible, and transferable without the guiding hand of a regional polity? The strategies that the communities employed were relatively unspecialized and lacking in intensity compared to those arrangements seen in the previous Late Bronze Age and later Iron Age II southern Levant. There are no signs that producers participated in regional markets or contributed to a larger centralized polity. Instead, production was designed in flexible ways to meet local subsistence demands in the precarious environmental settings in which communities were placed. Nor can the binary subsistence categories of nomadic pastoralism and sedentary agriculture accurately characterize production regimes. The communities were so dedicated to a sedentary existence that they invested substantially in their built environment, creating an infrastructure that sought to ensure their safety and subsistence. Grain harvesting occurred at limited levels, likely alongside the banks of the riparian zones, and produced food for humans and fodder for animals. Pastoralism and wild animal exploitation played an equally important role in meeting local subsistence needs. Communities in the region's semi-arid zones stationed themselves to have access to the wadi riparian econiches. Thus it was the need to access resources that determined settlements' locations rather than political boundaries or defensive priorities.

In Early Iron Age west-central Jordan, the nexus of human relationships contained within the community was maintained by households and their constituent members through their shared participation in production regimes. A set of cultural ideals about the need for such shared arrangements must have structured these relationships. The belief that households benefitted from their presence and participation in a community would have been a powerful and justifying ideology. Yet for those communities that inhabited the region's semi-arid zones, and faced scarcity and risk caused by limited and unpredictable amounts of natural resources, such a belief may still have had its limits. The repeated presence of storage technologies in individual households suggests that households were not willing to subscribe entirely to an ethic of sharing and collaboration. So before concluding that such a community ethic, whether discursively stated or just implicitly assumed, was entirely successful, one must also consider its limits, an issue that will be considered in the next chapter.

CHAPTER FIVE

Managing Community

What was the nature of leadership in Early Iron Age west-central Jordan? What role did wealth play in constituting this authority? Did the presence of leaders contribute to the communities' resilience or did it destabilize it? Were there limits to leaders' authority? This chapter will investigate these and other questions that pertain to the emergence of authority and inequality in the region's communities. Asking questions about small-scale societies such as those considered in this work returns the discussion to issues raised earlier, namely how societies moved between egalitarian and hierarchical relations over time, a feature of communal complexity. Determining whether these shifts occurred and explaining how they arose requires sensitivity to the micropolitics of everyday life in specific communities. Power and authority would not necessarily have been expressed in the discursive signatures which most discussions of ancient Near Eastern leadership depend on for evidence, such as monumental architecture and spectacular visual culture (Heinz and Feldman 2007). Rather, they could have been manifest in more subtle arrangements, the position and size of buildings, the circulation of food, and the willingness to cooperate in shared production activities. Nor should one expect leadership to emerge for the same reasons or unfold along the same trajectories in each instance. As Smith and Choi (2007) discovered in their simulations of leadership in small-scale societies, elites can emerge through unequal patron-client-like relationships that exploit inequalities between members. Alternatively, they can arise in moments when societies are most in need of guidance to manage resources and labor. Altogether, then, the nature of leadership, authority, and inequality cannot be merely assumed in Early Iron Age communities, as has often been the case in prior research (see the following discussion). Rather, it must be investigated in each instance using whatever materials are available.

Strategies of Authority in the Early Iron Age Levant

Most discussions of leadership and authority in Early Iron Age Levantine societies have focused on the political organization of early ancient Israel, combining the biblical narrative and the archaeological record of the central highland settlements, where the narrative places ancient Israel's development in the twelfth and eleventh centuries BCE. Scholars have been largely divided over such reconstructions, although their interpretations are nevertheless instructive for understanding what possibilities might exist. The oldest and most persistent interpretation is that early Israelite society exhibited an egalitarian, nearly acephalous, social structure characterized as a corporate personality that made no distinction between persons and the broader community in which they participated (Faust 2006:92–107; Johnson 1961, 1964; Robinson 1964).[1] Rather, individuals were bound within a kind of "psychic unity" where personal identities were projected onto the larger social collective. In turn, the social collective was projected onto the person. Moments in the biblical narrative illustrate this corporate personality in passages describing the covenant ceremonies between the Israelites and Yahweh; two examples are Levirate marriage obligations—where the wife of a deceased man marries her brother-in-law and names her firstborn son after her deceased husband—and collective punishment for the crimes of the individual or the few (e.g., Deuteronomy 13:12; Joshua 7:25–26; 2 Samuel 21:5–6).[2]

Despite this interpretation, it is difficult to ignore evidence for leadership in the written and, especially, the physical evidence. Some have drawn on social evolutionary categories to make sense of this evidence in ways that are similar to scholars described earlier who investigate early Moabite political organization (e.g., Dearman 1992; Mattingly 1992; Miller 1992). The biblical narrative's description of ancient Israel's development fits nicely with social evolutionary frameworks, after all. The narrative describes how Israelite society moved through increasingly complex stages of political organization.[3] Scholars have used the category of chiefdom to describe early Israel's political arrangements during the period between the Exodus and the Israelite polities. Chiefdoms exhibit economic, social, and political organization beyond that of tribe societies, but less than that of state societies. Ethnographic attestations of chiefdom societies indicate that leaders often base their authority on charisma, wealth, and tradition in order to manage subsistence practices and the distribution of materials and prestige items (Earle 1987:292–297; Rothman 1994). Such characterizations are reflected in the biblical narrative's description of the exploits of ancient Israel's earliest kings such as Saul and David who sought political power through charisma and force (Flanagan 1981). Scholars have attempted to link these descriptions to the physical evidence from the central highlands (Frick 1985; Miller 2005). After the Late Bronze Age city-state system's breakdown, early Israelite societies were organized as segmentary societies exhibiting political and economic centralization similar to tribes. As the Early Iron Age unfolded, the highland population increased. Frick cites advancements in agricultural technologies such as terracing, iron plows, and storage containers as prime movers in this growth. Such an increase would have required more complex forms of political and economic management, Frick reasons. At the apex of these new political structures were chiefs who managed agricultural and craft production, cooperated with and conducted warfare against their peers in neighboring societies, and maintained social order through religious ritual.[4]

Although a chiefdom perspective acknowledges the catalytic role that leaders played in reorganizing their societies, such an approach betrays what was likely a more complicated and uneven political landscape.[5] Both corporate personality and chiefdom perspectives gloss over the distinct anxieties in the biblical narrative concerning authority and leadership, particularly in those passages attributed to the Deuteronomistic School. Descriptions of the Early Iron Age found in the Books of Judges and Samuel depict instability prior to the development of the United Monarchy. Such anxieties are not surprising as the Deuteronomistic School's priority was to establish the legitimacy of kingship and the Davidic line of descent that took place in the later Iron Age II.[6] The early uncertainty served as a foil for the order and stability that the later monarchy supposedly instilled under the new territorial state. Despite the characterization of disorder, two distinct genres of authority are reflected in actors' leadership styles. The first, patrimonial authority, where leadership is ascribed according to age and gender, is prominent throughout the biblical narrative. Such authority is expressed in the biblical narrative as *zaqenim*, suprahousehold leadership councils. Although its use in the singular denotes an old man (e.g., *zaqen*, Genesis 18:11), the term also appears as a collective, best glossed as "elders," a collection of adult males drawn from individual households.⁷ Although variously constituted depending on the scale of political involvement, the elders performed an important leadership role in the early Israelite communities (McKenzie 1959; Reviv 1989). During the conquest and settlement of Canaan, the elders represent their tribes at regional assemblies such as the Shechem assembly described in Joshua 8. Elders also played an important role in governing everyday life in the early Israelite settlements. Several passages describe how elders adjudicated legal matters within and between families, often at the village gates, a neutral space in community civic life (e.g., Deuteronomy 21:19, 22:15, 25:7; Joshua 20:4). The elders' role did not diminish despite the rise of kingship during the later Iron II period, although they appear to have played an advisory capacity in the government (e.g., 1 Kings 8:1, 12:8).

The institution of the elders complements a broader understanding of patrimonial authority that scholars have used to characterize genres of authority in ancient Near Eastern life (Schloen 2001; Stager 1985) using Weber's (1968:1006–1069) classification of patriarchal authority. Ancient Near Eastern society rationalized authority in terms of nested patrimonial hierarchies. The basic unit in this hierarchy was the house of the father, the *bet 'ab*, an office held by the oldest adult male in each household. The metaphor of house and patrimony remained durable as the notion was applied in increasingly broader social contexts—the extended family, the community, and eventually, in the Iron II period, the kingdom. The institution of the *zaqenim*, with its authority based on age, rank, and gender, was a step above the household in the nested hierarchy of Early Iron Age patrimonial authority. Indeed, the description of elders suggests a certain degree of communalism, and it is possible to conjecture that each household, in principal, would have been represented during collective decision making.

The judge is the other mode of authority appearing in the biblical narrative of early ancient Israel. The judge, whose leadership skills are demonstrated throughout the Books of Judges and Samuel, is different from the *zaqenim* and is not based on patrimonial authority.⁸ Judges played a theological function in the greater narrative about ancient Israel. Yet behind these theological motives are several distinct features that contrast with patrimonial authority. Military leadership is one example. An early judge—and the only female—Deborah rallies the Israelite tribes to follow Barak in his battle with King Jabin of the Canaanites (Judges 4–5). Ehud similarly battles the Moabites, killing King Eglon in his palace (Judges 3:12–4:1). The most interesting instance is found in the biography of Gideon, sometimes referred to as Yerubbaal (Judges 6–8). Through a messenger,

Yahweh commissions Gideon to free the Israelites from the Midianites and Amalekites. With his army, Gideon pursues the Israelites' oppressors across the Jordan, where he eventually kills their leaders. In exchange for Gideon's military victories, the Israelites ask him to rule over them, "you and your son and your grandson also" (Judges 8:22), suggesting that Gideon's lineage would maintain a royal office. Gideon refuses, claiming that it is Yahweh who will rule the Israelites. Having earned his authority in battle, Gideon returns to "his own house" a wealthy, powerful man, capable of marrying several women, and living to an old age.[9]

Scholars have long sought to understand judges' authority from both historical and theological perspectives (Alt 1966:130–133; Boling 1975). Commentators (Hutton 1994; Malamat 1976; Weisman 1977) understand judges' authority within a broader discussion of charismatic authority—a type of leadership that Weber defines as erratic and ephemeral (Weber 1968:241–245). Several characteristics support this link between judges and charismatic authority, namely that authority is often ascribed through spontaneous means and from a divine source and exercised during periods of crises (Malamat 1976:161–162). Charismatic authority is not limited to age, gender, status, or place; judges are male and female, young and old, from both weak and strong tribes. Judges' authority rests upon neither formal administrative nor juridical precedent, but rather the privileges of power that the community bestows on a person.

It is noteworthy to observe that these two genres of authority in the biblical narrative—patrimonial and charismatic—coexist within the same social milieu. Their differences are significant: the ascribed and gendered nature of patrimonial authority contrasts with the accumulated authority that judges garnered through charismatic acts. This distinction might lead one to assume that the two genres did not function side by side. Yet the biblical narrative portrays their relationship as complementary in most instances, foregrounding the role of the judges as the narrative's protagonists while allowing the elders to play a supporting role in decision making. The biblical narrative does at times place the elders in a dependent role with judges. The elders ironically ask a judge to select a king rather than choose one themselves: when Samuel has grown old, the "elders of Israel" request that he appoint a king to govern over all of Israel (1 Samuel 8:4–5).

These textual representations of authority in the biblical narrative do not present tidy answers for understanding leadership in the Early Iron Age southern Levant. At the very least, these differences suggest that there were multiple paths to power. Complicating matters even further, of course, is that these representations in the biblical narrative were written down and subsequently edited in the centuries following the Early Iron Age, a point that was made in chapter 3. The crafting of these narratives furthermore occurred under political conditions that were different from those of the Early Iron Age. Within the territorial polities of the mid-first millennium BCE, kingship was the dominant mode of authority. The new office promoted itself through a patrimonial mode where the king's relationship to his constituents was likened to a father ruling over multiple households. The narrative does report that the institution of elders continued during this period, but these groups were organized at the local level and represented their community's concerns to the king (2 Samuel 5:3; 1 Kings 12:13). Therefore, the biblical narrative's representation of authority in the early Israelite communities was likely shaped from the writers' and editors' position in a later—and vastly different—cultural context. Given the uncertain circumstances of the narrative's production, the most conservative use of this information—short of disregarding it altogether— would be to generate questions that can be investigated in evidence external to the written source. If these patrimonial and charismatic genres of authority were indeed commonplace in the Early Iron Age southern Levant, and specifically in west-central Jordan, they will be apparent in the physical evidence.

Two pieces of evidence point to patrimonial and charismatic modes coexisting in Early Iron Age west-central Jordan. One is the Balu'a stele, a carved basalt stone (1.73 m × 0.7 m) that was discovered at the site of the same name in 1930 (Horsfield and Vincent 1932; Routledge and Routledge 2009) (fig. 5.1).[10] The stele depicts three figures engaged in an investiture scene. Reading the stele from right to left, a goddess or queen holding an ankh symbol in her right hand presents a royal figure to a male deity standing on the extreme left. In a scene mimicking a popular Egyptian New Kingdom image, the deity is investing the royal figure with authority. A brief inscription accompanying the stele is indecipherable, and several unsuccessful attempts to identify the script have been made.[11] The stele's investiture scene combines a variety of Canaanite and Egyptian styles, of which the costumes of the three figures are the most conspicuous. This scene using Egyptian and Canaanite iconography suggests that local leaders borrowed symbols of power to rationalize their authority on the local scene (Routledge 2004). This investiture scene also suggests that emergent leaders followed a pattern of emulation similar to the Canaanite palace-based elites of the Late Bronze Age. The king's costume in the stele is revealing of his identity. Scholars have pointed out that the king depicted in the Balu'a stele wears a headscarf typical of the Shasu (Drioton 1933; Giveon 1971; Ward and Martin 1964), a group described in Late Bronze Age written sources as nomadic peoples living east of the Jordan River. Although the Balu'a stele points to the presence of charismatic authority in west-central Jordan, particularly a local leader using international imagery to describe his divine sponsorship, the stele's date remains an open-ended question. Its discovery on Balu'a's surface and its damaged inscription make a date difficult to assign, although most scholars would place the object's crafting to the latter centuries of the second millennium based on its borrowing of Egyptian imagery.

A second piece of evidence is located in west-central Jordan's early Iron Age mortuary evidence. Early Iron Age communities interring the deceased took advantage of natural limestone caves that required only some modifi-

Figure 5.1. The Balu'a stele.

cation to convert them to extended family burial chambers. One tomb, Baq'ah Valley Cave A4, reveals much about Early Iron Age interment practices in the region (McGovern 1986:53–61).[12] The cave consisted of two parts, a forecourt and a burial cave. The excavators suggest that although erosional processes initially formed the forecourt, its shape and size suggest the area was widened during the cave's conversion into a tomb (McGovern 1986:55). A cobble surface lined the bottom of the forecourt, approximately five meters wide by five meters long. Six large boulders were positioned to the left of the tomb's entrance and were likely used to block up the entrance between interments. A ramp of cobble led into the tomb, measuring five to six meters in diameter. The tomb's arrangement suggests communal ideologies structured mortuary practices. Individuals are commingled with each other, and it is impossible to distinguish specific persons' interments in the tomb. Once a person's body had decomposed, his or her remains were integrated with the rest of the deceased.[13] But a closer look reveals that some evidence for social rank is present in two subtle lines of evidence. Prestige objects were present and included ceramic vessels, shells, beads, copper and iron jewelry, spindle whorls, a drop pendant, a cylinder seal, a stamp seal, a scarab, and a sickle blade (McGovern 1986, fig. 21). These objects suggest some individuals were given more elaborate burials than others. Another indication of rank is found in the twelve human crania that were arranged on a shelf in the tomb's northwest corner. This display suggests the community sought to commemorate particular persons of social import. Based on the biblical narrative's description, it is tempting to see this treatment as commemorative acts for members of a *zaqenim* council.

Despite their interpretive challenges, the Balu'a stele and the Baq'ah Valley Cave A4 strengthen the possibility that patrimonial and charismatic genres of authority operated simultaneously in Early Iron Age west-central Jordan, as the biblical narrative suggests was common in early Israelite society. But at the same time, is it necessary to characterize patrimonial and charismatic genres of authority in such polarized terms? Perhaps emergent leaders could draw on aspects of both modes to express their authority in the communities? Or perhaps both genres of authority coexisted, one being emphasized over the other depending on current circumstances set by political, economic, or environmental contingencies. In order to gain a better sense of how Early Iron Age authority was expressed, one must consider how wealth was defined and circulated in the social field that was the community.

Food as Wealth

One way to track how authority was organized in the Early Iron Age communities is to observe how wealth circulated among its members. Although production could create the wealth over which people negotiated social life in preindustrial societies, how such production was managed—by individuals, households, or the entire population—was central to the number and types of relationships between members. Through production routines and practices, communities converted local, naturally occurring resources into usable wealth such as food, tools, and buildings on which they subsisted. Intangible but equally important resources such as labor and charisma are likewise convertible into tangible resources such as buildings, agricultural infrastructure, and surplus agricultural products. When the production of wealth is observed within the field that is the community, it is then possible to understand how this wealth circulated between households, potentially answering questions such as: Were households responsible for managing their own production routines, or did households collaborate? Were households relatively equal in wealth, or did some hold sway over others?

Such questions regarding the circulation of wealth are complicated by the fact that production in marginal environments can yield unequal amounts of wealth that can subsequently contribute to inequalities between households. Recall that a number of communities examined in this work are positioned in the semi-arid zones of west-central Jordan, where production practices would have been more precarious than settlements in more temperate zones to the west and north. To reduce competition over scarce resources in the semi-arid zones, communities may manage production and the wealth it creates collectively. However, even if household and communal production co-occur, as the evidence presented earlier indicates, individual households might still accrue more wealth than their neighbors. The logic of this accumulation is based on the genuine possibilities of scarcity. During droughts, famine, and other periods of scarcity, households that accumulated surplus wealth increased their chances for survival. Such wealth, of course, can be shared with other, less-fortunate households, an exchange that can foster dependent relationships between households. However, such emergent asymmetrical relationships are not necessarily permanent features of social life. Rather, such debts and relationships of dependencies can be temporary, resolved through reciprocal gifts and acts in more fortunate times.

Although one may assume that different kinds of wealth circulated in symbolic and material forms, the circulation of food was arguably the most important—and potentially the most observable—in the communities' archaeological record.¹⁴ Food production and consumption was essential to the community's livelihood, and it dominated daily routines beyond that of agricultural chores and architectural repairs. Food's value depended on the conditions found in the socionatural system in which the community participated. A lean year of drought in which production activities were unsuccessful could dictate the conditions that structured food's circulation within and between households. During periods of scarcity, households could potentially accrue power through the distribution of food to less-fortunate households for the sake of demonstrating their generosity and shoring up reciprocal obligations. Households could also use their wealth to recruit new households to the community or to reaffirm relationships to discourage defection. By observing evidence associated with the storing, cooking, and sharing of food products, one can learn how this wealth was distributed across the community.

Scholars, including archaeologists and historians, have long observed how humans use commensal practices to convert food into different kinds of wealth or to garner power over their affiliates (Bray 2003b; Dietler and Hayden 2001; Goody 1998; Grottanelli and Milano 2004; Twiss 2007; Wiessner and Schiefenhövel 1996). These studies instruct that the sharing of food does not merely mark important holidays, accomplishments, and rites of passage for the larger community. Commensal events become venues in which relationships among people are forged through the evocative cultural practices of gifting and consumption. Like many gift exchanges, the sharing of food is bundled with messages and obligations that the recipient is obligated to interpret and sometimes reciprocate at later points in time (Mauss 1925). Supposedly benign events aimed at fostering communal cohesion could in fact be part of veiled strategies to accrue power through the public demonstration of generosity and wealth. In Yaeger's investigation of the Mesoamerican San Lorenzo community discussed in chapter 2, for instance, he interpreted the distribution of faunal remains, incense burners, and decorated serving vessels as evidence for communal feasts, possibly annual rites that involved the consumption of meat and the veneration of ancestors (Yaeger 2000:131). By participating in these feasts, members demonstrated their affiliation with the community in the same way as they did by collaborating in building and agricultural projects. Likewise, choosing not to participate in everyday and scheduled food production and consumption activities could signal a member's decision not to partake in communal life.

Commensal events were commonplace in ancient Near Eastern and Mediterranean societies, too. Evidence from adjacent Bronze and Iron Age societies helps to illustrate the roles food played in the commensal strategies of the Early Iron Age (Schmandt-Besserat 2001; Wright 2010a, 2010b). Written sources and visual culture (e.g., the Standard of Ur; Uruk Vase) attest to the tribute of food that was paid to palaces and temples at scheduled times of year, and to the lavish banquets thrown to commemorate success in warfare, treaties, the inauguration of a new temple or palace, and deities' feast days (Bottéro 1994; Lambert 1993; MacDonald 2008; Sasson 2004). Commensal practices have also been identified in the archaeological record of Near Eastern societies using a number of physical signatures linked to the production, storage, and consumption of food (cf., Hayden 2001, table 2.1; Lev-Tov and McGeough 2007; Lewis 2007; London 2009, 2011; Pollock 2003; Twiss 2007; Zuckerman 2007). The biblical narrative offers additional evidence for food's role in structuring social relationships during the Early Iron Age (Jenks 1992). Several passages discuss how making and sharing food was possibly the family's most important daily routine (e.g., Job 1:18–19; Psalms 128:2–3).

The biblical narrative also makes plain the symbolic importance of food, especially in passages that describe instances where food is shared between nonintimates. Upon a visit from three divine messengers, Abraham and Sarah prepared an elaborate meal of meat, bread, and milk (Genesis 18:1–9). Such generous acts demonstrated the host's hospitality and bolstered his reputation as selfless and wealthy enough to afford feeding individuals not under his immediate care. Food's symbolic importance is also obvious in its use in covenant ceremonies (e.g., Genesis 26:28–31, 31:51–54; Exodus 18:12; Joshua 9:3–27). Previously unaligned or conflicting individuals and families share a meal after taking an oath of allegiance. A basic feature of family solidarity, meal sharing implied a symbolic union, the creation of new familial bonds. But just as food carried a symbolic currency, so too did abstaining from food and rejecting invitations of hospitality. In First Samuel, Saul's son Jonathan, dismayed that his father had decided to kill David, "rose from the table in fierce anger and ate no food on the second day of the month, for he was grieved for David, and because his father had disgraced him" (1 Samuel 20:34). Jonathan's decision to leave his father's table and abstain from food communicated his anger over his father's decision.

The biblical narrative offers a context for understanding how food could mediate social relationships within and between households in the Iron Age Levant. Archaeological evidence from specific Early Iron Age contexts provides even more specificity. The paleobotanical and faunal evidence from the Early Iron Age communities that was discussed earlier indicates that the communities consumed a Mediterranean diet typical for Bronze and Iron Age societies in the southern Levant (Borowski 2004). This diet consisted of dairy products, grains, vegetables, fruit, pulses, and oils. Meat and fish were present, but not as commonly consumed. The lack of cold storage meant that fresh milk had to be quickly converted into products such as cheese, yogurt, and butter, and that meat products were smoked, dried, or salted to stave off spoilage. Grains would have been ground and baked in ovens to produce flat breads, and vegetables, fruits, pulses, and occasionally meats were combined to make stews.

Multiple physical signatures for commensal practices are identifiable in the Early Iron Age communities (Hayden 2001). Some of this evidence has already been described, such as the storage bins at al-'Aliya, Lahun, al-Mu'ammariyya, and al-'Umayri. Additional evidence includes the repetition of artifacts for food preparation and cooking in pillared buildings. Again, the best-preserved evidence for food production practices was found in the features and artifacts excavated in al-'Umayri's Building B (Clark 2002). The excavators have suggested that a surface (Locus 7K81:37) in Room B2, a corner room in the southeast corner of the building, was used for cooking, although this function depends on the interpretation of a feature (Locus 7K81:36) as a hearth (Clark 2002:95).[15] The room is relatively small, ranging between 1.5 and 2.2 meters wide and 4.2 meters long (Clark 2002:95). Although cooking practices were concentrated in this room, food may have been prepared in other activity areas throughout the building. The distribution of food production artifacts throughout Building B appears to support this possibility. Several basalt ground stone artifacts were found in the building, including loaf-shaped grinders, querns, mortars, and pestles (Herr and Platt 2002; Platt 2000; Platt and Herr 2002). Although they may have been put to use in alternative ways, scholars have widely agreed on their primary importance in food preparation activities such as the grinding of grain and the mixing of ingredients (Ebeling and Rowan 2004). Likewise, the excavation of several ceramic vessels suggests food production was primarily a household undertaking. These vessels include pots (e.g., Clark 2002, figs. 4.27.12 and 4.27.13) whose exteriors often demonstrate signs of burning that suggest they were placed on or near cooking fires. At least one such pot (Clark 2002, fig. 4.16.8) was discovered on Room B2's surface, strengthening the interpretation of this area as a cooking space. Likewise, ceramic kraters, appropriate for mixing and storing food, were excavated in the building (Clark 2002, fig. 4.15.5–4.15.9). There are other contexts where extant ovens, stone and ceramic vessels are found together in pillared buildings. At Lahun, ovens as well as ground stone and ceramic vessels are described in reports (Homès-Fredericq 1994, 1995, and 2000), and in one instance, a food production area is detailed (Homès-Fredericq 1992:188–191, fig. 16.4). Like the oven in al-'Umayri's Building B, an oven is located next to an entrance, likely for ventilation purposes. Also excavated in the room are a basalt grinding stone and grinder, as well as cooking pots and other ceramic vessels (Homès-Fredericq 1992:190).

Repeated patterns of storage and cooking in individual buildings suggest most food storage and daily food preparation and consumption were organized at the household level. The sharing of food within households was therefore one of the ways cohesion was maintained at the most immediate levels of the community. A well-stocked building was indicative of a household's wealth, reflecting its capacity to survive during the lean months of the year or to maintain itself during periods of scarcity. For analytical purposes, then, a building's size is an indicator of a household's material wealth. This link between building size and wealth is important for understanding how evenly the latter was distributed across the community. In fact, relative differences in building sizes and their constituent storage installations and food production centers suggest wealth was not equally distributed within communities, consequently a symptom of emergent inequality between households. When comparing building sizes at al-'Aliya, seven buildings range in area from 71 to 239 square meters (Routledge 2000:49, table 3). One building, Building 500, greatly surpasses its neighbors in size. Although its full extent is not yet known, this building was at least 239 square meters (fig. 5.2). Although a typical pillared building is recognizable in the complex (Rooms 501–503), several additional rooms surround it, only some of which have been documented (e.g., Rooms 504–509). Comparing the size of this building with others surrounding it reveals that these structures may be similar in design, but certainly not in size. Such differences strongly suggest that al-'Aliya and possibly the other Early Iron Age communities bore some degree of internal social differentiation. The construction of a large residence like Building 500 was not accidental. Rather, the owners were required to persuade their fellow community members to help acquire a larger than usual amount of building supplies and transport them to the settlement.

A closer look at Building 500's components indicates how the building owners were able to persuade their fellow community members to undertake a project that would only indirectly benefit them. A storage facility was

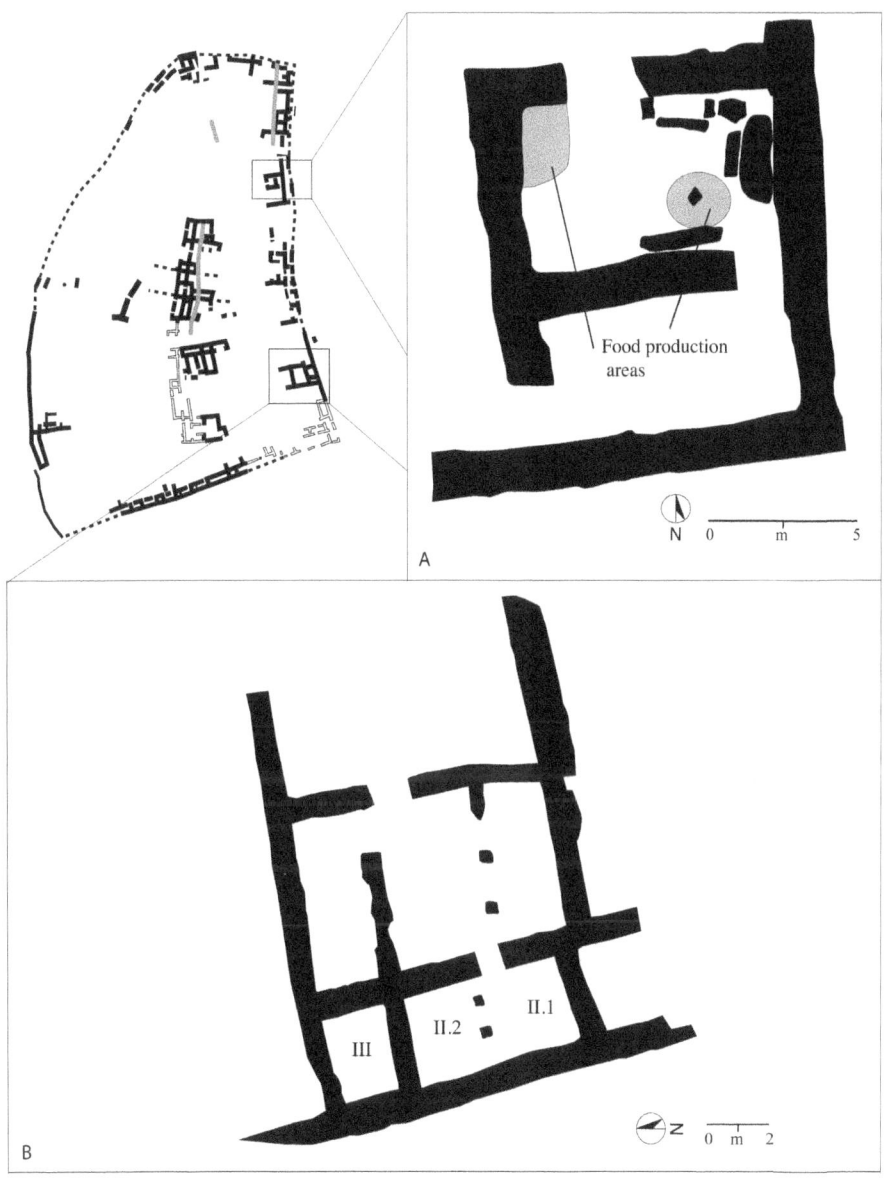

Figure 5.2. (A) The "Scarab House" and (B) Building 100 at Lahun. (*Sources*: Adapted from Homès-Fredericq 1992, fig. 16.4, and Homès-Fredericq 2000, fig. 3; © Equinox Publishing Ltd. 2011)

attached to the west side of the building that surpasses all other pillared building installations in size and elaborateness. Similar to the collective storage facilities in Building 100 and al-Muʿammariyya's citadel building, storage bins were located deep inside the building, suggesting that the contents required protection. One had to pass through a narrow corridor (Rooms 504b, 505–507) to access them. So far, two storage bins have been excavated. Room 504a, 1.94 meters wide and 2.12 meters long, is located alongside a large food production facility, Room 503. The recovery of carbonized barley in the fill levels immediately above the floor is yet another indication of the room's purpose. Another storage bin, Room 508, 4.4 meters wide and 2.4 meters long and bisected by a low wall, was located deep within the building and accessed only by passing through Rooms 504b, 505, 506, 507, and 508a. Storage jars similar in form and design to those found in the rear rooms of al-ʿUmayri's Building A and B were also recovered from these rooms. The eastern half of Rooms 505 and 509 may also have contained storage facilities, although these rooms have yet to be excavated. Thus, Building 500's disproportionately large storage facilities suggest agricultural produce was a practical and symbolic source of wealth in the community.

Building 500 also contained a food production installation larger than any other in the settlement (fig. 5.3). This installation includes three ovens located in a row against the northern wall of the room. The easternmost of these ovens is immediately adjacent to the main door of the house, probably to facilitate the release of smoke, and is protected by a windbreak formed by a single stone slab set on end separating the edge of the oven from the doorway. A large oven was formed by a low-fired cylindrical clay body five to six centimeters thick set on a base of wadi cobbles. The oven measures about forty-two centimeters in diameter at its mouth and about forty-eight centimeters in depth, with a shallow deposit of ashy materials laid over by compact calcareous fill. To the west was a platform of soot-blackened rocks set in compacted calcareous sediments. It appears to have been built at the same time as the ovens for use as a working surface. The two westernmost ovens differ from the other in that they are constructed of broken storage jar sherds set on a base of cobbles, with only the upper lips being constructed of low-fired clay oven material. Both of these ovens were filled with ashy sediments. Flotation of all of the oven sediments indicates that they are rich in both wood charcoal and carbonized seeds, especially grains.

Against the western and southwestern walls of the room are a series of installations that were related to the grinding of grain. One is a large (57 × 70 × 20–43 cm) basalt saddle quern that may have originally been larger as it is broken at one end. Immediately east of this quern are the

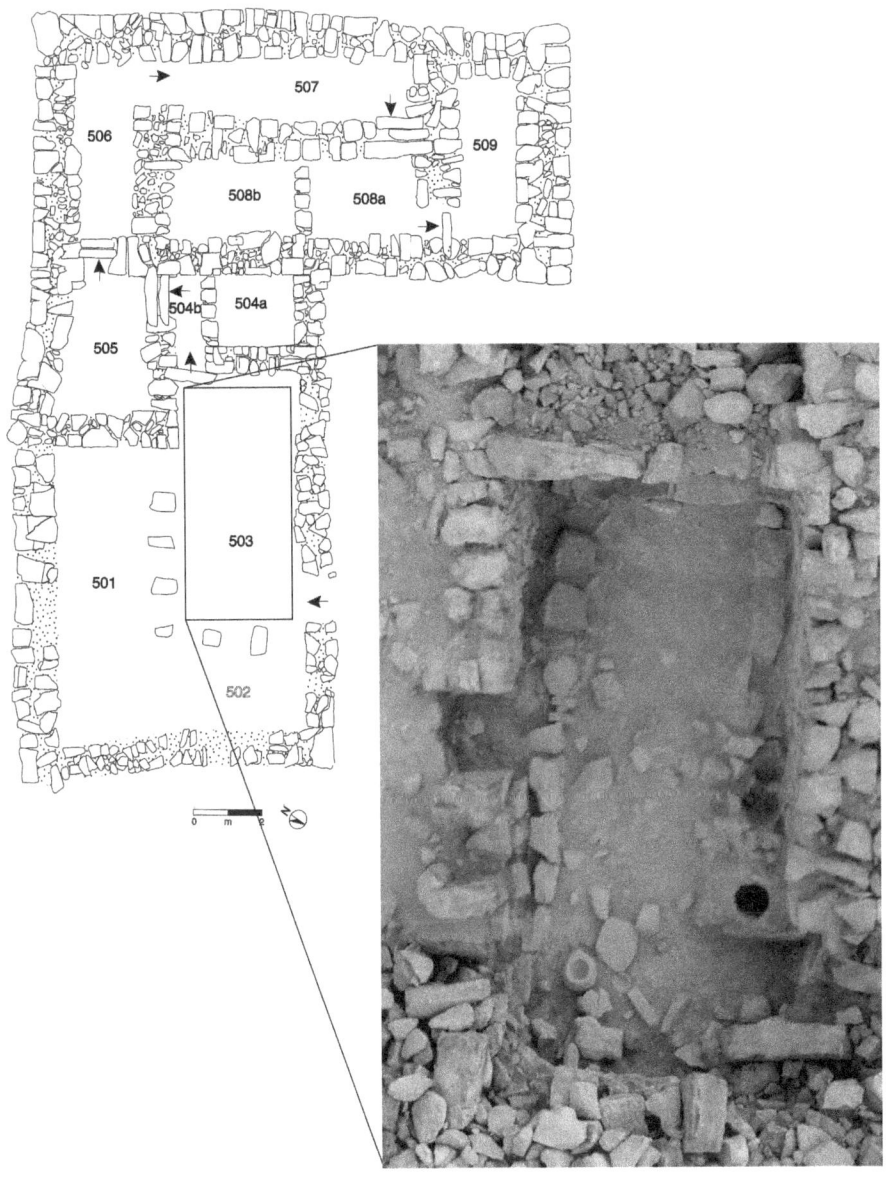

Figure 5.3. Al-'Aliya Building 500 and Room 503's kitchen. (*Source*: © Equinox Publishing Ltd. 2011)

remains of a poorly preserved oven or clay bin, built of low-fired clay set on a single circular stone slab base and measuring about seventy centimeters in diameter, but only preserved to fifteen centimeters in height. This area was covered over by ashy sediments, indicating the presence of burned materials. On the opposite side of the quern, against the western wall of Room 503, is a bench formed by a long limestone slab (140 × 40 × 15 cm) embedded in compacted sediments beside a basalt slab (56 × 28 × 30 cm). This suggests another grinding installation with an attached working platform. Two limestone slabs occupy the northwest corner of the room and appear to be benches similar to those found on the south side of the room.

Running parallel to the bases of the row of pillars that define the southern limits of Room 503 were six flat-lying limestone slabs set on small stones at a height of about thirty centimeters. In the southeast corner of Room 503, a further set of installations was discovered, including a large limestone mortar (45 cm diameter, 13 cm deep), a smaller, more finely made limestone bowl (21 cm diameter), and a rectangular piece of ground basalt located together in situ. Adjacent to these objects was an extremely compacted, possibly fire-hardened, surface and a low platform formed by oblong slabs laid on upright slabs. The eastern section cut along the line of pillars that defines the eastern edge of Room 503 indicates that a low wall about fifty centimeters in height served to separate Room 503 from Room 501 to the east.

For several reasons, this evidence suggests Room 503's primary purpose was the production of grain-based food, probably breads, for a large number of people. The size and contents of this food production installation compared to those at Lahun and al-'Umayri is conspicuous. Room 503 contains more ovens, ground stone tools, and vessels in a concentrated space. Furthermore, production activity areas dedicated to grinding, baking, and cooling appear organized into discreet and permanent spaces. Conversely, in the Lahun pillared building, food production activities other than cooking are difficult to discern and likely shared space with non-food producing activities. But the best evidence available is the installation's proximity to Building 500's unusually large storage facilities that was discussed earlier. Their positioning suggests that the large amount of grain stored in the building could be easily accessed for food preparation.

Feasting Strategies

Well-preserved contexts such as the kitchens and storage facilities described above offer the best contexts for reconstructing commensal practices in the Early Iron Age communities. Although this kitchen could certainly have serviced the needs of Building 500's immediate household, its size indicates that food could be produced in this room for consumption beyond the immediate household. Such occasions would have included feasts in which the entire community could participate on occasions such as weddings, births, and other rites of passage. Feasts following the end of large agricultural or building projects not only celebrated their completion but also rewarded those households that cooperated in the endeavor and helped build a sense of communal identity. Not least, the feast provided much-needed nourishment following the exertion of energy. The precise location of such feasting events has not been identified thus far in the archaeological record of the Early Iron Age communities. They likely took place in the large empty courtyards in the middle of many settlements, or in buildings that remain to be excavated.

In place of this contextual lacuna, one must look to other signatures of commensal practices in the communities' object assemblages. Ancient Near Eastern visual culture provides a window into the role that objects played in commensal events, a point that Zuckerman (2007) and Wright (2010a, 2010b) have made independently. Banquet scenes of royal elites surrounded by soldiers, musicians, food, and captives are commonly represented in Mesopotamian and Levantine visual culture (e.g., the Standard of Ur; Uruk Vase; Megiddo ivory, no. 2; Ashurbanipal's garden scene). These images indicate that objects were more than passive tools or markers of elite or cultural identity. Instead, they helped create the visual language that indexed the commensal act for participants. Objects were unassuming participants in the unfolding events that affirmed authority, cultural superiority, and remunerations for work. Vessels carried valuable contents to the occasion, displayed food for hosts and held food for guests, and mediated the act of eating. In fact, one can argue that objects first had to arrive on the scene before the commensal act could begin. Objects simultaneously played the dual role of host and guest in commensal events.

Such objects are identifiable in the Early Iron Age communities' ceramic vessel assemblages. Although the chemical and petrographic data are helpful in characterizing the general organization of vessel production, other lines of evidence can help identify which vessels were used in commensal practices. Commensal vessels can be identified within assemblages based on the abundance of certain forms designed for food consumption (e.g., bowls), or the production of select subassemblages made under specialized conditions (Hayden 2001, table 2.1). Other studies have identified commensal assemblages based on such characteristics (e.g., Bray 2003a; Cook and Glowacki 2003; Nelson 2003). In the Early Iron Age communities, alternatively, vessels were made under the same relatively unspecialized conditions, a point made in chapter 4. Most were likely used for multiple purposes, from serving food to storage, gathering, and food production. One exception, however, is a distinct subassemblage of painted bowls and kraters that stands out from the mainly undecorated majority (fig. 5.4).[16] The presence of decorated vessels defies normative expectations for an unspecialized vessel industry and calls out for further consideration. This subassemblage consists of twenty-one excavated samples (Porter 2011, table 1): fourteen from al-'Aliya, four from Balu'a, two from 'Aro'er, and one from Dhiban.[17] Decoration consists of the application of red pigments to the exteriors, rim, and occasionally, the interiors of vessels. Most designs consist of irregular lines varying in shape and length, running vertically or diagonally down from the rim. Occasionally, a horizontal band runs just below and parallel to the rim. The design's colors fall within reds and browns, although their original color cannot be determined precisely because of the pigments' interaction with the soils in which the vessel was buried. No complete vessels have been found, so it is impossible to determine if the preserved patterns were repeated throughout the bowl. The use of white slip under these decorations is present only some of the time. This pattern only appears on open vessels, bowls and kraters, two vessel forms used in the presentation and consumption of food.[18] Bowl forms included a medium-deep hemispherical bowl with a simple vertical rim and rounded lip and small, medium, and large bowls with simple vertical and outcurving rims and rounded lips (the most popular form in the Early Iron Age assemblage). Some variation exists within this category, such as a double-carinated bowl, a sharply carinated bowl, and bowls with thickened rims. Also, the assemblage consists of small kraters with thickened globular rims and gentle carinations, and medium kraters with externally thickened flattened rim profiles. One krater had a thickened globular rim, but two gentle carinations on the shoulder.

A select number of these decorated vessels were included in INAA and petrographic studies described in chapter 4. Nine vessels were analyzed using INAA, five of which fell into Group One, the dominant production group of the Early Iron Age communities. Two were excavated at Balu'a while another three were excavated at al-'Aliya. Another four vessels, two from Balu'a and two from al-'Aliya, went unassigned, likely part of other local production groups yet to be identified. Additionally, five vessels analyzed using petrographic techniques were classified into three of five

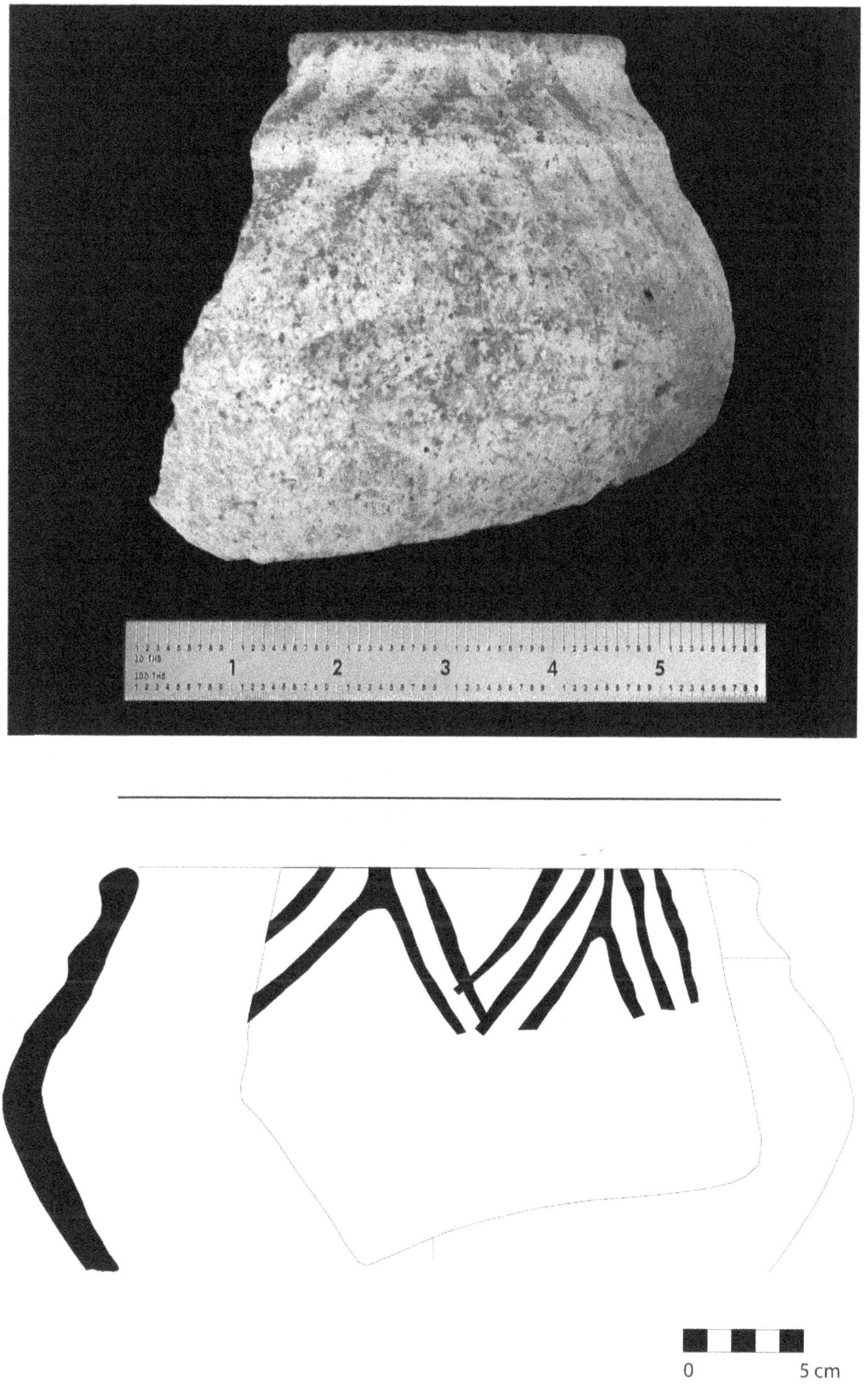

Figure 5.4. Illustration and profile drawing of bowl with red pigments.

groups (Routledge, Klassen, and Porter forthcoming). One appeared in Group One, two in Group Two, and two in Group Three. All three groups were populated with undecorated vessels of various forms and consisted of local clay and temper resources.[19] Additionally, the extent to which the chemical composition of the pigment was homogenous was measured using laser ablation–inductively coupled plasma–mass spectrometry (LA-ICP-MS hereafter) (Porter and Speakman 2008).[20] Like INAA, LA-ICP-MS measures the elemental composition of artifacts.[21] Eight samples were tested, although only three samples had pigments sufficiently preserved enough to be analyzed successfully. The results demonstrated that Early Iron Age pigments were somewhat similar in the amounts of each oxide and were relatively high compared to later Iron Age pigments that were tested. Although more pigment samples should be tested, these preliminary results suggest that producers used similar resources and recipes when making the pigment.

The painted assemblage's presence among a relatively unspecialized, undecorated corpus of ceramic vessels is conspicuous, raising a number of questions about its makers, users, and the role it played in the communities' commensal strategies. Some clues are apparent in the information regarding how these vessels were made. Producers formed decorated vessels using the same clay and temper recipes as undecorated vessels, and similar vessel forms were used for both undecorated and decorated genres. This pattern suggests that the act of decorating was integrated into broader vessel production routines rather than taking place in some specialized, possibly ritualized register of production. In other words, there seems to have been nothing particularly special about the materials used to craft decorated vessels. Additionally, the fact that producers based in at least four different Early Iron Age communities replicated a relatively similar pattern speaks to the broad appeal of the design across the region. If the decorated vessels had been crafted in a single workshop, then the design's replication could have been interpreted as a single workshop tradition. Instead, explanations for this design's regional circulation and replication exist in a handful of possibilities. Decorated vessels could have circulated to a new community where a producer encountered and then replicated the design on new vessels. Or, producers from different communities were in contact with each other enough to exchange knowledge about the design. This contact could have existed through the sharing of vessel production resources in the canyons or through visits to different communities. A final possibility could be that knowledge of ceramic production technologies and designs circulated between communities through the transfer of members. Such movements could have included the exchange of offspring in marriage alliances or the defection of households from one community to another one nearby.

Current knowledge of the decorated vessel assemblage prevents privileging one of these explanations over the other. Nevertheless, there seems to have been something attractive about this design that motivated unrelated producers to replicate it in similar ways. It is possible to imagine a scenario in which this design served as some expression of solidarity or affinity between communities. Making, owning, and using a vessel could have signaled one's membership in a larger supra-communal identity, possibly a sign of an Early Iron Age Moabite identity that would develop more fully by the ninth century BC under a territorial polity and expressed in written sources like the Mesha Inscription (Dearman 1989; Routledge 2000). Although scholars working within ethnicizing and historicizing frameworks described in chapter 3 may be attracted to such an interpretation, it still does not explain why ethnicity would need to be signaled in commensal events. A more relevant interpretation for these patterns is their semiotic role in commensal practices. If food was wealth to be exchanged in the Early Iron Age communities, as has been argued in this chapter, then the vessels that contained and presented it served as a type of value-enhancing package that accentuated its presentation. Visual simulations can help to model the presentation of the decorated vessels within two different commensal environments. In figure 5.5A, the vessels are illuminated by a fire at 1,126.85 degrees Celsius (1400 Kelvin) in a stone wall interior like those found in the early Iron Age communities; in figure 5.5B, the vessels are illuminated by an open-air fire burning at the same temperature.[22] These simulations reveal that the design's appearance on the vessels' exterior was visible to viewers sitting or standing near them. Food displayed inside and above the vessel would not have obscured the design, and may have played a complementary design role. Even when bowls were lifted to the face, the decoration would still have been visible to viewers.

Although the vessels' presentation is possible to envision, it is more difficult to interpret the meanings attached to the design. The choice of red pigment may have indexed the kind of materials that were to be presented in the vessel—red liquids, perhaps blood, being a candidate. However, red was a convenient pigment to produce using heavily levigated red soils typical in the landscape. Red slips and paints were second only to white in popularity, and they remained so throughout the Bronze and Iron Ages, as black was less common than red (Amiran 1970). The irregular streaky vertical and diagonal lines could have been an attempt to simulate a spilling of

Figure 5.5. Two simulations of the appearances of reconstructed vessels. (A) Vessels in a low-lit building interior. (B) Same vessels in a low-lit open courtyard context. (*Source*: Created by Andrew Wilson; © Equinox Publishing Ltd. 2011)

the contents down the vessel's sides. Such an image would have signaled a message of abundance, accentuating the symbolic value of the contents. That one could allow for such haphazard wasting of food during periods of scarcity was a conspicuous display of wealth. Whatever the design signified, the red paint on a plain brown, and especially white-slipped, background would have been a striking image under these low-light conditions that stood out against a relatively undecorated vessel assemblage. They, along with other co-present materials—the food that was served, the space that structured the hosts' and guests' interactions, the light, and the weather—helped to frame the setting and establish the sensorial cues that created the commensal event. Without these things assembled, the event could not achieve the hosts' desired effects.

The Limits of Authority and the End of Community

Given the precarious socionatural context in which the communities participated, one wonders how durable authority was, especially if it was justified on household wealth that consisted of organic, perishable remains that needed consistent replenishing? The answer to this question regarding the limits of authority can be discovered in the material remains of the community's final moments.

By the mid-tenth century BCE, the Early Iron Age communities of west-central Jordan were all abandoned, bringing to an end a less-than-two-centuries-long settlement system. This abandonment presents a paradox in need of explanation: the amount of energy and resources dedicated to building and maintaining settlements was inversely proportional to the amount of time in which these settlements were occupied. If communities invested so much time and labor in constructing a settlement infrastructure, a point that should be obvious by now, then why were most settlements abandoned after no more than a century of occupation, only three or four generations in length? This question resonates throughout the Early Iron Age southern Levant, especially in the central highlands, as so many settlements were occupied for limited amounts of time before they were abandoned, either temporarily or permanently. One might interpret this uneven settlement pattern across the Levant as symptomatic of the political chaos depicted in the biblical narrative. At al-'Umayri, the reason for the community's abandonment is clear. The excavation of destruction levels 1.5 to 2.0 meters thick in Buildings A and B contained stone ballistica, projectile points (Dubis 2002:222–226, figs. 11.1–11.2), and human remains (Chase 2002:220),[23] altogether suggesting that the Early Iron Age community was violently attacked and abandoned soon after (Clark 2002:100).[24]

Violent ends to settlements such as those at al-'Umayri, however, appear to be absent at the other Early Iron Age settlements that have been investigated in this work. Most settlements appear to have ended with little or no sign of upheaval. This abatement pattern is hardly surprising to scholars who use subsistence-based models to explain changing settlement patterns in the Levant (e.g., LaBianca 1990). Such an interpretation would suggest the communities exchanged sedentary for nomadic lifestyles and grew more dependent on pastoralism and less dependent on agricultural production over time. Causes for such changes in subsistence practices might include dramatic shifts in climate conditions, severe plagues, repeated seasons of famine, or unfavorable external political conditions. Although subsistence-based explanations for settlement abandonment could be valid, these prime movers are not readily apparent in the Early Iron Age. Recent examinations of climate change in the Early Iron Age southern Levant indicate the region was moister than previous centuries (Issar and Zohar 2004). Furthermore, aside from al-'Umayri's destruction, there is no sufficient evidence to suggest these communities were motivated to abandon sedentary life because of threats from external and more powerful political entities.

One additional explanation worth considering is that intersettlement conflict over territory and resources weakened communities. The loss of members and territory would have made it difficult for communities to recover from such conflicts and would have inadvertently made an impact on a community's production success. Unable to manage the sedentary subsistence routines put in place earlier, households may have had little choice but to abandon them and take up more mobile subsistence practices. Admittedly, this scenario is problematic as knowledge of the relationships between communities is limited to what has been explored in this chapter. Aside from al-'Umayri, which was abandoned around the time that the communities along the Wadi al-Mujib were founded further in the south, there is no physical evidence for conflict between the communities beyond that of the fortification systems that would have defended them during conflicts. Still, conflict was possible, and it is hoped that future archaeological investigations will clarify intercommunity relationships in more detail.

These different explanations for the end of sedentary life are all plausible scenarios. At the very least, they demonstrate the need for further investigation of individual settlements to discover the cause and course of events that led to their end. Al-'Aliya is a case in point. Evidence for the abatement process is visible in the excavated evidence from different buildings. Buildings 200 and 700 contained an unusually large amount of artifactual debris, particularly ceramic vessels and faunal remains, in post-occupation fill deposits (Routledge 2004, fig. 5.10). The buildings also appear to have been partially dismantled, their construction materials likely used for residences elsewhere in the settlement. These conditions contrast with other residences where evidence suggests buildings were abandoned hastily. Structures such as al-'Aliya's Buildings 100 and 500 remain architecturally intact and contain no sign of post-occupational debris. Both buildings contained in situ artifactual remains. As described earlier, Building 500's Room 503 contained a well-preserved food production installation that was abandoned soon after the last meal. Likewise, in both Buildings 100 and 500, agricultural surplus, an important source of wealth, remained unused in storage bins. The abatement conditions in other buildings, such as Building 400, were ominously "clean" of artifacts and building materials were left intact.[25] These conditions suggest building owners had more than enough time to pack up their belongings before their departure.

These three different abatement contexts across a single settlement do not lend themselves to blanket explanations based on violence or changes in subsistence practices. The investigation of production and authority presented earlier suggests another, more likely scenario. These emergent inequalities between households that were identified earlier in this chapter could have led disenfranchised households to leave the community and found new settlements or take up pastoral nomadism in the vicinity. Given the fragility of authority in the communities, leaders could not sufficiently coerce alienated constituents from dismissing themselves from the community in search of more favorable alternatives. Such a scenario squares with the evidence in Buildings 100 and 500, the largest and wealthiest buildings, that suggests they were abandoned last and under suspicious circumstances. Radiocarbon dating of organic evidence from the building placed the buildings' abandonment between 1001–921 BCE and 1011–941 BCE, respectively (2 sigma = 95.4 percent probability).[26] This flexibility in locality has important implications for understanding the mechanics of Early Iron Age community. Segments' abilities to attach themselves to new communities, as well as to dislodge themselves from old communities, in part explains the durability of settlement throughout the Early Iron Age. This pattern may have been more widespread across the region than previously recognized.

There is a paradox, however, when seeking to reconstruct the relationship between these Early Iron Age communities. Although the archaeological evidence suggests communities interacted with each other, at the same time, these communities were not always simultaneously settled. As described in chapter 3, the communities were instead founded episodically, as ceramic vessel evidence from Lahun and al 'Umayri dates from the late thirteenth and early twelfth centuries, whereas evidence from Balu'a, al-Mu'arradja, and al-'Aliya dates to the eleventh century. Considering this staggered settlement history alongside the similarities in architectural and artifact patterns strongly suggests that this pattern began in the northern half of west-central Jordan and gradually spread southward over the course of the Early Iron Age. Routledge has described this settlement pattern as a fissioning process in which segments abandoned communities and founded new communities nearby when conflicts between groups were irresolvable or communities grew too large (Routledge 2004:111–112). Inspired by Igor Kopytoff's (1987) explanation for settlement formation in central Africa, where mobility and flexible kinship practices made it possible for disenfranchised groups to aggregate into new collective arrangements, Routledge suggests that segments abandoned their previous community to join pre-existing communities or to establish new ones in adjacent territories.

This fissioning did not necessarily mean that old and new communities remained isolated, however. In instances where communities were positioned in close proximity to each other, everyday production routines such as animal herding and water collection created opportunities for social exchange between communities. Such informal occasions provided opportunities to exchange news and cultural knowledge about the landscape and subsistence practices. The investigation of the ceramic vessel industry supports the likelihood that communities maintained these kinds of relationships. Recall that analyses of the ceramic vessel industries indicated that the production resources of three communities—al-'Aliya, Balu'a and Lahun—overlapped in the Wadi al-Mujib canyon and its tributaries. Such an overlap in resources indicates that a degree of sharing and possibly collaboration took place between communities. Likewise, knowledge about clay sources, tempering practices, and production techniques was shared during these interactions.

Communities may have interacted in more formal relationships as well. Such interactions likely included collaboration in matters of subsistence or mutual defense. Collaborative relationships could be strengthened through regular feasts or marriage alliances involving younger members of the communities. However, relationships between communities were not always positive. Communities' extensive fortifications suggest that feuds and raids were common. Furthermore, relationships whereby one community grew dependent on another were certainly possible. If attacked, communities might have called on each other for help. During periodic droughts and famines, communities might have requested assistance from a more fortunate neighbor.

Does the possibility that communities were intertwined in a nexus of collaborative and, at times, dependent relationships allow one to conclude that the political complexity of Early Iron Age west-central Jordan was in some way on par with the biblical narrative's description of a territorial kingdom? Unfortunately, no—there is currently a lack of substantial evidence for these inter-community relationships (contra Finkelstein and Lipschits 2011). Furthermore, the absence of typical traits of a complex political entity—a clear settlement hierarchy, evidence for the collection and regional redistribution of agricultural surplus, and administrative evidence for kingship (e.g., palaces, prestige items, and royal tombs)—suggests that attempts to integrate communities in more complex political arrangements was rare, if not completely absent.

Conclusion

The evidence for emergent leadership does not offer an obvious choice between patrimonial and charismatic genres of authority to characterize west-central Jordan's Early Iron Age communities. Households were obviously the basic building blocks for the larger community, and one can imagine that members found ways to foster cohesion across households using kinship metaphors that may have, at first glance, reflected an ethos of corporateness that scholars have been wont to see in the evidence (e.g., Faust 2006). Yet regardless of such sentiments, the archaeological evidence suggests wealthier households did emerge in this corporate milieu. Given the potential for frequent periods of scarcity and the emphasis placed on food production and storage, these households would have been well poised to play a commanding role in the community's decision making. Such emergent inequalities did not necessarily spell the end of a communal ethos, however. These inequalities were likely rationalized through the nested hierarchies typical of ancient Near Eastern patrimonial societies (Schloen 2001). Whoever lived in al-'Aliya's Building 500 could have been understood in real and symbolic terms as a "father" to other households. But while patrimonial authority may have been the basis for a household's power over its neighbors, it need not have been the only form of authority. Exercises of social and symbolic capital associated with charismatic modes of authority would have complemented patrimonial modes. Constructing a visibly larger house, preparing and hosting commensal events demonstrating household wealth (and the willingness to spend it), and mobilizing other households in collective projects would have required leaders to circulate wealth to other households. The co-presence of patrimonial and charismatic genres in the Early Iron Age communities—and possibly other Bronze Age and Iron Age Near Eastern societies—suggests that authority cannot be reduced to a single category in the typologies that social science (e.g., Weber 1968) has instructed analysts to identify in their evidence. Instead, these genres of authority should be understood as strategies that leaders employed to maintain their authority in a landscape of shifting political, economic, and environmental contingencies.

This recognition of the dynamic role of leadership in the Early Iron Age communities leads to a larger question regarding the purpose of leadership in small-scale societies. Recent studies of agency in past societies often retrospectively focus on the corrosive effects of authority on the perceived "common good" until the organizational system this power has constructed collapses on itself (e.g., Dobres and Robb 2000). Such negative perspectives are potentially anachronistic, partly informed by contemporary society's experiences with twentieth-century despotism. But must an implicitly negative perception of leadership and its power necessarily be a default perception? The extent to which leaders contributed to a community's resilience presents a very different understanding of the role of leadership, particularly in marginal environments.

CHAPTER SIX

Conclusion

The Complex Community

At first glance, the Early Iron Age communities of west-central Jordan appear to have followed patterns relatively common among small-scale agropastoralist sedentary societies in the Near East. Each community organized its livelihood according to what it could produce from naturally available resources found in the nearby fields and riparian zones. The production routines that settlements followed—growing grains, raising herds, constructing buildings and fortifications, and making ceramic vessels—were relatively low in intensity, producing materials mainly for household and community consumption. Individual households could carry out only some of these routines on their own. When circumstances of convenience or necessity arose, households found ways to collaborate with each other in larger endeavors, such as communal herding, the construction of fortifications, and the defense of the community against outsiders. Yet this benign description of the community obscures a more complicated reality that becomes apparent upon a closer look at the evidence. Because many of these communities were founded in a landscape in which resources were distributed unevenly, this livelihood was consistently threatened by unpredictable environmental conditions. Especially in those communities situated in semi-arid zones such as al-'Aliya, Lahun, al-Mu'ammariyya, and al-Mu'arradja, the threat of scarcity was an omnipresent concern. Given these conditions, communities developed strategies and a supporting infrastructure to mitigate these uncertainties, particularly in the construction of storage facilities. From these efforts to produce and to store resources, namely food, wealth was generated that was unevenly distributed. Such differences indicate an emergent degree of inequality between households and a shift from relatively collaborative modes of decision making between households to ones in which more successful households held some power over their neighbors. This sway, however, had its limits, as evidence suggests individual households could and in fact did leave the community before the settlement's ultimate end.

This book has sought to understand the dynamics of these Early Iron Age communities in terms of communal complexity, a phenomenon, the reader will recall, in which small-scale societies possess flexible production routines and leadership strategies that allow them to adapt to shifting contingencies. Such a phenomenon can be potentially more common in marginal conditions in which resilience is threatened, propelling groups through adaptive cycles at unusually faster rates as they seek an organizational fit for the socionatural system in which they participate. Communal complexity draws from two frameworks archaeologists frequently use to understand preindustrial societies. One is a practice-based perspective that frequently appears in archaeological investigations of community (e.g., Canuto and Yaeger 2000; Knapp 2003; Varien and Potter 2008) and emphasizes how members' participation in scheduled routines fostered affiliation, the necessary sentiment for group cohesion. A practice-based perspective helped identify those routines in which Early Iron Age households collaborated with each other and how this collaboration created the nexus of relationships that became the community. This perspective also provided a framework to understand how households generated and accumulated wealth, and how this wealth circulated through the community.

Despite a practice-based perspective's usefulness for teasing out the minutiae of everyday routines and social relationships, the framework reaches its limits of utility when attempting to articulate the communities' development over time. These settlements did not spring up from nowhere fully formed in the landscape, nor did they collapse in a single moment. Rather, this process was gradual, with households accumulating in one location and then departing for other opportunities, breaking and building social bonds as they moved across the landscape. A number of questions pertaining to the communities' adaptive histories arise that a practice-based perspective cannot necessarily answer sufficiently because of its emphasis on daily, habitual routines. Consequently, a complex adaptive systems approach, the second framework informing communal complexity, is better equipped to answer such questions given its sensitivity to longer time horizons.

The Early Iron Age communities demonstrated several aspects of a complex adaptive system. The most salient is the trajectory of regional settlement patterns was nonlinear in its development and relatively low in overall intensity. Claims that west-central Jordan was organized in terms of a regional polity that could be characterized as a chiefdom, a kingdom, or a state (e.g., Finkelstein and Lipschits 2011; Mattingly 1992; Miller 1989; Timm 1989; Worschech 1990) are not supported by convincing evidence that would indicate that this settlement system was the result of a top-down administrative plan imposed upon the region. Instead, the evidence presented in this book suggests communities were independent entities that formed and dissolved across west-central Jordan in relatively irregular ways because of local contingencies that dictated subsistence and social life. These settlements were self-organizing, emergent phenomena that possessed the capacity to manage their own resources and to shift their decision-making strategies from egalitarian arrangements to more consolidated forms of leadership as the socionatural system in which they participated changed over time.

Each Early Iron Age community demonstrates slightly modified trajectories that sedentary life could follow in the region. Using these permutations, one can assemble specific model types that can simulate the different pathways a community could follow in its development. Such types can help researchers understand the ways in which groups' organizational structure unfolded as it passed through phases in an adaptive cycle. In a community's initial growth phase (the R phase), when groups can exploit new opportunities and resources, founding households gradually accumulated in one location. Whatever mobile characteristics households possessed prior to this phase declined as an implicit commitment to a sedentary lifestyle was made. Basic architectural components began to be constructed in the landscape, including some houses and impromptu fortifications designed to protect the new arrivals. Resource zones were identified in which households could organize subsistence practices and where herds could be watered, wild animals could be hunted and trapped, and naturally occurring plants could be gathered. As is typical of this phase, most planning took place on a short time horizon. Little thought was given to long-term viability of subsistence in this stage. Consequently, storage technologies were not yet constructed. Decision making at this time was likely a collaborative ad hoc effort among households that coordinated their activities with each other for mutual prosperity when convenient.

During the following conservation phase (the K phase), materials steadily accumulated on-site, leaders began to think in longer time horizons, and contingency plans were established based on scarcity projections. Communities initiated slightly more intensive production practices, particularly farming in the riparian zones, and more durable objects like ceramic vessels were crafted to assist with water transport from streams up the steep canyons to the settlements. Such sensibilities inspired more emphasis on the accumulation of surplus, leading to the construction of storage installations, stronger fortifications, and again, ceramic vessels to preserve liquids and grains in less permeable containers. During this phase, scheduled and collaborative production activities increased between households, partly because of new or more substantial kinship bonds fostered by marriage alliances and the growth of second-generation households that emerged from the founding generation. Participation in the construction of collective storage infrastructure and its subsequent management would have also integrated households into the community's shared sense of belonging. Inequalities in wealth between households also likely emerged during this phase, but it would not have necessarily had a great impact on the organization of community management and leadership.

It is worth considering at this point why Early Iron Age households would have participated in such sedentary endeavors that would have tethered them to a particular place. These formations that would eventually develop into the communities were likely unplanned organic ventures whose outcomes were probably just as uncertain as any other available alternative—nomadism, for example, or limiting settlement to a single household. Both options were certainly available to households, and instances of such settlement patterns exist in the region before and after the Early Iron Age. The answer probably lies in the likelihood that the community offered an appropriately scaled organizational venue for the marginal environmental circumstances that households faced. As a form based on face-to-face interactions, communities permitted households to organize different routines strategically, carrying out certain projects collectively that could not be easily accomplished by a single household alone. Communities' growth in the region's most optimal zones for resource exploitation also encouraged households to assemble themselves together. The historical circumstances of the Early Iron Age should also be considered. Lacking demands for output from larger state or imperial polities, communities had no reason to exceed certain levels of capacity. Altogether, the community offered a flexible social arrangement in which households could participate for their own livelihood until reaching a point in which collective life was no longer desirable. As the abatement evidence from al-'Aliya suggests, such departures could have been frequent.

Toward the end of a second conservation phase, ironically, as production practices become more regimented, and households become confident in their abilities, communities could grow too rigid in their organizational capacities to adapt to new circumstances. Consequently, communities could become less resilient despite their organizational complexity, especially if certain buffers against scarcity had not yet been put in place. An unanticipated shock to the community could test the community's resilience, sending it into the back loop of the adaptive cycle. In this release phase (the Omega phase), environment and human-induced disturbances such as drought, famine, and conflict could test the durability of infrastructure and production regiments the communities had established in the previous phase. During this phase, however, there would have been increased disparities in wealth between households. Households that had accumulated limited food surpluses in the previous phases would have depleted these reserves even further at this point. Such desperate households would therefore come to rely on more fortunate neighbors for assistance. It is also during this phase that reorganization in leadership took place. Households that had built a more durable resilience had a greater capacity to lead other households, making decisions that would potentially lead the community back into a growth phase. Leaders took on a greater managerial role, making decisions on production priorities, the management of any remaining collective wealth, and additional projects designed to sustain the community, and in particular, the leading households' assets. These leaders still depended on their less successful neighbors to carry out the collaborative projects that had been common in the earlier growth and conservation phases. Less fortunate households could abandon the community, believing that they would be better off pursuing nomadism, joining a neighboring community, or establishing a new one on their own with other disaffected households, hence beginning the adaptive cycle again. This consolidation in leadership likely contributed to a community's resilience. Leading households could have encouraged less fortunate households to remain attached to the community using a combination of patrimonial and charismatic genres of authority. More tangible strategies, however, would have been the circulation of leading households' wealth. Publicly performed acts such as feasts would have promoted the group's cohesion, rewarded participating households for their dedication, and further justified the leading households' abilities to manage the community through difficult times.

If and when the crisis subsided, the community could enter a final reorganization phase (an Alpha phase) when new practices and modes of management emerged. In this phase, communities could follow different trajectories. For one, substantial adjustments could be made that moved communities into a new adaptive cycle. Households could achieve a new awareness of their precarious situation that would lead them to dedicate more energy to constructing fortifications and storage facilities in a new growth phase. The leading households that emerged during periods of crisis could find it more difficult to justify their authority as dependent households once again achieved sustainable levels. Decision making likely returned to more equitable arrangements between households. Other trajectories were possible during the reorganization phase, of course, many of which involved households leaving the community for more sustainable options. Households that grew disaffected during the release phase over internal conflicts in community management could abandon it to found new ones in the region. This trajectory explains the fissioning pattern that Routledge observes in west-central Jordan's settlement system during the Early Iron Age (Routledge 2004:111–112). Alternatively, households could abandon sedentary life altogether, choosing nomadic subsistence practices in which they could move around the landscape to different environmental zones during optimal times of the year. Given the choices available to households on whether or not to continue communities, the decision to leave the community should not necessarily be cast in moral terms of failure or collapse. Rather, the choice to move one's livelihood into a new venue, sedentary or nomadic, was likely the best one available to actors concerned with subsisting in a marginal environment and working to navigate the shifting political and economic conditions of the region.

This narrative describing one potential way Early Iron Age communities could have moved through an adaptive cycle requires a few qualifications. The communities likely passed through not one, but several different adaptive cycles during the course of their existence. The first pass was likely a rapid boom-and-bust cycle in which households grew the settlement and subsistence began, but because of a lack of required features needed to mitigate crises, a community quickly moved into the back loop of an adaptive cycle. The next cycles could have been potentially slower. Projects designed to buffer against perceived crises were taken up in the growth and consolidation phases, staving off the back loop phases that would have threatened the community's sustainability. Communities also likely moved through adaptive cycles at different rates and for different reasons. Given that the evidence for each community's founding and abandonment is staggered over the Early Iron Age, one should not assume that all communities were experiencing the same conditions equally. Even more so, given the uneven microclimatic conditions across west-central Jordan, communities could have potentially experienced environmental shifts differently across the landscape. These distinct developmental histories suggest that some communities were potentially better off than others at certain moments in the Early Iron Age. The threat of attacks by more desperate communities was likely one of several justifications for constructing sizable fortifications around the settlements.

Yet another issue with this reconstruction plagues any regional investigation of cultural phenomena using archaeological materials: an unevenness in the quality and availability of evidence. In the settlements where excavation has been most abundant—al-'Aliya, Balu'a, Lahun, and al-Mu'arradja—the results are only partially published, primarily in book chapters, specialist reports, refereed journal articles, and websites. Reports presenting the recovered data in their fullest context are needed for these projects.[1] A plan of al-Mu'ammariyya's, and a better plan of al-Mu'arradja's, surface architecture would permit a more refined understanding of each settlement's spatial arrangements and would lay the groundwork for additional excavations. Survey data from the Dhiban Plateau also need to be published beyond the three existing preliminary reports in order to understand Early Iron Age settlement patterns in this important region (Ji and 'Attiyat 1997; Ji and Lee 1998, 2000). Likewise, settlements such as Khirbat al-Mudayna al-Mujib, a relatively unknown and inaccessible settlement positioned on the northwest corner of the Karak Plateau, needs investigation. Here, Worschech (1990: 54–59, figs. 16–17) recovered Early Iron Age remains during a surface survey. At the time of writing, additional Early Iron Age evidence was appearing in excavation projects at Dhiban (Routledge 2013) and Madaba (Harrison 2009) that should complement new data from ongoing excavations at al-'Umayri. This knowledge of Early Iron Age settlement activity in the northern half of west-central Jordan is essential as McGovern's research in the Baq'ah Valley remains the only substantially published Early Iron Age evidence from stratified settlement contexts north of 'Amman. Likewise, a lack of excavated data exists from the extreme southern half of west-central Jordan, the southern half of the Karak Plateau, and the Wadi al-Hasa. Several sites with Early Iron Age remains have been surveyed (Arikan 2012; Hill 2006; Miller 1991), and many remain potential candidates for excavation. All of this research north and south of the Wadi al-Mujib settlements will develop the current understanding of the region's settlement history during the late second millennium BCE and will provide insight into the diverse ways these communities adapted to the region's microclimates.[2]

Beyond collecting and making available new evidence, there is also a need to recover data at higher resolutions. What should be clear to the reader by now is that the region's Early Iron Age communities did not leave behind the abundant material remains to which archaeologists who investigate ancient Near Eastern societies are accustomed. Although these settlements are relatively accessible because of their preservation at or near the surface, their material records do not yield the written sources or the prestige objects, let alone the complete ceramic vessels, that typical historical reconstructions rely on for analysis. Therefore, the most valuable evidence can only be recovered using intensive sampling methods and high-resolution analytical techniques such as paleoethnobotanical, zooarchaeological, petrography, and microdebris analysis. Research at al-'Aliya and al-'Umayri has led the way in this respect, but more research is needed. Al-'Aliya's paleobotanical data set is limited to storage contexts that analysis suggests was used for animal fodder storage. Investigation of different contexts, such as the storage and food production facilities in Building 500, would provide a better understanding of human, rather than animal, consumption practices. Granted, even if all this evidence were available, one's ability to observe how these phases unfolded over time would be challenged given the nature of each settlement's preservation. Unfortunately, most settlements preserved only the final moments in household and community settlement activity, meaning that only the ends of each cycle, usually the back-loop phases, are available for study.[3]

Interpretive difficulties remain even when evidence from the final years of the Early Iron Age settlements is known. Currently available evidence from west-central Jordan's archaeological record makes it difficult to determine how these adaptive cycles unfolded during the tenth century, in the decades following the abandonment of the last-known settlement, al-'Aliya. The biblical narrative (e.g., 2 Samuel 8:2) suggests that during this time, the relatively new Israelite polity spread eastward into west-central Jordan and dominated much of the region. One would be tempted to dismiss this claim as political rhetoric common in the biblical narrative if it were not for the Mesha Inscription authored by a Moabite king claiming to have liberated much of west-central Jordan from ancient Israel's Omride Dynasty in the mid-ninth century BCE (Dearman 1989; Routledge 2004:133–153). Coinciding and following the writing of this inscription, physical evidence indicative of a political polity appears in the archaeological record of ninth- and eighth-century west-central Jordan that surpasses in scale the social complexity observed in the Early Iron Age (Routledge 2004:154–212).

What happened during this period between the abandonment of al-'Aliya (and possibly other settlements) and the rise of the Moabite polity in the second half of the ninth century? Several scenarios are possible, including the likelihood that ancient Israel's political dominance in the region motivated the abandonment of sedentary life. Alternatively, it is possible that sedentary life continued in settlements such as Adir, Karak, Qasr, and al-Rabba, four settlements in the Karak Plateau's interior where later building activity may not have preserved physical evidence for a late tenth- or early ninth-century occupation.[4] The inability to locate sedentary settlements during this period does not mean these communities ceased to exist, however. If indeed communities took up nomadic subsistence practices, households could still maintain relationships with each other. In this case, what would have changed was the setting in which these relationships occurred. No longer did fortification walls bind social life, and segments faced the challenge of amassing wealth while pursuing a lifestyle of increased mobility and seasonal migration. Mobility also decreased segments' abilities to organize projects that would have required the participation of disparately arranged households.

A strong indication that the region hosted a population during this relatively unknown period is the continuity in the genres of leadership and governance that was documented in the Early Iron Age communities. That is, many of the developments that appeared in the Early Iron Age—the ability to organize members and production routines, for example—foreshadow the more successful leadership strategies that arose in the ninth century BCE under a centralized Moabite polity. Although the mode of dominance did not change much, the scale at which this authority was recognized and administered did. By the ninth century, leaders were so emboldened that they had the power to integrate a variety of communities under a single polity, under the sponsorship of the Moabite god, Kemosh. How these leadership strategies that were only of limited success at the community level were more successful at the regional level will need further investigation as more evidence for tenth-century west-central Jordan comes to light.[5]

Rethinking the Community in the Early Iron Age Levant and Beyond

This book has repeatedly expressed dissatisfaction with disciplinary practices that use archaeological evidence to stitch together regional panoramic narratives that "make sense" in terms of the biblical narrative. Yet despite these protests, it is difficult to ignore the desire to narrate the time period and region in broader terms that are typical of culture history research. Generalizing statements, after all, are appreciated for classroom instruction and student textbooks that declare, "The Early Iron Age was a period of political and economic recovery that, at the same time, saw the emergence of new cultural identities." But in crafting such statements, must one then return to the Balkanized landscape of ethnic groups such as Philistines, Canaanites, and Israelites, a default ontology for narrating the time period?

Admittedly, these ethno-taxonomies do provide scholars with a common nomenclature to discuss their evidence. But it must be acknowledged that such a framework based on obsolete techniques of early twentieth-century culture area research can only partly describe social life. Rather, if one wishes to *explain* how human organizations developed—one important goal of archaeological research since the 1960s processual movement—then it is necessary to begin with the archaeological data, rather than the written sources, for the purpose of recognizing and interpreting diachronic patterns in the evidence. Furthermore, the use of historicizing and ethnicizing frameworks on Early Iron Age archaeological assemblages bears analytical consequences. Because these frameworks often ignore nuances for the sake of creating homogeneity within assemblages, they prevent the identification of local patterns that reveal different ways individual Early Iron Age settlements responded to the region's diverse environmental conditions. If the period was indeed as deflated in political and economic social complexity as it is often characterized (Bloch-Smith and Nakhai 1999), then one would predict more heterogeneity between settlements than is currently acknowledged. To recognize such diversity, the resolution at which Early Iron Age social life is studied must be narrowed considerably, as this book has attempted to do, so that slight differences within architectural and artifactual data can be observed in closer detail. On doing so, the subtle diversity of Early Iron Age society can be appreciated on its own terms, rather than for its abilities to uphold the biblical narrative or to meet the regional ethno-taxonomies to which the discipline clings.

Such fine-grained analyses produce a vast number of local iterations that together constitute a patchwork landscape of communities that defies the homogenizing tendencies of ethno-taxonomies. This patchwork raises an entirely new set of questions that can be asked of the evidence. So, for instance, the abundant southern coastal plain assemblage can be investigated to discover the myriad ways each Philistine settlement adapted to the coastal and marsh conditions in which they ensconced themselves.[6] Or, in settlements such as Megiddo strata VIB–VIA (Finkelstein, Ussishkin, and Halpern 2006; Harrison 2004), believed to be where Canaanite society continued in the aftermath of the Late Bronze Age collapse of the palace economies, one might ask how these communities adjusted to more diffuse political and economic arrangements, apparently without the administrative palatial elites? And in the central highlands, where most scholarly attention has sought to identify early ancient Israel's emergence, there are opportunities to look beyond the collared rim jars and "four-room" houses to appreciate how each community adapted its production practices to specific microclimatic conditions (Lev-Tov, Porter, and Routledge 2011). Alternatively, emphasis is placed on questions that can be pursued in individual archaeological contexts, questions of adaptation to local environmental conditions, the organization of production, the nature of social life, and emergent forms of leadership.

Of course, as has been reiterated throughout this book, if such diversity is to be accounted for, archaeologists need to make adjustments to their methodological practices. Alternative kinds of evidence, particularly at the microartifactual scale (e.g., paleoethnobotanical, faunal remains), need to be sampled from Early Iron Age settlements with greater consistency.[7] Published evidence needs reconsideration, paying greater attention to architectural arrangements or to the nonceramic artifacts (e.g., metal, stone) that go underappreciated compared to more abundant ceramic vessels and figurines. Emphasis must also be placed on regions, such as west-central Jordan, whose Early Iron Age evidence is underconsidered in syntheses. Recent research in southwestern Jordan, for example, has identified late second- and early first-millennia production centers associated with copper production (Levy et al. 2004; Levy, Ben-Yosef, and Najjar 2012). This new evidence has revised earlier claims that the region lacked settlement activity during the Early Iron Age; hence, investigators have wisely called for a reassessment of social complexity. Just as some regions need more intensive investigation, regions where evidence is already available need to be considered. Rarely considered alongside the southern Levantine evidence are the materials from the Early Iron Age settlements of the northern Levant, such as Afis, Charchemish, Hama, Sukas, and Tayinat (Akkermans and Schwartz 2003:360–377, fig. 11.3; Venturi 2010). Like their counterparts in the south, many of these and other settlements experienced decline in size or saw a complete abandonment at the end of the Late Bronze Age, only to see limited resettlement in the Early Iron Age that led to the development of Luwian and Aramaean states of the early first millennium BCE. Such differences suggest that northern Levantine societies recovered faster and followed different trajectories compared to southern Levantine societies. A cumulative effect of documenting this diversity across the region is an appreciation for the different rates and ways in which communities adapted to the new political, economic, and environmental conditions of the period. It therefore becomes possible to break down the monolithic narratives of "recovery" into more specific accounts that appreciate the contingencies in which these communities developed.

Broadening the scope of inquiry beyond the quest for history and ethnicity also has consequences for biblical archaeology, the discipline that has long held the Early Iron Age Levant as one of its mandates. First and foremost is delimiting what the biblical narrative can and cannot provide archaeological investigations. More than a century of scholarship has determined that biblical passages describing the Early Iron Age were not written down and edited until centuries after the period ended. Granted, the conditions through which Israelite scribes received and reinterpreted Early Iron Age "history" remains debated (e.g., Knoppers and McConville 2000). Still, there is enough uncertainty about the text that books such as Judges and First Samuel must be used judiciously when writing "histories" of late second-millennium society. But as this book has demonstrated, such a cautious view does not render the source completely useless. The biblical narrative can be used to inspire hypotheses that can be subsequently tested in more securely dated written sources and archaeological evidence. Such a technique has been used throughout this book when considering different aspects of Early Iron Age west-central Jordan, such as claims that the region was organized as a state, or the nature of leadership. In these and other instances, such questions were tested against evidence external to the biblical narrative with varying results. Ultimately, Early Iron Age Levantine history cannot be reduced to narratives of the early Israelites, or the Philistines, for that matter. Other groups lived beyond the central highlands, the southern coastal plain, and even west-central Jordan, some of whom still await discovery, some of whom will never offer up ethnic titles by which they can be labeled. The only way to discover such societies is to move beyond the regional ethno-taxonomies that biblical archaeology uses to delimit its inquiry.

Therefore, perhaps it is time to rescue the Early Iron Age Levant from biblical archaeology? Indeed, upon losing its status of "biblical exceptionalism," the Early Iron Age potentially becomes a case study for understanding societies at other moments in Levantine history. A distinct hallmark of the Early Iron Age compared to other Levantine epochs is the abundance of archaeological data collected from a time period of relatively deflated political and economic complexity, a so-called dark age. Such rich corpora of evidence are usually only available during periods when states and empires have stimulated regional economic development.

Conversely, the Early Iron Age provides opportunities to understand how Levantine societies developed during periods between episodes of increased political and economic complexity, in this case, the palace-administered city-states of the Late Bronze Age and the territorial states of the first millennium BCE. An immediate lesson is that Levantine archaeologists should suspect claims that such interstitial moments are characterized by an absence of sedentary life. Such assessments are often based on the presence or absence of settlement evidence in urban centers. What the Early Iron Age would instruct, however, is that evidence for sedentary life during such periods might be found in the rural settlements that are often believed to be abandoned during periods of decline or that are underconsidered in regional assessments. The potential continuity of rural communities throughout Levantine history harkens back to an earlier argument that they were the most persistent and common form of social organization in the region since the Neolithic Period.[8] Dense urban centers like the trading entrepôts along the Mediterranean Coast (e.g., Gaza, Byblos) and the cities positioned inland along commercial thoroughfares (e.g., Damascus, Aleppo, Jerusalem) were less normative forms of human settlement in the region.

The recognition of the community as a persistent form of social formation places Levantine archaeology in conversation with other archaeological culture areas in and beyond the Near East and Mediterranean Basin. The Early Iron Age Levant was only one of several regions—the Aegean, Anatolia, Cyprus, and Egypt—that recovered from the pan–Eastern Mediterranean collapse at the end of the Late Bronze Age. Panoramic studies in recent decades of the late second millennium have placed more emphasis on the region's collapse than on its recovery. It is time to place equal emphasis on the diverse ways Early Iron Age Eastern Mediterranean communities reestablished themselves following the Late Bronze Age collapse. Beyond the immediate region, however, what can Levantine archaeology contribute to global archaeological inquiry on preindustrial communities? The conceptual framework for this book has been inspired in large part by New World archaeological research (Canuto and Yaeger 2000), particularly in the American Southwest (Varien and Potter 2008). Admittedly, archaeologists working in the Levant have been reluctant to join such broader, cross-cultural conversations—or have not received the invitations to which they were entitled—for reasons too complex to discuss here. Yet the Levant does boast a substantial data set with which to investigate a wide range of human phenomena over several millennia, often with an abundant corpus of written sources and visual culture. Future investigations, therefore, should consider what unique perspectives the Levant offers the broader study of the preindustrial community.

In Praise of Small-Scale Societies

By now, some readers will have realized how the title of this chapter pays homage to another, older treatment of small-scale societies: cultural anthropologist Robert Redfield's classic 1955 monograph, *The Little Community: Viewpoints for the Study of a Human Whole*. Drawing on a lifetime of work in Latin American peasant societies, Redfield described Yucatan communities using different lenses that together spoke to his singular argument: societies, be they civilizations, states, or communities, must be studied using a wide array of perspectives ranging from the historical, ecological, and even psychological, in order to understand them as complete entities. The community offered Redfield a feasible scale to demonstrate his concern for holism, given its size and its accessibility to twentieth-century ethnographic field methods. Although written more than fifty years ago, and as a critique of mid-twentieth-century social scientific practices that are now considered somewhat passé in the twenty-first, Redfield's book consistently inspired this investigation of preindustrial Levantine communities.[9] In part, this influence was due to Redfield's willingness to take seriously the community as a mode of social organization (Redfield 1955:1).

Invoking Redfield's book in these final moments returns to a concern with which this book began—namely, the challenges one faces in studying past communities in a contemporary world in which the notion of "community" carries so much moral currency. Redfield, writing more than a half century ago, faced an entirely different set of concerns about the notion of community from the social sciences, particularly cultural anthropologists, as well as a rising public consciousness about mid-twentieth-century transformations, such as decolonization, and the effects of capitalism on the rural Global South. This book, however, has been researched and written under an entirely different set of contingencies. Like so much social archaeological writing since the early 1990s that has examined topics of gender, class, agency, identity, and other categories that concern contemporary society, this book has been challenged by the need to think in nonanachronistic terms about the community in past societies, societies very different from the one in which this book is read. Ignoring the usual caveat that archaeologists and their colleagues in the historical sciences cannot escape interpreting the past in terms of the present, this endeavor has sought to investigate empirically the material remains of a discrete set of social formations, all the while remaining conscious of contemporary meanings and experiences of community.

Charges of anachronism always introduce pessimism into historical inquiry. But perhaps some of this criticism can be reduced if one considers what contributions archaeologies of community can make to the modern world? Currently, in the first decades of the new century, there is a return to a desire for locally based, small-scale forms of social organization, despite public readers' ongoing fascination with "civilizations." What such discourses about communities suggest is that people believe that the organizations that form around intimate face-to-face relationships are well suited for solving problems in their neighborhoods and cities, from unemployment to recycling, crime, nutrition, and education. This move toward the local and the face-to-face is potentially a veiled rejection of the globalization ethic that was advanced at the end of the twentieth century, in which it was believed that a combination of markets and political organizations would provide solutions to humanitarian crises. But if indeed human societies are interested in organizing themselves around identities other than their citizenship in a nation, or their membership in a global religion, archaeologists have an opportunity to tell different stories about how past communities found common cause around tangible issues such as subsistence and survival.

The most pressing need currently is for more archaeologists to join inter- and multi-disciplinary conversations studying communities that live under rapidly changing climatic conditions (e.g., Hornborg and Crumley 2007; McIntosh, Tainter, and McIntosh 2000). Rising sea levels, for example, are challenging Pacific Islanders, and increasing aridity in sub-Saharan Africa is depleting soil and water resources, giving rise to a whole new classification of refugees, displaced not by war or unemployment, but by climate change. Such groups are now competing with each other and with federal governments and international corporations for what little resources are naturally available. Scholars long ago predicted that such communities on the edge of sustainability would adapt to these new circumstances by abandoning their settlements for urban industrialized centers, adopting new mobile subsistence patterns or vanishing altogether. But there is some indication that such communities are more resilient than previously believed, that they are capable of adapting to these new conditions rather than abandoning them for entirely different venues. In semi-arid Burkina Faso, for example, twentieth-century Mossi villages that were predicted to disappear have sustained themselves through livelihood diversification and the reorganization of household alliances (West 2009).

This story from Burkina Faso and others around the world (e.g., Hastrup 2009) presents the possibility that archaeology can contribute to discussions exploring how small-scale human social organization can be resilient in the face of challenging environmental and social conditions taking place in development, poverty, and environmental studies. In such collaborations, archaeologists can draw on their disciplinary sensitivities to the relationships between societies and their material worlds, as well as a long-held commitment to appreciating how groups adapt to and subsist in their environmental conditions. The most immediate lessons archaeologists have to offer is, obviously, that humans have inhabited challenging conditions for millennia—and will likely continue to do so despite the dire predictions of climate scientists. But one should not interpret these episodes on the edge as simply irrational missteps of unfortunate societies. Rather, such communities could have possessed their own internal logic that only the archaeological record can discern. Archaeologists can also offer such a study more complicated representations of past societies that go beyond the popular narratives of rise and collapse. As was seen in the Early Iron Age communities of west-central Jordan, the course of development passed through several adaptive cycles in which communities made substantial adjustments to all facets of their organization, from the ways food was produced, to the organization of decision-making bodies. As archaeology has and continues to make offerings to the very pressing issues that concern the modern world, what contributions the discipline can make to the amelioration of global poverty and climate refugees are only beginning to be considered. It is hoped that this study of a historically remote collection of Middle Eastern communities living at the limits of sustainability serves as an example of a step in this direction.

Notes

Acknowledgments

1. There are several instances in this book where data have been summarized due to constraints of space. The reader is encouraged to consider Porter (2007) alongside this book where certain data sets are presented and interpreted in greater detail. Of course, some of the ideas in this earlier treatment of the materials have been refined in this book or disregarded altogether. Additional presentations of data can be found in Lev-Tov, Porter, and Routledge (2010), Porter (2010, 2011), and at Open Context (www.opencontext.org), a web-based research data publication website where portions of the data described in this book are archived.

Chapter One

1. See esp. Bauman (2001); Blanchot (1988); Block (2008); Delanty (2003); Nancy (1991); and Putnam (2000).
2. These sentiments partly explain why the notion of community is often subtly laden with nostalgia when deployed in academic and public discourse.
3. Like Durkheim and Tönnies, Weber in *Economy and Society* made a distinction between community and society based on the type of relationship between individuals (1968:40–43). Communal relationships (*Vergemeinschaftung*), Weber argued, are based on the group's subjective feelings that it belongs together and are distinguished from associative relationships (*Vergesellschaftung*) based on individuals' rationally agreed-upon interests, values, or terms common in society.
4. In this book, semi-arid environments are defined as those regions with high temperatures and annual precipitation levels hovering around the minimum amounts needed for rain-fed agricultural production, usually between 250 and 300 mm per year (Wallén 1967).

5. The geographic terms "Middle East" and "Near East" require clarification. "Middle East" is used to denote the region east of the Mediterranean Sea and west of the Persian Gulf (but including Iran), south of the Caucasus region, and north of the Arabian Sea. "Near East," an older toponym for relatively the same region, is used in this work to refer to the region's societies prior to 1918 CE, as in the expressions "Ancient Near East," "Classical Near East," and "Islamic Near East." All of these terms are problematic and make it difficult to define the limits of the region with any precision. For genealogies of these terms, see Davison (1960); Keddie (1973). "Near Eastern archaeology" is the name of the discipline charged with studying the region's human history from the Paleolithic Era until the early twentieth century CE.

6. The genealogy of the community concept in the modern Middle East is not vast, but nevertheless interesting. Mid-twentieth-century examples (Antoun 1972; Nieuwenhuijze 1962; Tannous 1944) described a complex nexus of social organization dependent on subsistence, kinship, religion, and authority. Although these researchers observed the ways these different aspects fit together to create a community, they offered static representations of village social life, leaving the reader to wonder how supposedly isolated societies changed over time. Rosenfeld's critique observed that many studies lacked analytical rigor, failed to place their subjects in proper spatio-temporal frameworks, and did not emphasize conflict or social change (Rosenfeld 1972:45, 53). See Peters's diachronic research in a Lebanese village (Peters 1963, 1972) and Cohen's investigation of the effects that the reorganization of rural Palestine under the new state of Israel had on Arab village settlements (Cohen 1965) for other, more nuanced readings of the Middle Eastern community.

7. The Levant is defined in this work as the region located between the eastern end of the Mediterranean Sea and the western edge of the Arabian Desert, falling within the borders of Lebanon, Palestine, and Israel, and the western portions of Syria and Jordan. Readers familiar with the traditional chronological nomenclature of Levantine archaeology will observe that a more ambiguous category, the "Early Iron Age," is used throughout this book instead of the more traditional "Iron Age I." As it will become clear soon, the communities discussed in this book potentially began before 1250 BCE, the largely accepted start date of the time period, and extended well into the tenth century, past the traditional cutoff date for the standard Iron Age I terminology, 1000 BCE. Consequently, this book takes a relatively agnostic position in debates about Iron Age Levantine chronology that have plagued the discipline for more than a decade (e.g., Levy and Higham 2005) and instead prefers to express time in terms of specific centuries (i.e., "the eleventh century").

8. For a more detailed discussion of this literature, see Porter (2007:53–109).

Chapter Two

1. For different treatments of the community concept in archaeological research, principally the category's reception in New World archaeology, see Varien and Potter (2008) and Yaeger and Canuto (2000). For a different treatment of this discussion by the author, see Porter (2007:29–51).

2. According to Yaeger (2000), the San Lorenzo community consisted of twenty mound groups, the overwhelming majority being residential units. The architectural

and artifactual evidence suggests a relative evenness in the community's social hierarchy. Political and economic authority was likely concentrated in nearby Xunantunich, a much larger settlement center. The destinies of the two settlements were intertwined, as both settlements declined around 900 AD.

3. The literature on the debate over the nature of pueblo social organization is extensive and spans several decades. Overviews of the issues with accompanying bibliography can be found in Hegmon 2005. For responses and suggestions on this matter, see also Feinman, Lightfoot, and Upham (2000); McGuire and Saitta (e.g., McGuire and Saitta [1996]; Saitta [1997]; Saitta and McGuire [1998]); Rautman (1998).

4. Research on complexity and complex adaptive systems is a transdisciplinary pursuit spanning several fields in the social and natural sciences. For a recent statement, see, for example, Holling (2001); Levin (2002). Lansing (2003) describes its limited reception in anthropology in a review of research, although the approach is generally growing in popularity in the social sciences (e.g., Epstein 2006; Miller and Page 2007). Archaeologists, too, have contributed to the investigation of complex adaptive systems, with most research based in the prehistoric American Southwest (e.g., Kohler and Gumerman 2000; Gumerman and Gell-Mann 1994). Much of this research both in and beyond archaeology is being supported by the Santa Fe Institute (www.santafe.edu). For a provocative critique of complexity research, particularly agent-based simulations techniques, see Helmreich (1998).

5. Noting the basic instability between community doxa and discourse is not to say that complex adaptive systems research has ignored the role of agents and agency. Rather, agent-based modeling is commonly employed to understand how human actions and relationships partly shaped the larger systems in which they took place (Kohler and Gumerman 2000). The agentive role of individuals was often ignored or downplayed in earlier attempts to apply systems theory in archaeological research (e.g., Flannery 1972), and became a common point of critique for such thinking (Brumfiel 1992) during archaeology's postprocessual turn in the 1990s. Yet what is striking about agent-based modeling techniques is how well they can complement contemporary archaeological concerns with agency and practice (Dobres and Robb 2000). From this project's perspective, one principal difference lies in each approach's use of metaphor and narrative. Whereas agent-based modeling adopts an empirical tone to describe actors, practice-based approaches narrate a situation with a more embodied language of personhood. So rather than see conflicts between these various techniques, this work considers them complementary in many ways.

6. Resilience thinking has become a key component in discussions about how socionatural systems sustain themselves in the face of adversity. For introductory statements, see Gunderson, Allen, and Holling (2009), Gunderson and Holling (2002), and Walker and Salt (2006), the last of which is written for a public audience. The Resilience Alliance website (www.resalliance.org) also contains information and sources from a multidisciplinary perspective. Archaeological contributions to resilience theory have been gradually appearing since Redman's (2005) sensible call and the term's appearance in a recent collection (McAnany and Yoffee 2010) that questions Jared Diamond's book on collapse (2005). See also Fisher, Hill, and Feinman (2009).

7. For further details and discussion of adaptive cycles and thresholds, see Holling and Gunderson (2002, esp. fig. 2.1). Walker and Salt (2006), likewise, describe cycles and thresholds using real-world examples.

8. The isolation of an organization, such as a community or a state, for the sake of identifying its adaptive cycles and thresholds must of course be recontextualized in the socionatural system in which it participates. After all, it is only one complex adaptive system among many potential others that are in conversation with each other. These systems are linked to each other in what resilience studies define as a broader pattern of panarchy (Gunderson and Holling 2002).

9. Schwartz and Falconer's (1994) volume is an interesting venue for this discussion as several studies are based in this investigation's study area, the Middle East. This work also raises several problems that characterize the archaeological investigation of community, more broadly. See Porter (2007:32–34) for a discussion.

10. Only recently has it been recognized that prehistoric sedentary communities lived in a much broader geographical scope than those societies that followed them in historical periods. For example, in the arid eastern half of Jordan (e.g., the Jafr and Azraq drainage basins), fluvial environments that once hosted lakes and marshes are today dry or nearly so (Cordova 2007, fig. 2.6). For detailed, evidence-based descriptions of these environmental changes, see Arikan (2012); Cordova (2007), esp. chap. 6; Hill (2006); and Rosen (2007).

Chapter Three

1. The written source popularly known today as the Bible will be drawn on throughout this book as it is an important and problematic source for Early Iron Age Levantine societies. The portions of the text that are collectively titled by Christian audiences as the "Old Testament" will instead be called the "Hebrew Bible" in order to appreciate the fact that the majority of the text was written in biblical Hebrew. The Hebrew Bible will also be described interchangeably at times as the "biblical narrative." Translations of the text used in this book are either the author's or originate from the New Revised Standard Version (NRSV) (e.g., Metzger and Murphy 1991) that most scholars consider a credible translation.

2. The literature on the history and archaeology of the Middle Bronze Age southern Levant is vast. See Burke (2008) and Cohen (2002). For classic, but dated overviews of the period, see Dever (1987); Ilan (1995); and Weinstein (1975).

3. For discussions of Late Bronze Age economic organization, see McGeough (2007); Monroe (2009); Routledge and McGeough (2009); and Schloen (2001). For the circulation of prestige objects, see Feldman (2006).

4. Overviews of the later Iron Age include Herr (1997); Holladay (1995); Joffe (2002); Mazar (1990); Routledge (2004); and Stern (2001), among many others.

5. The quality of excavation techniques and publication quality vary across the evidence. In the past, excavations focused on the recovery of macro-remains such as architecture and ceramic vessels. Only recently has it become somewhat normative to recover faunal evidence and botanical evidence, although sampling strategies still remain poorly planned.

6. See Soggin (1981) and Boling (1975) for commentaries offering critical discussions of the Book of Judges.

7. But see also excavation projects in other regions, such as southern Jordan (e.g., Levy et al. 2004; Levy, Ben-Yosef, and Najjar 2012).

8. The Song of Deborah is one often-cited example of a passage with archaic vocabulary and grammatical structure that led scholars to date the text to the Early Iron Age. Oral compositions such as the Song of Deborah were eventually written down as early as the tenth century (Soggin 1989:201) and as late as the eighth century BCE (Schniedewind 2004, esp. p. 63). For additional discussions on textual composition in recent commentaries, see McCarter (1980:12–30, 1984) for the Books of 1 and 2 Samuel; Nelson (1997:2–3) for the Book of Joshua; and Niditch (2008:6–8) for the Book of Judges.

9. The other ways that scholars have conceived of Early Iron Age social life, particularly in terms of subsistence, production, kinship, and authority, will be discussed further in chapters 4 and 5.

10. The western limit of this study is the western edge of the region's plateaus and does not extend into the Jordan Valley itself. Given that environmental conditions and Early Iron Age settlement patterns differ in this region, it deserves treatment on its own terms.

11. Miller (1989) interestingly suggests that the editors of Numbers may have arranged these episodes with the purpose of demonstrating that the Israelites held a legitimate claim to the area north of the Arnon River.

12. Glueck (1940:28) wrote, "For the present, it has been possible to establish the presence of two outstanding civilizations in Transjordan during its early history. The one is the Early Bronze Age civilization. The other is the Iron Age civilization. Between these there was apparently in much of the land, particularly in central and southern Transjordan, a serious decline in the history of permanent sedentary occupation, lasting from about the end of the nineteenth to the beginning of the thirteenth century B.C."

13. In a recent return to Glueck's "maximalist" interpretation of the evidence, Finkelstein and Lipschits (2011) argue for an Early Iron Age Moabite polity with an administrative center at Baluʻa. Given how little is known currently about the size and composition of Early Iron Age Baluʻa, it is difficult to agree with their argument.

14. James Sauer (1986:10) pointed out in his critique that Glueck had been correct in his identification of several Early Iron Age settlements in west-central Jordan.

15. But see Worschech (2009:65–66) for a more recent interpretation of west-central Jordan during the Early Iron Age.

16. J. Andrew Dearman's summary comment is typical: "A significant percentage of Moab's population was pastoralist in the Bronze and Iron Ages. For much of the Late Bronze and Iron Ages, the political and economic life in the region did not include many walled settlements. . . . The Iron Age phenomenon of an increase in village life and regional stems of fortified outposts and watchtowers does not reach its culminating point until Iron II" (Dearman 1992:73). And J. Maxwell Miller writes, "Yet these physical circumstances alone hardly make a case for an early Iron Age Moabite monarchy and neither, I submit, can a case be made on the basis of the currently available epigraphical and archaeological evidence. This notion originated with, and in my opinion still depends upon, an uncritical reading of the Hebrew Bible. This is not to deny that there probably were kingdoms or chiefdoms of sorts in Moab during the early Iron Age, or to contend that a unified territorial monarchy would have been impossible at that time. My point is simply that the notion is open to serious question and should not be allowed to predetermine the way we interpret the epigraphical and archaeological evidence" (Miller 1989:84).

17. For a discussion of the utility of chiefdom models, see chap. 5 of this book.

18. Only recently and in a limited way have scholars working in the region acknowledged the complicated discussions taking place in cultural anthropology over the nature of segmentary mechanics (e.g., Bienkowski 2009; Routledge 2004). Discussions over the rather perfect picture of segmentary mechanics painted by Evans-Pritchard are numerous and impossible to recount here in their entirety (Dresch 1988; Munson 1989; Peters 1963; Rosen 1979). The discussion is divided between scholars who understand segmentary lineage as either a description of social organization that manifests itself in society or a social ideal that is reflected in indigenous discourse, but its basis in actual social relationships is randomly attributed (Dresch 1986; Caton 1987).

19. The house of Micah is the best example of a family that fails to conform to the Israelite ideal (Judges 17–18). With his father deceased, Micah is left to care for his entire family, including his domineering mother and his son (and their wives) as well as a Levite priest who "became like one of his own sons" (Judges 17:11) and "the men who lived near Micah's house" (Judges 18: 22). In this example, kin terms play less of an organizing role than they do as metaphors expressing alliances, dominance, and loyalty.

20. Scholars (e.g., Kitchen 1992) have commonly identified Shutu with the "sons of Seth" mentioned in Numbers 24:17, a passage that suggests this group was an antecedent to the Moabites: "A scepter shall rise out of Israel; it shall crush the borderlands of Moab, and the territory of all the Sethites." Passages such as Deuteronomy 2:10–11 and 2:20–23 as well as Numbers 13:18–23 describe other groups such as the Emim, Zamzumim, and the Rephaim living in the area prior to the Moabites and Ammonites. Of course, the late dates of these compositions call their reliability into question.

21. Scholars have debated the extent to which Middle Kingdom Egypt dominated the southern Levant during this period, citing the written sources such as that just described in the text and Egyptian material culture as evidence of Egypt's imperial practices in the region (Mazar 1968; Rainey 1994). Others find the historical evidence unconvincing for an imperial presence and the material evidence only proof of contact, not dominance, between the two regions (Redford 1992, 1996; Weinstein 1975).

22. Middle and Late Bronze Age settlements in the Wadi al-Hasa, the southern edge of west-central Jordan, were limited in number according to systematic landscape surveys. See Hill (2006:40–43, 113–114) for discussion.

23. The Hebrew Bible provides additional support for Moab's early existence in Numbers 21:10–20 and 33:5–39 as well as Deuteronomy 2, which describe the Israelites' early encounters with the Moabites, living south of the Arnon, the Wadi al-Mujib. That Moab's territory had been reduced in size soon before the Israelites arrived is suggested in Numbers 21:26, recording how the Amorite Sihon had fought the Moabites and conquered the area north of the Arnon. While the Israelites attacked Sihon and claimed his territories for themselves, the biblical writers go to great lengths to demonstrate that the Israelites respected the territorial integrity of Moab and did not campaign south of the Arnon, actions that Yahweh forbade of them. These narratives, many if not all of which were composed several centuries later when Moab's border expanded northward following Mesha's expulsion of the northern kingdom of Israel, appear to be making the case that land north of the Arnon rightly belong to the Israelites who won the territory fairly from the Amorites in earlier centuries (Miller 1989). This matter was all the more urgent to the biblical writers as Num-

bers 32 reports that the tribes of Reuben and Gad settled in the area won from King Sihon. That the Gadites lived in the region is corroborated in line ten of the ninth-century Mesha Inscription that reports that they were living in Atarot before Mesha expelled them.

24. In the Wadi al-Hasa, the Early Iron Age is better attested than are the earlier Middle and Late Bronze Ages, according to landscape surveys (Hill 2006:43–44). Still, the extent of the settlement system needs further investigation as follow-up excavations at sites identified in survey revealed no substantial Early Iron Age settlement activity (Bienkowski et al. 1997).

25. Given limitations of space, it is not possible in this work to describe the settlements and survey results bearing ephemeral evidence for the Early Iron Age. Only the best excavated and published evidence has been chosen for analysis. For the fullest and most recent treatment of early (and later) Iron Age materials from the region, the reader is directed to Gass (2009, esp. pp. 213–294). Herr (2009) and Ji (1995) are two additional syntheses bearing some interpretation of settlement patterns.

26. 'Aro'er is a small site located 4 km east of the Madaba-Karak highway, on the edge of the Wadi al-Mujib. Under the sponsorship of the Casa di Santiago de Jérusalem, Emilio Olávarri conducted three excavation seasons at 'Aro'er between 1964 and 1966 (Olàvarri 1965, 1969, 1993). Evidence for Early Iron Age occupation is limited to a partially exposed Level V house, Loci 204, 206, and 208 in Trench D. The Level V ceramic assemblage is similar to other Early Iron Age settlements in the region, notably al-'Aliya, Balu'a, and al-Mu'arradja. Until excavations are completely published, little can be said to characterize the settlement's extent and the role it played in the region with any accuracy.

27. Balu'a is located on the northern edge of the Karak Plateau, at the entrance to the Wadi Balu'a. In 1987, Udo Worschech of the Friedensau Adventist University began excavations at the site, with Friedbert Ninow of the same institution taking over the directorship in recent years (Worschech 1989, 1990; Worschech and Ninow 1994, 1999; Worschech, Rosenthal, and Zayadine 1986). Unfortunately, later Iron Age, Roman, and Middle Islamic building activities have obscured the Early Iron Age settlement, making it difficult to characterize the settlement's size and design accurately. Two additional buildings, Field A Hauskomplex and Field E Hauskomplex, although assigned to the later Iron Age period, have yielded enough ceramic evidence to suggest that these buildings were originally founded in the Early Iron Age period. Most Early Iron Age ceramic vessels were excavated in the silos and subterranean features associated with the buildings.

28. Lahun is an elliptically shaped Early Iron Age village of 1.6 ha resting on the northern edge of the Wadi al-Mujib (Homès-Fredericq 1992, 1994, 1995, 1997, 2000; Swinnen 2009). Between 1978 and 2000, the Belgian Committee of Excavations conducted excavations at Lahun under the direction of Denyse Homès-Fredericq. Aside from these published sources, this discussion of Lahun draws on the most recent excavation summary at http://www.lehun-excavations.be/late%20bronze-iron%20age.htm.

29. Al-'Aliya is another elliptically shaped village of 2.2 ha located 19 km northeast of modern Karak. Between 1994 and 2004, Bruce Routledge conducted five excavation seasons at the site (Routledge 2000, 2004; Routledge and Porter 2007). The settlement is located on a high promontory overlooking the juncture of the Wadis al-Mukhayris and al-Nukhayla.

30. Al-Mu'arradja is an elliptically shaped village of 1 ha, located 5 km north of al-'Aliya and 4 km south of Balu'a. In 1976 and again in 1982, Emilio Olàvarri conducted two excavation seasons at al-Mu'arradja (Olàvarri 1977–1978, 1983). The settlement is perched on a promontory above the Wadi al-Mukhayris.

31. Al-Mu'ammariyya is a site of unknown size, situated north of Balu'a and south of Lahun. Friedbert Ninow carried out three seasons of excavation there in 2002, 2003, and 2005 (Ninow 2004, 2006). Aside from nearby Roman ruins, the settlement dates to a single period, the Early Iron Age.

32. Sahab is an Early Iron Age settlement of unknown size located 12 km southeast of 'Amman. Under the supervision of Moawiyyah Ibrahim, Jordan's Department of Antiquities conducted excavations for three seasons, 1968, 1972, and 1973, at the site (Ibrahim 1972, 1974, 1975). Domestic architecture dating to the Early Iron Age was well represented on the west and north sides of the settlement in Areas A, B, D, E, E/W, H, and G. Two buildings were almost completely exposed in Areas B (Ibrahim 1974, pl. 15) and D (Ibrahim 1974, pl. 18), both of which demonstrate a pattern of long rectangular rooms. In Area A, multiple storage jars with diagnostic collared rims were excavated on the floor of a domestic building (Ibrahim 1987). The modern community living above the materials limited the extent to which these areas could be exposed.

33. Tall al-'Umayri is an Early Iron Age settlement of unknown size located 15 km south of 'Amman. Under the auspices of the Madaba Plains Project, Larry G. Herr and Douglas Clark have supervised excavations at the site for several seasons (Geraty et al. 1989; Herr et al. 1991, 1997, 2000, 2002). Early Iron Age materials are distributed throughout the tall, but are concentrated and best understood in Fields A and B.

34. In addition, several excavated settlements present limited evidence for Early Iron Age occupation. In most cases, evidence datable to the early Iron Age—usually ceramic vessel materials—are recovered in secondary debris contexts not associated with the surfaces of architectural units. In other instances, Early Iron Age materials are identified in contexts mixed with earlier or later materials. A final persisting issue is the poor quality or lack of published information that precludes a better assessment of excavated materials. Settlements bearing one or more of these issues include Abu Kharakha (Parker 1987), the 'Amman Citadel (Dornemann 1983), the 'Amman Roman Theatre (Hadidi 1970), Dhiban (Tushingham 1972; Winnett and Reed 1964), Hesban (Ray 2001), 'Iraq al-Amir (Lapp 1989), Khirbat al-Mudayna al-Mujib (Worschech, Rosenthal, and Zayadine 1986; Worschech 1990), and Safut (Wimmer 1987). These contexts are poorly stratified and published, yet are worth mentioning as they speak to the widespread distribution of Early Iron Age settlements across west-central Jordan. See Gass (2009) for a fuller treatment of this more ephemeral evidence.

35. Yet as Homès-Fredericq (1992:188, 190) suggests, a local craftsman who did not speak or read Egyptian could have cut the scarab, as the god's name, "Amun-Re," is spelled incorrectly. The artist may have used popular Egyptian imagery that circulated in the region during and after it was under Egyptian control. Ultimately, the scarab is only somewhat helpful in assigning narrow dates to Lahun's Early Iron Age settlement.

36. Bayesian modeling of Oxford AMS (accelerator mass spectrometry) radiocarbon dates using OxCal determined that the date of house construction at al-'Aliya

took place between 1105 and 1016 BCE (2 sigma=95.4 percent probability). Fifteen dates were taken from seven roof beams and one from reed matting on a building floor. These dates using the InCal 04 atmospheric curve supersede the problematic beta-counted dates from Laval University published in Routledge (2000:47–48, fig. 8; B. Routledge, personal communication with author, 2013).

37. Similar ceramic vessel assemblages from secure eleventh- and early tenth-century strata occur at Deir Allah (Phases A–E) in the Jordan Valley and at various sites west of the Jordan Valley including Beer Sheba VII–VI, Gezer XI–X, Hazor Xb–IXb, 'Izbet Sartah II–I, Megiddo VI–V, Qasile XII–X, and Ta'anach IIA and IIB.

Chapter Four

1. Just who constituted a "household" or a "family" in the Iron Age Levant has seen much discussion between scholars, with little agreement over composition (Faust 2000; Halpern 1996; Meyers 1997; Schloen 2001; Stager 1985). Bronze Age and Iron Age written sources describe the *bet*, the "house," as materially and symbolically constituted as a nested patrimonial hierarchy of institutions that could be rationalized at different levels of organization, from the modern notion of the "nuclear family" upward to the "extended family," and eventually to the polity, where the ruler is understood to be a "father" over his constituent "sons." The current work assumes that such nested hierarchies functioned in the Early Iron Age communities of west-central Jordan, but such discourses of affiliation were deployed inconsistently in everyday life and were subject to rupture, especially during periods of stress. See Porter (2007:77–84) for additional discussion on kinship and patrimonialism in the Iron Age Levant.

2. The settlement history of 'Izbet Sartah, an Early Iron Age settlement located northeast of Rosh Ha'ayin in modern Israel, illustrates how this transition toward increasing sedentarization took place (Finkelstein 1986).

3. Hopkins's (1985, 1987) research in the central highlands, however, was unique in its consideration of the Early Iron Age evidence for production. He argued that because of variance in amount or quality of soil, precipitation, and vegetation, agricultural strategies were in large part determined by a settlement's situated environmental context (1985:266–267). Given that subsistence challenges demanded a disproportional amount of time and labor, permanent agricultural installations such as cisterns and terraces were not regular features of central highland agricultural practices. Instead, communities employed risk-reduction strategies that helped to ensure a regular agricultural yield in an unstable environment. Hopkins points out the variety of storage technologies, including ceramic vessels, buildings, and subsurface installations that communities constructed to store food in periods of drought or famine.

4. Production in the ancient Near East and particularly in the Early Iron Age Southern Levant has most often been discussed in terms of peasant societies. Near Eastern scholars (e.g., Diakonoff 1974; Liverani 1979; Zaccagnini 1983) studying the economies of earlier Bronze Age societies have debated the extent to which Karl Marx's Asiatic mode of production and Karl Wittfogel's (1957) "Oriental" despotism are useful for modeling Bronze Age society. For a review of this argument and a critique of its findings, see Schloen (2001:189–194). In the Early Iron Age southern Levant, production has been indirectly considered in the application of peasant village

models to agro-pastoralists (Mendenhall 1962, 1976, 1983; Gottwald 1979, 1983). These attempts, however, have drawn on definitions of peasants as subordinated egalitarian social groups within larger political-economic systems that fit better with more recent historical phenomena such as feudalism and capitalism (e.g., Redfield 1941; Scott 1976; Wolf 1966) and less well with the disparately organized Early Iron Age southern Levant. Furthermore, these studies dwell almost exclusively on the problematic written evidence and spend little time considering the physical evidence for production in the archaeological record. For the author's critique, see Porter (2007:72–75).

5. See Routledge (2000:60–63) for a discussion of determining demography at al-'Aliya. For a broader discussion of household demography in ancient Israel, see Schloen (2001:135–183).

6. Scholars (e.g., Faust and Bunimovitz [2003]; Harding [2004]; Holladay [1992]; Shiloh [1970]) have gone to great lengths to define the functions of individual rooms.

7. At Sahab and al-'Umayri, fortification systems manifest themselves in different configurations, likely because the plans from earlier Bronze Age settlements are repaired in the Early Iron Age. At Sahab, Early Iron Age materials are associated with a large wall constructed during the Late Bronze Age in Area E (Ibrahim 1974, 1975). At al-'Umayri, a Middle Bronze fortification system was repaired in the early Iron Age and a wall between 1.6 and 2.0 meters thick was constructed at its crest (Herr 2000:172). Like other Early Iron Age settlements, the back rooms of pillared buildings double as a casemate room.

8. A published plan of al-Mu'ammariyya is not yet available, but Ninow (2004:257) writes that "the approach to al-Mu'ammariyya leads through a western pathway winding its way up the slopes of Jabal al-Muammariyya, surrounding the site and leading up to a saddle from which a small path leads to a gate situated in the southern city wall near the citadel."

9. Based on a thirty-year average, temperatures during the summer months range between 15° C in April and 25° C in August (Ferguson and Hudson 1986, table 2.1). The southern Levant has grown increasingly warmer and drier since the beginning of the Holocene 11,500 years ago (Issar and Zohar 2004). Climate data garnered from the analysis of stalagmites in Soreq Cave (Israel) (Bar-Matthews et al. 1999) and fluctuations in the level of the Dead Sea (Frumkin et al. 1991) together suggest that starting around 1600 BCE, a relatively warmer and drier phase began and peaked between 1500 and 1400 BCE (Issar and Zohar 2004). Following this period, humidity increased and eventually temperatures cooled, achieving its maximum around 1100 BCE. The climate again warmed after 1000 BCE. The relative lack of environmental proxy data from west-central Jordan makes it difficult to make observations about Late Holocene conditions with further precision.

10. See Cordova (1999, 2000, 2007; Cordova et al. 2005) for more detailed discussion of the region's soils. In summary, RMS have a high clay content (50 to 70 percent) that permits water to infiltrate the soil, trapping and storing precipitation. RMS are basic in chemical composition, have high levels of potassium and calcium, and are consequently most suitable for agricultural production. YMS are not as favorable for the precipitation of calcium carbonates, the formation of clay, and iron staining. YMS's chemical composition is lower in basic elements and essential nutrients. YMS

contain less clay and, consequently, less precipitation infiltrates the soil. YSS contain very low amounts of clay; they develop in thin beds adjacent to desert areas and on alluvial and colluvial deposits or recently exposed bedrock.

Erosion explains the uneven distribution of soil quality (van Andel, Zangger, and Demitrack 1990). Soils grow destabilized and erode into wadi canyons where stream action carries deposits downstream, creating a palimpsest of sediment beds adjacent to wadi streams and in alluvial fans. Close inspection of these sediment deposits reveal that the rate, as well as the circumstances, of deposition are not uniform across the region and require local investigation (Cordova 1999, 2000). With its introduction in the Neolithic period (Köhler-Rollefson 1988) and its intensification in the Early Bronze Age (Rosen 1986), agricultural practices have stimulated widescale environmental degradation. Therefore, soil erosion and deforestation was already a wide-scale problem in the region before the Early Iron Age period (Cordova 2007:192–195).

11. At Hesban, wheat, barley, lentils, and grapes were reported from Iron Age contexts, although unfortunately, this evidence is not differentiated between the early and later Iron Ages (Gilliland and Fisk 1986, fig. 7.1).

12. Granted, additional analysis of these wetland weed species is necessary before this claim can be made with confidence (Simmons, personal communication, 2013).

13. Simmons (2000:21) reported that the absence of olives is likely due to the issue that olive pits tend not to float, making them difficult to collect when separating paleobotanical evidence from their dirt context.

14. Producers could also practice management strategies that sought to rejuvenate soil nutrition, decrease erosion on hillside slopes, and store sediments (Schnurrenberger and Cole 1997). Because agricultural practices often deplete nutrients necessary for productivity, producers often leave select fields fallow for a cycle or two in order to restore moisture levels. Animals that are grazed on fields contribute their manure to restore soil nutrients. In addition to fallowing, crops can be rotated around field plots in order to avoid the depleted state in which the successive planting of a single crop leaves soils. The high nitrogen levels that pulses possess made them an ideal crop for alternating with nitrogen-depleting crops such as wheat.

15. Three vegetation zones, Mediterranean, Irano-Turanian, and Saharo-Sindian, are documented in west-central Jordan (al-Eisawi 1985; Lacelle 1986b). The Mediterranean zone predominates on the plateaus' western halves with characteristic oak (*Quercus calliprinos*) and pine species (*Pinus halepensis*), cypress trees (*Cypressus sempervirens*), cultivated fruit and nut tress (e.g., pears, figs, olives, pistachios, almonds), and vines (Crawford 1986). Covering the entire area is nonforest vegetation such as *Rhamnus palestinus*, *Calicotome villosa*, and *Sarcopterium spinosum*—spiny and unpalatable species on which sheep and goats graze. The second and third vegetation zones, the Irano-Turanian and Saharo-Sindian zones, are found on the western descent to the Jordan Valley as well as the eastern edge of the plateau. Vegetation in these regions is indicative of climates receiving less than 200 mm of annual precipitation and includes communities of steppe forests (e.g., pistachio trees (*Pistacia atlantica*), thorny and broomlike brushwoods, and dwarf shrubs (*Anabis syrica*) (Zohary 1962:131–146).

The lack of moisture during the summer is stressful on west-central Jordan's flora. Only species bearing water conservation features survive to regenerate in winter

(Lacelle 1986b; Younker 1989; Zohary 1962:178–207). Plants that begin growing during west-central Jordan's mild winters and complete their reproductive cycles before the summer drought are most suitable to regional conditions (Lacelle 1986b:105–106). During summer, these plants die back and leave only their seeds, bulbs, and tubers for repropagation when moisture again becomes available at winter's beginning. Plants producing seeds are best as the seeds can survive severe droughts and later sprout once precipitation commences. Additionally, plants shedding their larger leaves for smaller leaves in warmer months limit their transpiration and conserve water. Other characteristic plants that thrive in the region are those that tolerate the xeric soil while maintaining photosynthetic processes such as plants in the Phlomis, Salvia (sage), and Centaury (Centaurea) families. The annual soil recharge is so limited that very little moisture is retained for plants to use during arid periods. Consequently, successful herbs and shrubs develop shallow but extensive root systems, increasing the amount of moisture a plant can absorb.

The current vegetational landscape is only a shadow of that which west-central Jordan's Iron Age communities would have encountered (Cordova 2007:62–94). Prior to the first episode of intensive agricultural production in the Early Bronze Age, trees characteristic of Mediterranean vegetational zones such as Aleppo pine, pistachio, and deciduous Tabor oaks formed a lush primordial forest (LaBianca 1997). Pollen cores drawn from the Sea of Galilee and the southern end of the Dead Sea suggest that this vegetational landscape gradually contracted beginning in the Middle Bronze period and continued through the Iron Age (Baruch 1990:284, see core subzone X2). Forest clearing, intensified cultivation practices, and animal grazing are some of the anthropogenic practices that led to this contraction.

16. This pattern may have more to do with the type and quality of contexts from which samples were recovered. Paleobotanical evidence from al-'Aliya's domestic contexts that has yet to be analyzed will likely reveal more regarding the human consumption of wild cultivars.

17. For a complete publication of al-'Aliya's faunal evidence, including methods of analysis, see Lev-Tov, Porter, and Routledge (2010). Excavated faunal remains are also available from the Iron Age levels of Hesban (LaBianca and von den Driesch 1995, table 5.21), although two problems hamper the use of these data in the current investigation. First, later Iron Age building activities destroyed much of the Early Iron Age settlement, leaving only a handful of secure Early Iron Age deposits for analysis. Second, early and later Iron Age evidence are not differentiated in the presentation of data.

18. Although each of these collections permits insight into animal husbandry practices, each collection bears its own inherent problems. At Hesban, the context for most of the materials are secondary deposits that were disturbed by later Iron II building activities. Materials from the collection are limited to only the best season, 1976, because of sampling and processing errors (von den Driesch and Boessneck 1995:67). At al-'Umayri, the studied materials are not selected from all excavated Early Iron Age deposits, but rather from a refuse bin associated with Buildings A and B (Peters, Pöllath, and von den Driesch 2002:306). This material is useful in that it provides an excellent window into the food consumption practices of a limited number of residences, but it is in no way representative of the entire community. Finally, the faunal assemblage is relatively limited at al-'Aliya and Hesban, containing only 652 and 1,502 items, respectively, compared to 4,184 in the al-'Umayri collection. At Hesban, the

limited amount is due again to the fact that the context for most materials was excavated in secondary deposits disturbed by later Iron II building activities. At al-'Aliya, the number of samples is small despite the fact that several residences were excavated over the course of two seasons (1998 and 2000). Eighty-five percent of the faunal evidence was very small and difficult to identify beyond the general categories of mammal, fish, or bird (Lev-Tov, Porter, and Routledge 2010). The one camel bone is likely a later intrusive element.

19. Number of identified species (NISP) is a raw count of the number of specimens that the analyst successfully assigned to a species type. This number does not reflect the minimum number of individuals (MNI) in each collection. NISP counts are favored over MNI counts for this work because the data from all three collections are reported in NISP counts.

20. Recall that this conclusion is based on a limited sample of sheep and goat bones ($n = 122$).

21. Granted, this observation is based on a sample size of fifteen specimens, as the authors are well aware (von den Driesch and Boessneck 1995:317).

22. Another strategy, the construction of anthropogenic structures that collected soils and runoff precipitation, required greater coordination, planning, and cooperation between community members. Archaeological surveys have identified several types of anthropogenic structures in the vicinity of early Iron Age settlements (e.g., Ibach 1987; Younker 1991), although determining their precise construction dates is challenged by their reuse during settlement episodes in later centuries. Most prevalent are the cisterns and reservoirs that were hewn into the bedrock in order to collect and store precipitation before it could infiltrate soils, drain into wadis, or evaporate (Cole 1989; Oleson 2001). Animals could be watered, and water could be transported from these sites to communities for cooking, drinking, and ceramic vessel production. Aside from water storage structures, several types of soil-retaining structures were built in the landscape. Stone terrace walls, constructed on hill slopes and often positioned on the lips of exposed bedrock, were other common anthropogenic structures (Christopherson and Guertin 1995). Eroded soil and runoff precipitation would accumulate behind the walls, creating a deep, moist matrix for planting crops. Embankments built perpendicular to wadi tributary floors were a second category of soil-retaining structures. These embankments permitted soil to accumulate against the walls and reduce gully erosion. Embankments also slowed the velocity of runoff precipitation and, hence, increased the amount of soil infiltration. Another feature were dams placed directly on the wadi floors, again strategically placed to prevent gullying and promote the accumulation of soils.

Although these anthropogenic features preserved and increased cultivatable land and provided some guarantee of an annual yield, their construction and maintenance required a dedication of time and labor, necessitating the attention of and cooperation between multiple community members beyond that of the household. Cooperation in these labor projects, much like the cooperation in the construction of fortifications, was an opportunity for members to participate in the community's social life and demonstrate their worthiness as members deserving of full benefits. Conversely, failure to participate in agricultural projects meant failure to participate in the community and a general disregard for the community's sustainability.

23. The lack of a scale on the blueprint of the building prevents the measurement of these rooms except in a single case (Ninow 2004, fig. 4). Ninow's figure 12's scaled drawing of R11 suggests the room was approximately 3 m wide by 2 m long.

24. The total area of Building 100 may be indeed larger than these measurements. An unexcavated structure abuts Building 100's north side. Future excavations of this structure will determine its relationship to Building 100.

25. See Locus 7J99.8 (Herr and Platt 2002:97, fig. 4.35). On either side of the north edge of this flagstone paving were bases that the excavators suggest supported a curtained wood superstructure that further protected the room's contents.

26. See Locus 2G86:29 (Bruce Routledge, personal communication, 2013).

27. A more detailed presentation of the ceramic vessel evidence can be found in Porter (2007:216–317).

28. The number of whole vessels found in excavation is limited compared to other Near Eastern archaeological sites where ceramic artifacts are usually the most abundant category. This limited number may mean that vessels were valuable, baskets were more common, or households that abandoned the site were careful to take vessels with them. The general size of the assemblage is limited. The settlements appear to share a relatively similar ceramic vessel assemblage with secure eleventh- and early tenth-century strata at Deir 'Alla (Phases E–H) in the Jordan Valley and at various settlements west of the Jordan Valley, including Beer Sheba Strata VII–VI, Gezer Strata XI–X, Hazor Strata Xb–IXb, 'Izbet Sartah Strata II–I, Megiddo Strata VI–V, Qasile Strata XII–X, and Ta'anach Strata IIA and IIB. For a catalog of these and other ceramic vessels from the Early Iron Age settlements, including their published parallels at other settlements, see Porter (2007:241–252) and Routledge (2000:47, 2008).

29. A handful of Late Bronze Age and Iron Age vessel workshops such as Lachish Cave 4034 (Tufnell 1958), Megiddo Tomb 37 (Guy and Engberg 1938), Hazor Buildings 6063 and 6225 (Yadin and Angress 1960), Ashdod Area D (Dothan 1971; Dothan and Porath 1982), and Sarepta Sounding X (Pritchard 1975) have been excavated (Killebrew 1996). Both the single and double wheels were used interchangeably in the Iron Age. The single, or simple, wheel required two people to operate it successfully, whereas the double wheel eliminated the need for a second person. Some examples of single wheels were excavated in the Hazor LBIIA workshop (Yadin and Angress 1960) and Gezer (Macalister 1912). Evidence for such pits is identified in the workshops at Lachish Cave 4034 (Tufnell 1958, Pits C and D) and Megiddo, Tomb 37 (Guy and Engberg 1938, Pit H). Archaeological evidence indicates Iron Age kilns were limited to horizontal and vertical designs, the latter being the most popular (Killebrew 1996; Wood 1990:26–33).

30. Although unable to discern whether paste recipes or shaping practices changed first, Franken (1969:74–75) is correct in observing a symbiotic relationship between the two variables. Lean clay pastes are best suited for mold and coiling techniques and are ideal when constructing vessels in section and applying accessory pieces such as handles. Compared to those made from plastic clays, vessels composed from lean clays dry faster as pockets created by nonplastic materials permit evaporation; additionally, lean clay withstands sudden changes in firing temperatures.

31. Although no sufficient reason explaining why the use of slips and pigments declined in the Iron Age has been put forth, it is clear that the two decorative techniques are related. Franken and London (1995) have demonstrated that the salt scum

forming on the vessel's exterior is a result of the high saline content in clay pastes. If the vessel is not scraped between drying and painting, the scum prevents pigments from adhering to the vessel wall. Even when pigments are successfully applied, residual salt scums can interfere with pigment color both before and during firing. The vessel producers may protect pigment color and shape with the application of a thick slip. While their application was a popular and perhaps necessary practice during the Middle and Late Bronze Ages, the white slips applied to early Iron Age vessels are often thinner and often only used when pigments are included.

32. INAA is a procedure that characterizes the elemental composition of material by measuring gamma-ray emissions from the isotopes of an irradiated sample (Glascock 1992; Glascock and Neff 2003; Neff 2000). The gamma rays that exude from isotopes were measured using semiconductor detectors. By measuring the amounts of gamma-ray activity, the elemental concentrations of each sample are determined. These raw data are subjected to multivariate statistical packages that help to identify samples that share chemical compositions. Samples were analyzed at the Archaeometry Laboratory of the University of Missouri's Research Reactor in 2003. For a detailed description of sampling and testing techniques and instrumentation, visit http://archaeometry.missouri.edu.

33. But the small number of samples and the problematic architectural contexts make it difficult to explain this diversity.

34. Primary contexts include monomineralic clays born of the chemical weathering of parent rock found toward the upper half of soil horizons. Clay horizons also contain sand and silt grains, organic remains, and unweathered particles, and are exposed following erosion or through deliberate mining. Once extracted, clays from primary contexts require extensive preparation, including sifting and levigating, to create a uniform recipe and remove unwanted inclusions. Secondary clay contexts are clay deposits that are born of soil erosion and transport. As they are eroded off the plateaus and into wadi canyons, soils are transported downstream. As soil travels, alluvial forces separate grains according to size and weight. Unlike their heavier counterparts such as sand and gravel that travel closer to the streambed, clay is held in suspension in flows with high speed. Only upon slowing does it drop out of the streamflow. Once water comes to a complete standstill, clay falls out of suspension and is the last of the sediment to settle, leaving available clay deposits on the surface. Seasonal streams that transport sediment materials at varying speeds during the winter create secondary clay deposits in the late spring and through the summer, providing a ready source of clay for ceramic production. See Velde and Druc (1999:59–74) for a general description of the origin of clay resources in fluvial environments.

Chapter Five

1. Attempts to apply corporate personality perspectives to the evidence have seen consistent critique since their introduction. Yet discussions of ancient Israel's supposed egalitarian ethos continues (Faust 2006:92–107). The use of the corporate personality model to characterize ancient Israelite society is developed in separate critiques by J. R. Porter (1965) and John W. Rogerson (1970). Both authors raise their doubts concerning Robinson's claim that the individual and the group were so easily

collapsible in ancient Israel. Porter reexamines many of Robinson's examples (e.g., Joshua 7) against the backdrop of ancient Israelite legal codes, concluding that the group is punished for the sins of the individual in only exceptional circumstances—bloodguilt or disobeying Yahweh, for instance—in which the Israelite legal codes in the Books of Leviticus and Deuteronomy did not legislate. In most criminal cases, Israel's legal codes recognized the person's role and considered him or her worthy of punishment (Porter 1965:366).

Rogerson draws forth an interesting point that has implications for the present study. He writes that "in spite of the dropping of corporate personality there are certain parts of the Old Testament where there is a tension between the collective and the individual that has to be explained" (Rogerson 1970:57). Rogerson considers the possibility that early Israelite society bore more conflict than originally imagined. This tension between the individual and the social unit was drawn out even further in Joel S. Kaminsky's (1995) treatment of a related issue, corporate responsibility. Kaminsky argued that ancient Israelites rationalized corporate responsibility in terms of their covenant with Yahweh. Corporate responsibility and punishment were reported frequently in the Pentateuch and Deuteronomist history. In making this claim, Kaminsky argues against scholars such as Robinson (1964) and Andersen (1969) who suggest that Israelite society evolved from a corporate legal perspective in the premonarchical period to one based on the individual during the United and Divided Kingdoms. Instead, Kaminsky suggests that individual and corporate responsibilities existed alongside each other as late as the postexilic period. The awareness of the tensions between the person and the group in ancient Israel speaks to the point made in this chapter about leadership in communal complexity.

2. Robinson drew on many of the same social scientific epistemologies that inspired early definitions of the community described in chapter 1. Robinson (1964:6–7) based his claims about ancient Israel's corporate personality on Lévy-Bruhl's (1925) and Durkheim's (1915) discussions of the primitive mind. Robinson cites Lévy-Bruhl's description of the "law of participation" in Australian Aboriginal society, where individuals and collectives (e.g., ancestors) are considered one and the same. Robinson claims that Israelite society shared this ability to collapse the categories of the individual and the society.

3. Under such a schema, Israelite society was organized at the level of tribe during and after the Exodus, but after two centuries, territorial polities emerged with borders, institutionalized leadership, and bureaucracies in what are often characterized as state-level societies (e.g., Master 2001; Routledge 2004; Joffe 2002).

4. This use of a chiefdom perspective was refined using settlement size and location data to reveal incongruities in political organization across the landscape that suggest political complexity in the central highland communities evolved at different rates (Miller 2005).

5. Frick, for example, describes early ancient Israel's evolution from tribe to chiefdom to state as a series of external environmental, historical, and social factors that together propelled communities toward greater social complexity. Such visions of Early Iron Age societies as passive entities reacting to changing circumstances ignore the possibilities that persons and groups played a role in this political and economic development. Such an understanding is a result of evolutionary models' tendency to forego intra-site settlement analysis in favor of regional settlement size and distribution.

Miller's analysis, on the other hand, is helpful in identifying relationships between settlements, but stops short of identifying the internal relationships that structured individual communities. Most problematic, however, are Frick's and Miller's analyses of leadership and authority in early ancient Israel. Although the emergence of community leaders is often featured in their discussions, the two authors concentrate more on the *office* of leadership rather than on how such leaders emerge. They assume that leaders appeared ex nihilo in ancient Israelite communities and their authority was met with little resistance, a vision similar to that presented in the biblical narrative.

6. See the discussion of the Deuteronomistic School in chapter 3.

7. The collective meaning appears 115 times in the biblical narrative's description of all stages of ancient Israel's history.

8. Judges filled a leadership vacuum in the biblical narrative of early Israel. They first appeared after Joshua's death (Joshua 24:29) and continued to appear up until Samuel appoints Saul king over a unified ancient Israel (1 Samuel 9–11).

9. Along with military leadership, judges offered wisdom and advice in legal matters. Deborah held court "under the palm of Deborah . . . and the Israelites came up to her for judgment" (Judges 4:5). The Bible's description of Samuel, in particular, illustrates the extent to which judges played a religious role in early Israelite cultic practice. The soon-to-be-appointed first king of ancient Israel, Saul, while searching for his donkeys, visits Samuel in an unnamed town (1 Samuel 9–10). The Bible describes Samuel as a seer whose purpose in the visit is to bless the community's sacrifice before a religious festival. Following the feast, Samuel anoints Saul the first king of Israel. Samuel's dual role as religious leader and kingmaker suggests the office of the judge not only exercised authority in religious matters but also in assigning authority to individuals.

10. Some scholars (e.g., Zayadine 1991) have also thought the Rujm al-ʻAbd, or the "Shihan warrior" stele, should be dated to the Late Bronze Age, an assumed contemporary to the Baluʻa stele. Yet, there is plenty of evidence to place this stele in the stone-carved relief traditions of the first millennium BCE (Routledge 2004:178).

11. See Routledge (2004:82, 84) and Routledge and Routledge (2009) for reviews of various attempts to translate and date the Baluʻa stele.

12. Other published studies of tombs with early Iron Age materials include the Abu Shunnar Tomb (Thompson 1986), the Jebal Nuzah Tomb (Dajani 1966), Madaba Tomb A (Harding 1953), the Nebo tomb (Saller 1965–1966), Sahab Tomb A (Albright 1932) and C (Dajani 1970), and the Umm Dimis tomb (Worschech 2003). Most of the region's known tombs were used over several centuries, if not millennia, making it difficult to assign reliable *terminus post quem* and *terminus ante quem* dates to tomb groups. At times, when the occasional tomb was used within a narrow window of time (e.g., Madaba Tomb A), evidence that would suggest absolute dates is lacking. Baqʻah Valley Cave A4 is therefore the best preserved and most secure evidence for Early Iron Age interment practices in west-central Jordan.

13. Mortuary practices that reflect and reproduce the social life of the community were not exclusive to the Early Iron Age. For a discussion of the roles that mortuary practices played in Early Bronze Age communities in the southern Levant, for example, see Chesson (1999).

14. Another sign that food was a key source of wealth is the marked absence of finished prestige goods excavated in the Early Iron Age communities. Although an

argument from silence, the absence of such objects suggests that households lacked access to prestige items in which their wealth could be displayed or justified to others.

15. This interpretation of the southeast room is called into question as the excavation report indicates that objects associated with food production were distributed throughout the building, suggesting that these activities were not necessarily confined to one particular location in the room. Most conspicuous is the discovery of basalt ground stone tools that were discovered in the rear room of the building, an area already discussed as primarily used for storage (Clark 2002:97–98). From this information, one should not conclude that activity areas are impossible to identify in Iron Age residences, but rather, analysis is dependent on preservation as well as higher resolution excavation and analytical techniques. For a recent attempt to discern activity areas in late Iron Age residences, see Harding (2004).

16. See Porter (2011, figs. 6.1–6.3) for profile drawings of all known examples, and table 1 for accompanying registration numbers, ware descriptions, diameters, and additional information for each vessel.

17. Additional published studies with decorated vessels may exist. Brown (1991:194) described two Early Iron Age bowls (Nos. 188, 190) with dripped red paint decoration in her catalog of ceramic materials from the Karak Plateau survey materials. Brown reported, "The red paint that appears occasionally among Iron I wares is found on two bowl fragments, Nos. 188 and 190. The former shows only faint traces of paint on the rim: the latter, being better preserved, has a deep red-painted rim and dripped red paint on the interior" (1991:194). Another possible attestation may occur in the Tell Deir Alla Phase E materials (Franken 1969, figs. 55, 59, 79). Another two may have been recovered from Worschech's survey of Dafyan, a chronologically mixed settlement near Karak (Worschech 1985, figs. 18.18.4–18.18.5; 1990:10:52–53). One more example may be present in a mixed-period burial cave at Umm Dimis, north of Balu'a (Worschech 2003, fig. 78).

18. Swinnen (2009, figs. 22, 23) published a rimless two-handled jar decorated with a painted geometric design on a white-slipped background from Early Iron Age Lahun. This jar's design is only somewhat reminiscent of the decorated vessel design considered in this work and is therefore not included in the corpus.

19. Although the compositional groups formed by INAA and the petrofabric groups formed by petrographic analysis are different in sample composition, they both point to a similar conclusion that vessel production was local and relatively unspecialized.

20. A bivariate plot comparing the samples' iron and magnesium oxide levels is presented in Porter and Speakman (2008:241) and Porter (2011, fig. 9).

21. During LA-ICP-MS, a laser microprobe removes a small portion of sample and ionizes it using an argon gas plasma. The sample is then introduced into the mass spectrometer where the ions are separated according to their mass/charge ratio. Ions pass through a detector where their atomic mass ranges are measured and recorded. Like INAA, raw data are subjected to multivariate statistical packages that help to identify samples that share chemical compositions. Samples were analyzed at the Archaeometry Laboratory of the University of Missouri's Research Reactor in 2003. For a detailed description of LA-ICP-MS techniques and instrumentation, visit http://archaeometry.missouri.edu.

22. It is possible to gauge the color of fire based on its temperature, between about 1200 Kelvin and 1930 Kelvin. A hotter fire would burn white and then blue; a colder

flame would burn red. Light simulations are growing popular in archaeological research; see, e.g., Dawson et al. (2007); Papadopoulos (2011). Color versions of these images can be viewed in the online version of Porter (2011) and at Open Context (www.opencontext.org).

23. Chase (2002) reports that the minimum number of individuals is two adults (at least one male), a juvenile around fifteen years of age, and one child.

24. Current excavations suggest that al-'Umayri was occupied again in the Early Iron Age, although only in a much limited way (Herr et al. 2002:17).

25. In a similar context at Lahun, House 18's backroom, likely designated for storage, was blocked up just prior to abandonment, presumably so that its owners could return at a later time to retrieve its contents (Swinnen 2009, fig. 24).

26. Bayesian modeling of fourteen dates using OxCal determined these dates. Samples were taken from burnt barley grains from storage bins in each building. These dates using the InCal 04 atmospheric curve supersede the problematic beta-counted dates from Laval University published in Routledge (2000:47–48, fig. 8); (B. Routledge, personal communication with author, 2013).

Chapter Six

1. The comprehensive publications of the Tall al-'Umayri Project stand out as an other exception, of course.

2. Additionally, many Early Iron Age settlements are located in regions that are today witnessing increased agricultural development and settlement expansion, especially those on either side of the Wadi al-Mujib. Such development, when coupled with a lack of security, threatens these sites' preservation and will impede future research. Additional documentation of surface architecture, limited sampling to recover datable materials, and subsequent analysis were quite feasible at the time of writing.

3. Of course, additional questions and themes could be investigated with the materials at hand. For example, recent discussions in global archaeology on the nature of personhood can offer new ways to think about how identities such as gender were manifest in the communities. Such an understanding could provide additional ways to think about how people made sense of themselves and their role in various social forms beyond that of a membership in an ethnic group as the biblical narrative suggests. Additionally, there is a need to understand how architectural spaces of settlements mediated relationships between persons and between households. Such a study could be combined with an investigation of the sensorial landscape within and around the communities that considered how various human senses mediated the experience of being in the community. All of these ideas are potential avenues for future research.

4. While such a hypothesis is reasonable to conjecture, very little evidence for Early Iron Age occupation was found in pedestrian surveys at Karak and Qasr. At Karak, Miller (1991:59–60, 89) recovered only fifteen Early Iron Age sherds, and at Qasr, two sherds.

5. This issue may eventually be resolved as archaeologists working in west-central Jordan use radiometric techniques to date cultural levels. See Harrison and Barlow (2005) for one attempt to reinterpret Iron Age cultural levels at Tall Madaba. Recent excavations at 'Ataruz northwest of Dhiban and southwest of Madaba may

indeed contain settlement episodes dating to the decades prior to the Mesha Inscription (Ji 2012).

6. See Yasur-Landau's (2010:282–330) synthesis of the twelfth-century Philistine settlement on the coastal plain for one such step in this direction.

7. The increased use of the archaeological sciences in field excavations is already bringing about these adjustments in the field at important sites such as Dor, Megiddo, Khirbat al-Nahas, and Tell al-Safi (Gath). In part, these changes can be explained by the increased use of portable instrumentation that can be used directly in field excavation. Still, there remains a need to employ consistent sampling strategies in the collection of these data across all excavated contexts, rather than nonrandom judgment sampling of convenient contexts such as hearths. Most noticeable is the need for sifting excavated soils at consistent rates and with appropriately small mesh sizes.

8. See Maeir, Dar, and Safrai (2003) for the results of a conference on the rural landscape of ancient Israel that presented examples of sedentary settlements from the Early Bronze Age to the Middle Islamic Period.

9. For another use of Redfield's ideas, namely his "Great" and "Little" traditions framework, in southern Levantine archaeology, see LaBianca and Witzel (2007).

References

Adams, Robert McC. 1966. *The Evolution of Urban Society: Early Mesopotamia and Prehispanic Mexico*. Chicago: Aldine.
Aerial Photographic Archive for Archaeology in the Middle East (APAAME). www.classics.uwa.edu.au/aerial_archaeology.
Ahituv, Shemuel. 1978. Economic Factors in the Egyptian Conquest of Canaan. *Israel Exploration Journal* 28(1–2): 93–105.
Akkermans, Peter, and Glenn Schwartz. 2003. *The Archaeology of Syria: From Complex Hunter-gatherers to Early Urban Societies (c. 16000–300 BC)*. Cambridge: Cambridge University Press.
Albright, William F. 1932. An Anthropoid Clay Coffin from Sahab in Transjordan. *American Journal of Archaeology* 36(3): 295–306.
———. 1934. Soundings at Ader, a Bronze Age City of Moab. *Bulletin of the American Schools of Oriental Research* 53:13–18.
———. 1939. The Israelite Conquest of Canaan in the Light of Archaeology. *Bulletin of the American Schools of Oriental Research* 74:11–23.
———. 1941. The Land of Damascus between 1850 and 1750 B.C. *Bulletin of the American Schools of Oriental Research* 83:30–36.
———. 1943. The Gezer Calendar. *Bulletin of the American Schools of Oriental Research* 92:16–26.
———. 1949. *The Archaeology of Palestine*. Baltimore: Penguin.
Alt, Albrecht. 1966. *Essays on Old Testament History and Religion*. Oxford: Blackwell.
Amiran, Ruth. 1970. *Ancient Pottery of the Holy Land*. New Brunswick, NJ: Rutgers University Press.
van Andel, Tjeerd, Eberhard Zangger, and Anne Demitrack. 1990. Land Use and Soil Erosion in Prehistoric and Historical Greece. *Journal of Field Archaeology* 17(4): 379–396.
Andersen, Francis. 1969. Israelite Kinship Terminology and Social Structure. *Bible Translator* 20(1): 29–39.

Antoun, Richard T. 1972. *Arab Village: A Social Structural Study of a Transjordanian Peasant Community.* Bloomington: Indiana University Press.

Arensberg, Conrad M. 1961. The Community as Object and as Sample. *American Anthropologist* 63(2): 241–264.

Arensberg, Conrad M., and Solon T. Kimball. 1940. *Family and Community in Ireland.* Cambridge, MA: Harvard University Press.

———. 1965. *Culture and Community.* New York: Harcourt Brace & World.

Arikan, Bülent. 2012. Don't Abhor Your Neighbor for He Is a Pastoralist: The GIS-based Modeling of the Past Human-Environment Interactions and Landscape Changes in the Wadi el-Hasa, West-Central Jordan. *Journal of Archaeological Sciences* 39:2908–2920.

Barker, Graeme. 1996. *Farming the Desert: The UNESCO Libyan Valleys Archaeological Survey.* Paris: UNESCO.

Barker, Graeme, and David Gilbertson, eds. 2000. *The Archaeology of Drylands: Living at the Margin.* London: Routledge.

Bar-Matthews, Miryam, Avner Ayalon, Aaron Kaufman, and Gerald J. Wasseerburg. 1999. The Eastern Mediterranean Paleoclimate as a Reflection of Regional Events: Soreq Cave, Israel. *Earth and Planetary Sciences* 166(1–2): 86–95.

Barth, Fredrik. 1962. Nomadism in the Mountain and Plateau Areas of South West Asia. In *The Problems of the Arid Zone: Proceedings of the Paris Symposium of Arid Zone Research XVIII.* 341–355. Paris: UNESCO.

Baruch, Uri. 1990. Palynological Evidence of Human Impact on the Vegetation as Recorded in Late Holocene Lake Sediments in Israel. In *Man's Role in the Shaping of the Eastern Mediterranean Landscape*, ed. Sytze Bottema, Gertie Entjes-Nieborg, and Willem van Zeist, 283–293. Rotterdam: A. A. Balkema.

Bauman, Zygmunt. 2001. *Community: Seeking Safety in an Insecure World.* Cambridge: Polity Press.

Beardsley, Richard K., Preston Holder, Alex D. Krieger, Betty J. Meggers, John B. Rinaldo, and Paul Kutsche. 1956. Functional and Evolutionary Implications of Community Patterning. In *Memoirs of the Society for American Archaeology*, ed. Richard B. Woodbury, 11:129–157. Salt Lake City: Society for American Archaeology.

Bell, Gertrude. 1907. *Syria: The Desert and the Sown.* New York: E. P. Dutton.

Bendor, Shunya. 1996. *The Social Structure of Ancient Israel.* Jerusalem: Simor.

Betts, Alison V. G., ed. 1991. *Excavations at Jawa, 1972–1986: Stratigraphy, Pottery, and Other Finds.* Edinburgh: Edinburgh University Press.

Bhabha, Homi K. 1994. *The Location of Culture.* New York: Routledge.

Bienkowski, Piotr. 2009. "Tribalism" and "Segmentary Society" in Iron Age Transjordan. In *Studies on Iron Age Moab and Neighbouring Areas in Honour of Michèle Daviau*, ed. Piotr Bienkowski, 7–26. Louvain, BE: Peeters.

Bienkowski, Piotr, Russell Adams, R. A. Philpott, and Leonie Sedman. 1997. Soundings at ash-Shorabat and Khirbat Dubab in the Wadi Hasa, Jordan: The Stratigraphy. *Levant* 29:41–70.

Blanchot, Maurice. 1988. *The Unavowable Community.* Barrytown, NY: Station Hill Press.

Blanton, Richard. 1998. Beyond Centralization: Steps toward a Theory of Egalitarian Behavior in Archaic States. In *Archaic States*, ed. Gary Feinman and Joyce Marcus, 135–172. Santa Fe, NM: School of American Research.

Blanton, Richard, Gary Feinman, Stephen Kowalewski, and Peter Peregrine. 1996. A Dual-Processual Theory for the Evolution of Mesoamerican Civilization. *Current Anthropology* 37(1): 1–14.

Bloch-Smith, Elizabeth, and Beth Alpert Nakhai. 1999. A Landscape Comes to Life: The Iron Age I. *Near Eastern Archaeology* 62(2): 62–92, 101–127.

Block, Peter. 2008. *Community: The Structure of Belonging*. San Francisco: Berrett-Koehler.

Boling, Robert G. 1975. *Judges: Introduction, Translation, and Commentary*. Garden City, NY: Doubleday.

———. 1988. *The Early Biblical Community in Transjordan*. Sheffield, UK: Almond Press.

Borowski, Oded. 1987. *Agriculture in Iron Age Israel*. Winona Lake, IN: Eisenbrauns.

———. 1998. *Every Living Thing: Daily Use of Animals in Ancient Israel*. Walnut Creek, CA: AltaMira Press.

———. 2004. Eat, Drink, and Be Merry: The Mediterranean Diet. *Near Eastern Archaeology* 67(2): 96–107.

Bottéro, Jean. 1994. Boisson, Banquet, et Vie Sociale en Mésopotamie. In *Drinking in Ancient Societies*, ed. Lucio Milano, 3–13. Padua: Sargon.

Bourdieu, Pierre. 1977. *Outline of a Theory of Practice*. Cambridge: Cambridge University Press.

———. 1984. *Distinction: A Social Critique of the Judgment of Taste*. Cambridge: Harvard University Press.

———. 1990. *The Logic of Practice*. Stanford: Stanford University Press.

Braemer, Frank. 1982. *L'Architecture Domestique du Levant à l'Âge du Fer*. Paris: Éditions Recherche sur les Civilisations.

Bramlett, Kent. 2004. A Late Bronze Age Cultic Installation at Tall al-'Umayri, Jordan. *Near Eastern Archaeology* 67(1): 50–51.

Bray, Tamara L. 2003a. To Dine Splendidly: Imperial Pottery, Commensal Politics, and the Inca State. In *The Archaeology and Politics of Food and Feasting in Early States and Empires*, ed. Tamara L. Bray, 93–142. New York: Kluwer Academic/Plenum.

———, ed. 2003b. *The Archaeology and Politics of Food and Feasting in Early States and Empires*. New York: Kluwer Academic/Plenum.

Breasted, James Henry. 1906. *Ancient Records of Egypt: Historical Documents from the Earliest Times to the Persian Conquest*. Chicago: University of Chicago Press.

Brown, Robin. 1991. Ceramics from the Kerak Plateau. In *Archaeological Survey of the Kerak Plateau*, ed. J. Maxwell Miller, 169–279. Atlanta: Scholars Press.

Brumfiel, Elizabeth. 1992. Distinguished Lecture in Archaeology: Breaking and Entering the Ecosystem—Gender, Class, and Faction Steal the Show. *American Anthropologist* 94(3): 551–567.

Brumfiel, Elizabeth, and Timothy Earle. 1987. Specialization, Exchange, and Complex Societies: An Introduction. In *Specialization, Exchange, and Complex Societies*, ed. Elizabeth Brumfiel and Timothy Earle, 1–9. Cambridge: Cambridge University Press.

Burke, Aaron. 2008. *"Walled Up to Heaven": The Evolution of Middle Bronze Age Fortification Strategies in the Levant*. Winona Lake, IN: Eisenbrauns.

Byrne, Ryan. 2007. The Refuge of Scribalism in Iron I Palestine. *Bulletin of the American Schools of Oriental Research* 345:1–31.

Canuto, Marcello, and Jason Yaeger, eds. 2000. *The Archaeology of Communities: A New World Perspective.* London: Routledge.

Carrier, James G. 1995. *Gifts and Commodities: Exchange and Western Capitalism since 1700.* London: Routledge.

Caton, Steven. 1987. Power, Persuasion, and Language: A Critique of the Segmentary Model in the Middle East. *International Journal of Middle Eastern Studies* 19: 77–101.

Chase, Joan. 2002. Report on the Human Bones from Tall al-'Umayri 1992–1996. In *Madaba Plains Project 5: The 1994 Season at Tall al-'Umayri and Subsequent Studies*, ed. Larry Herr, Douglas Clark, Lawrence Geraty, Randall Younker, and Øystein LaBianca, 206–221. Berrien Springs, MI: Andrews University Press.

Chesson, Meredith. 1999. Libraries of the Dead: Early Bronze Age Charnel Houses and Social Identity at Urban Bab edh-Dhra', Jordan. *Journal of Anthropological Archaeology* 18:137–164.

Christopherson, Gary L., and D. Phillip Guertin. 1995. Soil Erosion, Agricultural Intensification, and Iron Age Settlement in the Region of Tall al-'Umayri, Jordan. Paper presented at the annual meetings of the American Schools of Oriental Research, Philadelphia, PA. http://www.casa.arizona.edu/MPP/Um_erosion/erosion_pap.html.

Clark, Douglas. 1997. Field B: The Western Defense System. In *Madaba Plains Project 3: The 1989 Season at Tell el-'Umeiri and Vicinity and Subsequent Studies*, ed. Larry G. Herr, Lawrence Geraty, Øystein LaBianca, Randall Younker, and Douglas Clark, 53–98. Berrien Springs, MI: Andrews University Press.

———. 2000. Field B: The Western Defense System. In *Madaba Plains Project 4: The 1992 Season at Tall al-'Umayri and Subsequent Studies*, ed. Larry G. Herr, Douglas Clark, Lawrence Geraty, Randall Younker, and Øystein LaBianca, 59–94. Berrien Springs, MI: Andrews University Press.

———. 2002. Field B: The Western Defense System. In *Madaba Plains Project 5: The 1994 Season at Tall al-'Umayri and Subsequent Studies*, ed. Larry Herr, Douglas Clark, Lawrence Geraty, Randall Younker, and Øystein LaBianca, 48–116. Berrien Springs, MI: Andrews University.

———. 2003. Bricks, Sweat, and Tears: The Human Investment in Constructing a "Four-Room" House. *Near Eastern Archaeology* 66(1–2): 34–43.

Clark, Douglas, and Gloria London. 2000. Investigating Ancient Ceramic Traditions on Both Sides of the Jordan. In *The Archaeology of Jordan and Beyond: Essays in Honor of James B. Sauer*, ed. Lawrence Stager, Joseph Greene, and Michael Coogan, 100–110. Winona Lake, IN: Eisenbrauns.

Clark, Geoffrey, Michael Neeley, Burton MacDonald, Joseph Schuldenrein, and Khairieh 'Amr. 1992. Wadi al-Hasa Paleolithic Project—1992: Preliminary Report. *Annual of the Department of Antiquities of Jordan* 36:13–23.

Clark, Geoffrey, Deborah Olszewski, Joseph Schuldenrein, Nazmieh Rida, and Jamies Eighmey. 1994. Survey and Excavation in Wadi al-Hasa: A Preliminary Report of the 1993 Field Season. *Annual of the Department of Antiquities of Jordan* 38:41–55.

Cleveland, Ray L. 1954–1956. The Excavation of the Conway High Place (Petra) and Soundings at Khirbet Ader. In *Annual of the American Schools of Oriental Research*, vols. 34–35. Baltimore: J. H. Furst.

Cohen, Abner. 1965. *Arab Border-Villages in Israel: A Study of Continuity and Change in Social Organization.* Manchester: Manchester University Press.

Cohen, Anthony P. 1985. *The Symbolic Construction of Community*. London: Routledge.
Cohen, Ronald, and Elman R. Service, eds. 1978. *Origins of the State: The Anthropology of Political Evolution*. Philadelphia: Institute for the Study of Human Issues.
Cohen, Susan L. 2002. *Canaanites, Chronologies, and Connections: The Relationship of Middle Bronze IIA Canaan to Middle Kingdom Egypt*. Winona Lake, IN: Eisenbrauns.
Cole, Jon. 1989. Available Water Resources and Use in the el-'Umeiri Region. In *Madaba Plains Project 1: The 1984 Season at Tell el-'Umeiri and Vicinity and Subsequent Studies*, ed. Lawrence Geraty, Larry Herr, Øystein LaBianca, and Randall Younker, 41–50. Berrien Springs, MI: Andrews University Press.
Cook, Anita, and Mary Glowacki. 2003. Pots, Politics, and Power: Huari Ceramic Assemblages and Imperial Administration. In *The Archaeology and Politics of Food and Feasting in Early States and Empires*, ed. Tamara L. Bray, 173–202. New York: Kluwer Academic/Plenum.
Coon, Carleton S. 1951. *Caravan: The Story of the Middle East*. New York: Holt.
Coote, Robert. 1990. *Early Israel: A New Horizon*. Minneapolis: Fortress Press.
Coote, Robert, and Keith Whitelam. 1987. *The Emergence of Early Israel in Historical Perspective*. Sheffield, UK: Almond Press.
Cordova, Carlos. 1999. Landscape Transformation in the Mediterranean-Steppe Transition Zone of Jordan: A Geoarchaeological Approach. *The Arab World Geographer* 2(3): 182–201.
———. 2000. Geomorphological Evidence of Intense Prehistoric Soil Erosion in the Highlands of Central Jordan. *Physical Geography* 21(6): 538–567.
———. 2007. *Millennial Landscape Change in Jordan: Geoarchaeology and Cultural Ecology*. Tucson: University of Arizona.
Cordova, Carlos, Chris Foley, April Nowell, and Michael Bisson. 2005. Landforms, Sediments, Soil Development, and Prehistoric Site Settings on the Madaba-Dhiban Plateau, Jordan. *Geoarchaeology* 20(1): 29–56.
Costin, Cathy L. 1991. Craft Specialization: Issues in Defining, Documenting, and Explaining the Organization of Production. In *Archaeological Method and Theory*, 3, ed. Michael Schiffer, 1–56. Tucson: University of Arizona Press.
Crawford, Patricia. 1986. Flora of Tell Hesban and Area, Jordan. In *Hesban 2: Environmental Foundations*, ed. Øystein LaBianca and Larry Lacelle, 75–98. Berrien Springs, MI: Andrews University Press.
Cross, Frank Moore. 1973. *Canaanite Myth and Hebrew Epic: Essays in the History of the Religion of Israel*. Cambridge, MA: Harvard University Press.
Crowfoot, John W. 1934. An Expedition to Balu'ah. *Palestine Exploration Fund Quarterly Statement* 66:76–84.
Dajani, Rafik. 1966. Jabal Nuzha Tomb at Amman. *Annual of the Department of Antiquities of Jordan* 11:48–52.
———. 1970. A Late Bronze–Iron Age Tomb Excavated at Sahab, 1968. *Annual of the Department of Antiquities of Jordan* 15:29–34.
D'Altroy, Terence N., and Timothy K. Earle. 1985. Staple Finance, Wealth Finance, and Storage in the Inka Political Economy. *Current Anthropology* 26(2): 187–206.
Davison, Roderic H. 1960. Where Is the Middle East? *Foreign Affairs* 38(4): 665–675.

Dawson, Peter, Richard Levy, Don Gardner, and Matthew Walls. 2007. Simulating the Behaviour of Light Inside Arctic Dwellings: Implications for Assessing the Role of Vision in Task Performance. *World Archaeology* 39(1): 17–35.

Dearman, J. Andrew, ed. 1989. *Studies in the Mesha Inscription and Moab*. Atlanta: Scholars Press.

———. 1992. Settlement Patterns and the Beginning of the Iron Age in Moab. In *Early Edom and Moab: The Beginning of the Iron Age in Southern Jordan*, ed. Piotr Bienkowski, 65–75. Sheffield, UK: J. R. Collis.

Delanty, Gerard. 2003. *Community*. Routledge: London.

Dever, William G. 1981. The Impact of the 'New Archaeology' on Syro-Palestinian Archaeology. *Bulletin of the American Schools of Oriental Research* 242:15–29.

———. 1987. The Middle Bronze Age: The Zenith of the Urban Canaanite Era. *The Biblical Archaeologist* 50(3):148–177.

———. 2003. *Who Were the Early Israelites and Where Did They Come From?* Grand Rapids, MI: Wm. B. Eerdmans.

Diakonoff, I. M. 1974. *Structure of Society and State in Early Dynastic Sumer*. Los Angeles: Undena.

Diamond, Jared. 1997. *Guns, Germs, and Steel: The Fates of Human Societies*. New York: W. W. Norton.

———. 2005. *Collapse: How Societies Choose to Fail or Succeed*. New York: Viking.

Dietler, Michael, and Brian Hayden, eds. 2001. *Feasts: Archaeological and Ethnographic Perspectives on Food, Politics, and Power*. Washington, DC: Smithsonian Institution Press.

Dobres, Marcia-Anne, and John E. Robb, eds. 2000. *Agency in Archaeology*. London: Routledge.

Doolittle, William E. 1988. Intermittent Use and Agricultural Change on Marginal Lands: The Case of Smallholders in Eastern Sonora, Mexico. *Geografiska Annaler* 70(2): 255–266.

Dornemann, Rudolph. 1983. *The Archaeology of the Transjordan in the Bronze and Iron Ages*. Milwaukee: Milwaukee Public Museum.

Dothan, Moshe. 1971. Ashdod II–III: The Second and Third Seasons of Excavations, 1963, 1965. *'Atiqot* 9–10.

Dothan, Moshe, and Yosef Porath. 1982. Ashdod IV: Excavation of Area M. *'Atiqot* 15.

Dothan, Trude. 2008. *Deir el-Balah: Uncovering an Egyptian Outpost in Canaan from the Time of the Exodus*. Jerusalem: Israel Museum.

Dresch, Paul. 1986. The Significance of the Course Events Take in Segmentary Systems. *American Ethnologist* 13(2): 309–324.

———. 1988. Segmentation: Its Roots in Arabia and Its Flowering Elsewhere. *Cultural Anthropology* 3(1): 50–67.

von den Driesch, Angela, and Joachim Boessneck. 1995. Final Report on the Zooarchaeological Investigation of Animal Bone Finds from Tell Hesban, Jordan. In *Hesban 13: Faunal Remains*, ed. Øystein LaBianca and Angela von den Driesch, 65–108. Berrien Springs, MI: Andrews University Press.

Drioton, Etienne. 1933. A Propos de Stèle du Balou'a. *Revue Biblique* 42:353–365.

Dubis, Elzbieta. 2002. Metal Objects. In *Madaba Plains Project 5: The 1994 Season at Tall al-'Umayri and Subsequent Studies*, ed. Larry Herr, Douglas Clark, Lawrence Geraty, Randall Younker, and Øystein LaBianca, 222–229. Berrien Springs, MI: Andrews University Press.

Durkheim, Émile. 1893. *The Division of Labour in Society.* Basingstoke, UK: Macmillan.
———. 1915. *The Elementary Forms of the Religious Life: A Study in Religious Sociology.* London: Allen & Unwin.
Dyson-Hudson, Rada, and Neville Dyson-Hudson. 1980. Nomadic Pastoralism. *Annual Review of Anthropology* 9:15–61.
Earle, Timothy K. 1987. Chiefdoms in Archaeological and Ethnohistorical Perspective. *Annual Review of Anthropology* 16:279–308.
Ebeling, Jennie, and Yorke Rowan. 2004. The Archaeology of the Daily Grind: Ground Stone Tools and Food Production in the Southern Levant. *Near Eastern Archaeology* 67(2): 108–117.
al-Eisawi, Dawud. 1985. Vegetation in Jordan. In *Studies in the History and Archaeology of Jordan*, ed. Adnan Hadidi, 2:45–57. Amman: Jordanian Department of Antiquities.
Epstein, Joshua M., ed. 2006. *Generative Social Science: Studies in Agent-based Computational Modeling.* Princeton, NJ: Princeton University Press.
Escobar, Arturo. 1995. *Encountering Development: The Making and Unmaking of the Third World.* Princeton, NJ: Princeton University Press.
Evans-Pritchard, E. E. 1940. *The Nuer: A Description of the Modes of Livelihood and Political Institutions of a Nilotic People.* London: Oxford University Press.
———. 1949. *The Sanusi of Cyrenaica.* Oxford, UK: Clarendon Press.
Eyre, Christopher J. 1995. The Agricultural Cycle, Farming, and Water Management in the Ancient Near East. In *Civilizations of the Ancient Near East*, ed. Jack M. Sasson, 175–189. Peabody, MA: Hendrickson.
Faust, Avraham. 2000. The Rural Community in Ancient Israel during Iron Age II. *Bulletin of the American Schools of Oriental Research* 317:17–39.
———. 2006. *Israel's Ethnogenesis: Settlement, Interaction, Expansion and Resistance.* London: Equinox.
Faust, Avraham, and Shlomo Bunimovitz. 2003. The Four Room House: Embodying Iron Age Israelite Society. *Near Eastern Archaeology* 66:22–31.
Feinman, Gary. 2000a. Corporate/Network: A New Perspective on Leadership in the American Southwest. In *Hierarchies in Action: Cui Bono?*, ed. Michael Diehl, 152–180. Carbondale, IL: Southern Illinois University.
———. 2000b. Dual-Processual Theory and Social Formations in the Southwest. In *Alternative Leadership Strategies in the Prehispanic Southwest*, ed. Barbara J. Mills, 207–224. Tucson: University of Arizona Press.
———. 2001. Mesoamerican Political Complexity: The Corporate-Network Dimension. In *From Leaders to Rulers*, ed. Jonathan Haas, 151–175. New York: Kluwer Academic/Plenum.
Feinman, Gary M., Kent G. Lightfoot, and Steadman Upham. 2000. Political Hierarchies and Organizational Strategies in the Puebloan Southwest. *American Antiquity* 65(3): 449–470.
Feinman, Gary M., and Joyce Marcus, eds. 1998. *Archaic States.* Santa Fe, NM: School of American Research.
Feldman, Marian. 2006. *Diplomacy by Design: Luxury Arts and an "International Style" in the Ancient Near East, 1400–1200 BCE.* Chicago: University of Chicago Press.
Ferguson, Kevin, and Tim Hudson. 1986. Climate of Tell Hesban and Area. In *Hesban 2: Environmental Foundations*, ed. Øystein LaBianca and Larry Lacelle, 7–22. Berrien Springs, MI: Andrews University Press.

Finkelstein, Israel. 1986. *'Izbet Sartah: An Early Iron Age Site Near Rosh Ha'ayin, Israel*. Oxford, UK: Archaeopress.
———. 1988. *The Archaeology of the Israelite Settlement*. Jerusalem: Israel Exploration Society.
Finkelstein, Israel, and Oded Lipschits. 2011. The Genesis of Moab: A Proposal. *Levant* 43(2): 139–152.
Finkelstein, Israel, and Nadav Na'aman, eds. 1994. *From Nomadism to Monarchy: Archaeological and Historical Aspects of Early Israel*. Jerusalem: Israel Exploration Society.
Finkelstein, Israel, David Ussishkin, and Baruch Halpern, eds. 2006. *Megiddo IV: The 1998–2002 Seasons*. Tel Aviv: Institute of Archaeology, Tel Aviv University.
Fisher, Christopher T., J. Brett Hill, and Gary M. Feinman, eds. 2009. *The Archaeology of Environmental Change: Socionatural Legacies of Degradation and Resilience*. Tucson: University of Arizona Press.
Flanagan, James G. 1989. Hierarchy in Simple "Egalitarian" Societies. *Annual Review of Anthropology* 18:245–266.
Flanagan, James W. 1981. Chiefs in Israel. *Journal for the Study of the Old Testament* 20:47–73.
Flannery, Kent V. 1972. The Cultural Evolution of Civilizations. *Annual Review of Ecology and Systematics* 2:399–426.
Franken, Henrikus J. 1969. *Excavations at Tell Deir 'Alla I: A Stratigraphical and Analytical Study of the Early Iron Age Pottery*. Leiden: Brill.
Franken, Henrikus J., and Gloria London. 1995. Why Painted Pottery Disappeared at the End of the Second Millennium B.C.E. *Biblical Archaeologist* 58(4): 214–222.
Frick, Frank S. 1985. *The Formation of the State in Ancient Israel: A Survey of Models and Theories*. Sheffield, UK: Almond Press.
Fried, Morton. 1967. *The Evolution of Political Society: An Essay in Political Anthropology*. New York: Random House.
Frumkin, Amos, Mordechai Magaritz, I. Carmi, and Israel Zak. 1991. The Holocene Climatic Record of the Salt Caves of Mount Sedom, Israel. *The Holocene* 1(3): 191–200.
Gass, Erasmus. 2009. *Die Moabiter: Geschichte und Kultur eines Ostjordanischen Volkes im 1. Jahrtausend v. Chr.* Wiesbaden: Harrassowitz.
Geraty, Lawrence, Larry Herr, Øystein LaBianca, and Randall Younker, eds. 1989. *Madaba Plains Project 1: The 1984 Season at Tell el-'Umeiri and Vicinity and Subsequent Studies*. Berrien Springs, MI: Andrews University Press.
Gerstenblith, Patty. 1983. *The Levant at the Beginning of the Middle Bronze Age*. Philadelphia: American Schools of Oriental Research.
Gibbon, Edward. 2003 (1776–1789). *The Decline and Fall of the Roman Empire*. New York: Random House.
Giddens, Anthony. 1984. *The Constitution of Society: Outline of the Theory of Structuration*. Cambridge, UK: Polity Press.
Gilliland, Dennis. 1986. Paleoethnobotany and Paleoenvironment. In *Hesban 2: Environmental Foundations*, ed. Øystein LaBianca and Larry Lacelle, 121–142. Berrien Springs, MI: Andrews University Press.

Gilliland, Dennis, and Lanny Fisk. 1986. Paleoethnobotany and Paleoenvironment. In *Hesban 2: Environmental Foundations*, ed. Øystein LaBianca and Larry Lacelle, pp. 123–142. Berrien Springs, MI: Andrews University Press.

Gitin, Seymour, Amihai Mazar, and Ephraim Stern, eds. 1998. *Mediterranean Peoples in Transition: Thirteenth to Early Tenth Centuries B.C.E.* Jerusalem: Israel Exploration Society.

Giveon, Raphael. 1971. *Les Bédouins Shosou des Documents Égyptiens*. Leiden: Brill.

Glanzman, William D., and Stuart J. Fleming. 1986. Fabrication Methods. In *The Late Bronze and Early Iron Ages of Central Transjordan: The Baq'ah Valley Project, 1977–1981*, ed. Patrick McGovern, 164–177. Philadelphia: University Museum.

Glascock, Michael. 1992. Characterization of Archaeological Ceramics at MURR by Neutron Activation Analysis and Multivariate Statistics. In *Chemical Characterization of Ceramic Pastes in Archaeology*, ed. Hector Neff, 11–26. Madison, WI: Prehistory Press.

Glascock, Michael, and Hector Neff. 2003. Neutron Activation Analysis and Provenance Research in Archaeology. *Measurement Science & Technology* 14:1516–1526.

Glavanis, Kathy, and Pandeli Glavanis, eds. 1990. *The Rural Middle East: Peasant Lives and Modes of Production*. Birzeit, PS: Birzeit University.

Glueck, Nelson. 1934. Explorations in Eastern Palestine I. In *Annual of the American Schools of Oriental Research*, vol. 14. Philadelphia: American Schools of Oriental Research.

———. 1935. Explorations in Eastern Palestine II. In *Annual of the American Schools of Oriental Research*, vol. 15. New Haven, CT: American Schools of Oriental Research.

———. 1939. Explorations in Eastern Palestine III. In *Annual of the American Schools of Oriental Research*, vols. 18–19. New Haven, CT: American Schools of Oriental Research.

———. 1940. *The Other Side of the Jordan*. New Haven, CT: American Schools of Oriental Research.

———. 1951. Explorations in Eastern Palestine IV. In *Annual of the American Schools of Oriental Research*, vols. 25–28. New Haven, CT: American Schools of Oriental Research.

Goody, Jack. 1998. *Food and Love: A Cultural History of East and West*. New York: Verso.

Gottwald, Norman. 1979. *The Tribes of Yahweh: A Sociology of the Religion of Liberated Israel, 1250–1050 B.C.E.* Maryknoll, NY: Orbis Books.

———. 1983. Early Israel and the Canaanite Socio-Economic System. In *Palestine in Transition: The Emergence of Ancient Israel*, ed. David Noel Freedman and David Frank Graf, 25–37. Sheffield, UK: Almond Press.

Greene, Joseph, and Khairieh 'Amr. 1992. Deep Sounding on the Lower Terrace of the Amman Citadel: Final Report. *Annual of the Department of Antiquities of Jordan* 36:113–144.

Grottanelli, Cristiano, and Lucio Milano, eds. 2004. *Food and Identity in the Ancient World*. Padua: Sargon.

Gumerman, George, and Murray Gell-Mann, eds. 1994. *Understanding Complexity in the Prehistoric Southwest*. Reading, MA: Addison-Wesley.

Gunderson, Lance H., Craig R. Allen, and C. S. Holling, eds. 2009. *Foundations of Ecological Resilience*. Washington, DC: Island Press.

Gunderson, Lance H., and C. S. Holling, eds. 2002. *Panarchy: Understanding Transformation in Human and Natural Systems*. Washington, DC: Island Press.

Guy, P. L. O., and Robert M. Engberg. 1938. *Megiddo Tombs*. Chicago: University of Chicago Press.

Haas, Jonathan. 1982. *The Evolution of the Prehistoric State*. New York: Columbia University Press.

Hadidi, Adnan. 1970. The Pottery from the Roman Forum at Amman. *Annual of the Department of Antiquities of Jordan* 15:11–15, 43–45.

Halpern, Baruch. 1996. Sybil, or the Two Nations? Archaism, Kinship, Alienation, and the Elite Redefinition of Traditional Culture in Judah in the 8th–7th Centuries B.C.E. In *The Study of the Ancient Near East in the Twenty-First Century: The William Foxwell Albright Centennial Conference*, ed. Jerrold Cooper and Glen Schwartz, 291–338. Winona Lake, IN: Eisenbrauns.

Hanson, Paul D. 2001. *The People Called: The Growth of Community in the Bible*. Louisville: Westminster John Knox Press.

Harding, G. Lankester. 1953. *Four Tomb Groups from Jordan*. London: Palestine Exploration Fund.

Harding, James W. 2004. Understanding Domestic Space: An Example from Iron Age Tel Halif. *Near Eastern Archaeology* 67(2): 71–83.

Harrison, Timothy. 2004. *Megiddo 3: Final Report of the Stratum VI Excavations*. Chicago: Oriental Institute of the University of Chicago.

———. 2009. "The Land of Medeba" and Early Iron Age Madaba. In *Studies on Iron Age Moab and Neighbouring Areas in Honour of Michèle Daviau*, ed. Piotr Bienkowski, 27–45. Louvain, BE: Peeters.

Harrison, Timothy, and Celeste Barlow. 2005. Mesha, the Mishor, and the Chronology of Iron Age Madaba. In *The Bible and Radiocarbon Dating: Archaeology, Text, and Science*, ed. Thomas Levy and Thomas Higham, 179–190. London: Equinox.

Hasel, Michael. 1994. Israel in the Merneptah Stela. *Bulletin of the American Schools of Oriental Research* 296:45–61.

Hastrup, Kirsten, ed. 2009. *The Question of Resilience: Social Responses to Climate Change*. Copenhagen: Royal Danish Academy of Sciences and Letters.

Hayden, Brian. 2001. Fabulous Feasts: A Prolegomenon to the Importance of Feasting. In *Feasts: Archaeological and Ethnographic Perspectives on Food, Politics, and Power*, ed. Michael Dietler and Brian Hayden, 23–64. Washington, DC: Smithsonian Institution Press.

Hayden, Brian, and Aubrey Cannon. 1982. The Corporate Group as an Archaeological Unit. *Journal of Anthropological Archaeology* 1(2): 132–158.

Hegmon, Michelle. 2005. Beyond the Mold: Questions of Inequality in Southwest Villages. In *North American Archaeology*, eds. Timothy Pauketat and Diana DiPaolo Loren, 212–234. Malden, MA: Blackwell.

Heinz, Marlies, and Marian Feldman, eds. 2007. *Representations of Political Power: Case Histories from Times of Change and Dissolving Order in the Ancient Near East*. Winona Lake, IN: Eisenbrauns.

Helmreich, Stefan. 1998. *Silicon Second Nature: Culturing Artificial Life in a Digital World*. Berkeley: University of California Press.

Helms, Svend W. 1981. *Jawa: Lost City of the Black Desert*. Ithaca, NY: Cornell University Press.
Hendrix, Ralph E., Philip R. Drey, and J. Bjørnar Storfjell. 1997. *Ancient Pottery of Transjordan: An Introduction Utilizing Published Whole Forms*. Berrien Springs, MI: Andrews University Press.
Hennessy, J. Basil. 1966. Excavation of a Late Bronze Age Temple at Amman. *Palestine Exploration Quarterly* 98:155–162.
Herr, Larry G., ed. 1983. The Amman Airport Excavations, 1976. In *Annual of the American Schools of Oriental Research*, vol. 48. Winona Lake, IN: Eisenbrauns.
———. 1997. The Iron Age II Period: Emerging Nations. *Biblical Archaeologist* 60(3): 114–151, 154–183.
———. 2000. The Settlement and Fortification of Tell al-'Umayri in Jordan during the LB/Iron I Transition. In *The Archaeology of Jordan and Beyond: Essays in Honor of James B. Sauer*, ed. Lawrence Stager, Joseph Greene, and Michael Coogan, 167–179. Winona Lake, IN: Eisenbrauns.
———. 2009. Jordan in the Iron I Period. In *Studies in the History and Archaeology of Jordan*, ed. Fawwaz al-Khraysheh, 10:549–561. Amman: Department of Antiquities of Jordan.
Herr, Larry, Douglas Clark, Lawrence Geraty, Øystein LaBianca, and Randall Younker, eds. 2002. *Madaba Plains Project 5: The 1994 Season at Tall al-'Umayri and Subsequent Studies*. Berrien Springs, MI: Andrews University Press.
Herr, Larry, Douglas Clark, Lawrence Geraty, Randall Younker, and Øystein LaBianca, eds. 2000. *Madaba Plains Project 4: The 1992 Season at Tall al-'Umayri and Subsequent Studies*. Berrien Springs, MI: Andrews University Press.
Herr, Larry G., Lawrence Geraty, Øystein LaBianca, and Randall Younker, eds. 1991. *Madaba Plains Project 2: The 1987 Season at Tell el-'Umeiri and Vicinity and Subsequent Studies*. Berrien Springs, MI: Andrews University Press.
———. 1997. *Madaba Plains Project 3: The 1989 Season at Tell el-'Umeiri and Vicinity and Subsequent Studies* Berrien Springs, MI: Andrews University Press.
Herr, Larry G., and Elizabeth Platt. 2002. The Objects from the 1989 Season. In *Madaba Plains Project 5: The 1994 Season at Tall al-'Umayri and Subsequent Studies*, ed. Larry Herr, Douglas Clark, Lawrence Geraty, Randall Younker, and Øystein LaBianca, 358–399. Berrien Springs, MI: Andrews University Press.
Higginbotham, Carolyn R. 2000. *Egyptianization and Elite Emulation in Ramesside Palestine: Governance and Accommodation on the Imperial Periphery*. Leiden: Brill.
Hill, J. Brett. 2006. *Human Ecology in the Wadi al-Hasa: Land Use and Abandonment through the Holocene*. Tucson: University of Arizona Press.
Hoffmeier, James K., and Alan Millard, eds. 2004. *The Future of Biblical Archaeology: Reassessing Methodologies and Assumptions*. Grand Rapids, MI: Wm. B. Eerdmans.
Holladay, John S., Jr. 1992. House, Israelite. In *The Anchor Bible Dictionary*, ed. David Noel Freedman, 3:308–318. New York: Doubleday.
———. 1995. The Kingdoms of Israel and Judah: Political and Economic Centralization in the Iron II A–B (ca. 1000–750 BCE). In *The Archaeology of Society in the Holy Land*, ed. Thomas Levy, 368–398. New York: Facts on File.
Holling, C. S. 2001. Understanding the Complexity of Economic, Ecological, and Social Systems. *Ecosystems* 4(5): 390–405.

Holling, C. S., and Lance H. Gunderson. 2002. Resilience and Adaptive Cycles. In *Panarchy: Understanding Transformations in Human and Natural Systems*, ed. Lance H. Gunderson and C. S. Holling, 25–62. Washington: Island Press.

Homès-Fredericq, Denyse. 1992. Late Bronze and Iron Age Evidence from Lehun in Moab. In *Early Edom and Moab: The Beginning of the Iron Age in Southern Jordan*, ed. Piotr Bienkowski, 187–202. Sheffield, UK: J. R. Collis.

———. 1994. *Preliminary Report of the Twelfth Season of the Belgian Excavations in Jordan*. Brussels: Belgian Committee of Excavations in Jordan.

———. 1995. *Preliminary Report of the Thirteenth Season of the Belgian Excavations in Jordan*. Brussels: Belgian Committee of Excavations in Jordan.

———. 1997. *Decouvrez Lehun et la Voie Royale / en de Koningsweg*. Brussels: Belgian Committee for Excavations in Jordan.

———. 2000. Excavating the First Pillar House at Lehun (Jordan). In *The Archaeology of Jordan and Beyond*, ed. Lawrence Stager, Joseph Greene, and Michael Coogan, 180–195. Winona Lake, IN: Eisenbrauns.

Hope, Robert. 1897. Moab and the Moabites. PhD diss., University of Pennsylvania.

Hopkins, David C. 1985. *The Highlands of Canaan: Agricultural Life in the Early Iron Age*. Sheffield, UK: Almond Press.

———. 1987. Life on the Land: The Subsistence Struggles of Early Israel. *Biblical Archaeologist* 50(3): 178–191.

Hornborg, Alf, and Carole L. Crumley, eds. 2007. *The World System and the Earth System: Global Socioenvironmental Change and Sustainability since the Neolithic*. Walnut Creek, CA: Left Coast Press.

Horowitz, Aharon. 1979. *The Quaternary of Israel*. New York: Academic Press.

Horsfield, George, and Hughes Vincent. 1932. Un Stèle Egypto-Moabite au Balou'a. *Revue Biblique* 41:417–445.

Hutton, Rodney R. 1994. *Charisma and Authority in Israelite Society*. Minneapolis: Fortress Press.

Ibach, Robert D., Jr. 1987. *Hesban 5: Archaeological Survey of the Hesban Region*. Berrien Springs, MI: Andrews University Press.

Ibrahim, Moawiyah. 1972. Archaeological Excavations at Sahab, 1972. *Annual of the Department of Antiquities of Jordan* 17:23–36, 117–123.

———. 1974. Second Season of Excavation at Sahab, 1973. *Annual of the Department of Antiquities of Jordan* 19:55–61, 187–198.

———. 1975. Third Season of Excavations at Sahab, 1975. *Annual of the Department of Antiquities of Jordan* 20:69–82, 169–178.

———. 1987. Sahab and Its Foreign Relations. In *Studies in the History and Archaeology of Jordan*, ed. Adnan Hadidi, 3:73–81. Amman: Department of Antiquities of Jordan.

Ilan, David. 1995. The Dawn of Internationalism: The Middle Bronze Age. In *The Archaeology of Society in the Holy Land*, ed. Thomas Levy, 297–315. New York: Facts on File.

Issar, Arie S., and Mattanyah Zohar. 2004. *Climate Change: Environment and Civilization in the Middle East*. Berlin: Springer.

Jacobs, Linda. 1983. Survey on the South Ridge of the Wadi 'Isal, 1981. *Annual of the Department of Antiquities of Jordan* 27:245–274.

Jenks, Alan. 1992. Eating and Drinking in the Old Testament. In *The Anchor Bible Dictionary*, ed. David Noel Freedman, 250–254. New York: Doubleday.

Ji, Chang-Ho. 1995. Iron Age I in Central and Northern Transjordan: An Interim Summary of Archaeological Data. *Palestine Exploration Quarterly* 127:122–140.

———. 1997. A Note on the Iron Age Four-Room House in Palestine. *Orientalia* 66: 387–413.

———. 2012. The Early Iron Age II Temple at Hirbet 'Atarus and Its Architecture and Selected Cultic Objects. In *Temple Building and Temple Cult: Architecture and Cultic Paraphernalia of Temples in the Levant (2.-1. Mill. B.C.E.)*, ed. Jens Kamlah, 203–221. Wiesbaden: Harrassowitz Verlag.

Ji, Chang-Ho, and Taysir 'Attiyat. 1997. Archaeological Survey of the Dhiban Plateau, 1996: A Preliminary Report. *Annual of the Department of Antiquities of Jordan* 41:115–128.

Ji, Chang-Ho, and Jong Keun Lee. 1998. Preliminary Report of the Survey on the Dhiban Plateau, 1997. *Annual of the Department of Antiquities of Jordan* 42: 549–571.

———. 2000. A Preliminary Report on the Dhiban Plateau Survey Project, 1999: The Versacare Expedition. *Annual of the Department of Antiquities of Jordan* 44: 493–506.

Joffe, Alexander H. 2002. The Rise of Secondary States in the Iron Age Levant. *Journal of the Economic and Social History of the Orient* 45(4): 425–467.

Johnson, Aubrey R. 1961. *The One and the Many in the Israelite Conception of God.* Cardiff: University of Wales.

———. 1964. *The Vitality of the Individual in the Thought of Ancient Israel.* Cardiff: University of Wales.

Kaminsky, Joel S. 1995. *Corporate Responsibility in the Hebrew Bible.* Sheffield, UK: Sheffield Academic Press.

Keddie, Nikki R. 1973. Is There a Middle East? *International Journal of Middle Eastern Studies* 4(3): 255–271.

Killebrew, Ann E. 1996. Pottery Kilns from Deir el-Balah and Tel Miqne-Ekron. In *Retrieving the Past: Essays on Archaeological Research and Methodology in Honor of Gus W. Van Beek*, ed. Joe D. Seger, 135–162. Winona Lake, IN: Eisenbrauns.

———. 2005. *Biblical Peoples and Ethnicity: An Archaeological Study of Egyptians, Canaanites, Philistines, and Early Israel, 1300–1100 B.C.E.* Leiden: Brill.

Kitchen, Kenneth A. 1964. Some New Light on the Asiatic Wars of Ramesses II. *Journal of Egyptian Archaeology* 50:47–70.

———. 1992. The Egyptian Evidence on Ancient Jordan. In *Early Edom and Moab: The Beginning of the Iron Age in Southern Jordan*, ed. Piotr Bienkowski, 21–34. Sheffield, UK: J. R. Collis.

Knapp, A. Bernard. 2003. The Archaeology of Community on Bronze Age Cyprus: Politiko "Phorades" in Context. *American Journal of Archaeology* 107(4): 559–580.

Knauf, Ernst Axel. 1992. The Cultural Impact of Secondary State Formation: The Cases of the Edomites and Moabites. In *Early Edom and Moab: The Beginning of the Iron Age in Southern Jordan*, ed. Piotr Bienkowski, 47–54. Sheffield, UK: J. R. Collis.

Knoppers, Gary, and J. Gordon McConville, eds. 2000. *Reconsidering Israel and Judah: Recent Studies on the Deuteronomistic History.* Winona Lake, IN: Eisenbrauns.

Koenig, Y. 1990. Les Textes d'Envoutement de Mirgissa. *Revue d'Egyptologie* 41:101–125.

Kohler, Timothy, and George Gumerman, eds. 2000. *Dynamics in Human and Primate Societies: Agent-Based Modeling of Social and Spatial Processes.* New York: Oxford University Press.

Kohler, Timothy, and Sander E. van der Leeuw, eds. 2007. *The Model-Based Archaeology of Socionatural Systems.* Santa Fe, NM: School of Advanced Research.

Köhler-Rollefson, Ilse. 1988. The Aftermath of the Levantine Neolithic Revolution in the Light of Ecological and Ethnographic Evidence. *Paléorient* 14:87–93.

Köhler-Rollefson, Ilse, and Gary Rollefson. 1990. The Impact of Neolithic Subsistence Strategies on the Environment: The Case of 'Ain Ghazal, Jordan. In *Man's Role in the Shaping of the Eastern Mediterranean Landscape,* ed. Sytze Bottema, Gertie Entjes-Nieborg, and Willem van Zeist, 3–14. Rotterdam: A. A. Balkema.

Kolb, Michael J., and James E. Snead. 1997. It's a Small World after All: Comparative Analyses of Community Organization in Archaeology. *American Antiquity* 62(4): 609–628.

Kopytoff, Igor. 1987. The Internal African Frontier: The Making of African Political Culture. In *The African Frontier: The Reproduction of Traditional African Societies,* ed. Igor Kopytoff, 3–84. Bloomington: Indiana University Press.

Kuijt, Ian, ed. 2000. *Life in Neolithic Farming Communities: Social Organization, Identity, and Differentiation.* New York: Kluwer.

LaBianca, Øystein. 1990. *Hesban 1: Sedentarization and Nomadization: Food System Cycles at Hesban and Vicinity in Transjordan.* Berrien Springs, MI: Andrews University Press.

———. 1997. A Forest That Refuses to Disappear: Cycles of Environmental Degeneration and Regeneration in Jordan. Unpublished report to the National Geographic Society. http://www.casa.arizona.edu/MPP/ngs_report/ngs_rep.html.

———. 1999. Excursus: Salient Features of Iron Age Tribal Kingdoms. In *Ancient Ammon,* ed. Burton Macdonald and Randall Younker, 19–23. Leiden: Brill.

LaBianca, Øystein, and Angela von den Driesch, eds. 1995. *Hesban 13: Faunal Remains.* Berrien Springs, MI: Andrews University Press.

LaBianca, Øystein, and Kristen Witzel. 2007. Nomads, Empires, and Civilizations: Great and Little Traditions and the Historical Landscape of the Southern Levant. In *On the Fringe of Society: Archaeological and Ethnoarchaeological Perspectives on Pastoral and Agricultural Societies,* eds. Benjamin A. Saidel and Eveline J. van der Steen, 63–74. Oxford: Archaeopress.

LaBianca, Øystein, and Randall Younker. 1995. The Kingdoms of Ammon, Moab, and Edom: The Archaeology of Society in Late Bronze/Iron Age Transjordan (ca. 1400–500 BCE). In *The Archaeology of Society in the Holy Land,* ed. Thomas Levy, 399–411. New York: Facts on File.

Lacelle, Larry. 1986a. Bedrock Geology, Surficial Geology, and Soils. In *Hesban 2: Environmental Foundations,* ed. Øystein LaBianca and Larry Lacelle, 25–58. Berrien Springs, MI: Andrews University Press.

———. 1986b. Ecology of the Flora of Tell Hesban and Area, Jordan. In *Hesban 2: Environmental Foundations,* eds. Øystein LaBianca and Larry Lacelle, 75–98. Berrien Springs, MI: Andrews University Press.

Lambert, Wilfred G. 1993. Donations of Food and Drink to the Gods in Ancient Mesopotamia. In *Ritual and Sacrifice in the Ancient Near East,* ed. J. Quaegebeur, 191–201. Leuven, BE: Peeters Publishers and Department of Oriental Studies.

Lamprichs, Roland. 1998. *Abu Snesleh: Ergebnisse der Ausgrabungen 1990 und 1992*. Rahden: Marie Leidorf.
Lancaster, William, and Fidelity Lancaster. 1995. Land Use and Population in the Area North of Karak. *Levant* 27:103–124.
Lansing, J. Stephen. 2003. Complex Adaptive Systems. *Annual Review of Anthropology* 32:183–204.
Lapp, Nancy. 1989. 'Iraq el-Amir. In *Archaeology of Jordan: Field Reports: Surveys and Sites A–K*, ed. Denyse Homès-Fredericq and J. Basil Hennessy, 2:280–297. Louvain, BE: Peeters.
Lapp, Paul. 1965. The 1962 Excavations at 'Araq el-Emir. *Annual of the Department of Antiquities of Jordan* 10:37–42.
Larson, Daniel. 1996. Population Growth, Agricultural Intensification, and Culture Change among the Virgin Branch Anasazi, Nevada. *Journal of Field Archaeology* 23(1): 55–76.
van der Leeuw, Sander, and Charles L. Redman. 2002. Placing Archaeology at the Center of Socio-natural Studies. *American Antiquity* 67(4): 597–605.
Lemche, Niels Peter. 1998. *The Israelites in History and Tradition*. Louisville: Westminster John Knox Press.
Leonard, Albert, Jr. 1989. The Late Bronze Age. *Biblical Archaeologist* 52(1):4–39.
Levin, Simon A. 2002. Complex Adaptive Systems: Exploring the Known, the Unknown, and the Unknowable. *Bulletin of the American Mathematical Society* 40(1): 3–19.
Levine, Baruch A. 2000. *Numbers 21–36: A New Translation with Introduction and Commentary*. New York: Doubleday.
Lev-Tov, Justin, and Kevin McGeough. 2007. Examining Feasting in Late Bronze Age Syro-Palestine through Ancient Texts and Bones. In *The Archaeology of Food and Identity*, ed. Katheryn Twiss, 85–111. Carbondale: Southern Illinois University Press.
Lev-Tov, Justin, Benjamin Porter, and Bruce Routledge. 2010. Measuring Local Diversity in Early Iron Age Animal Economies: A View from Khirbat al-Mudayna al-'Aliya (Jordan). *Bulletin of the American Schools of Oriental Research* 361:67–93.
Levy, Thomas E., ed. 2010. *Historical Biblical Archaeology and the Future: The New Pragmatism*. London: Equinox.
Levy, Thomas E., Russell B. Adams, Mohammad Najjar, Andreas Hauptmann, James D. Anderson, Baruch Brandl, Mark A. Robinson, and Thomas Higham. 2004. Reassessing the chronology of Biblical Edom: New Excavations and ^{14}C Dates from Khirbat en-Nahas (Jordan). *Antiquity* 78: 865–879.
Levy, Thomas E., Erez Ben-Yosef, and Mohammad Najjar. 2012. New Perspectives on Iron Age Copper Production and Society in the Faynan Region, Jordan. In *Eastern Mediterranean Metallurgy and Metalwork in the Second Millennium BC*, ed. Vasiliki Kassianidou and George Papasavvas. London: Oxbow.
Levy, Thomas E., and Thomas Higham, eds. 2005. *The Bible and Radiocarbon Dating: Archaeology, Text and Science*. London: Equinox.
Lévy-Bruhl, Lucien. 1925. *How Natives Think*. New York: A. A. Knopf.
Lewis, Krista. 2007. Fields and Tables of Sheba: Food, Identity, and Politics in Early Historic Southern Arabia. In *The Archaeology of Food and Identity*, ed. Kathryn Twiss, 192–217. Carbondale: Southern Illinois University Press.

Liebmann, Matthew, and Uzma Rizvi, eds. 2008. *Archaeology and the Postcolonial Critique*. Lanham, MD: AltaMira Press.
Liverani, Mario. 1979. "Irrational" Elements in the Amarna Trade. In *Three Amarna Essays*, ed. M. L. Jaffe, 93–105. Malibu, CA: Undena.
London, Gloria. 2009. Feasting at Tall al-'Umayri in the Second Millennium BC. In *Studies in the History and Archaeology of Jordan*, ed. Fawwaz al-Khraysheh, 10:899–916. Amman: Department of Antiquities of Jordan.
———. 2011. Late Second Millennium BC Feasting at an Ancient Ceremonial Centre in Jordan. *Levant* 43(1): 15–37.
Macalister, Robert S. 1912. *The Excavation of Gezer*. London: Palestine Exploration Fund.
MacDonald, Nathan. 2008. *Not Bread Alone: The Uses of Food in the Old Testament*. Oxford: Oxford University Press.
Maeir, Aren, Shimon Dar, and Ze'ev Safrai. 2003. *The Rural Landscape of Ancient Israel*. Oxford: Archaeopress.
Magness-Gardiner, Bonnie, and Steven Falconer. 1994. Community, Polity, and Temple in a Middle Bronze Levantine Village. *Journal of Mediterranean Archaeology* 7:127–164.
Malamat, Abraham. 1976. Charismatic Leadership in the Book of Judges. In *Magnalia Dei: The Mighty Acts of God: Essays on the Bible and Archaeology in Memory of G. Ernest Wright*, ed. Frank Moore Cross, Werner E. Lemke, and Patrick D. Miller, Jr., 152–168. Garden City, NY: Doubleday.
Marcus, Joyce, and Jeremy A. Sabloff, eds. 2008. *The Ancient City: New Perspectives on Urbanism in the Old and New World*. Santa Fe, NM: School for Advanced Research.
Marfoe, Leon. 1979. The Integrative Transformation: Patterns of Sociopolitical Organization in Southern Syria. *Bulletin of the American Schools of Oriental Research* 234:1–42.
Marx, Karl. 1859. *A Contribution to the Critique of Political Economy*.
Marx, Karl, and Friedrich Engels. 1848. *The Communist Manifesto*. London: Penguin Books.
Master, Daniel M. 2001. State Formation Theory and the Kingdom of Ancient Israel. *Journal of Near Eastern Studies* 60(2): 117–131.
Matthews, Victor. 1978. *Pastoral Nomadism in the Mari Kingdom (ca. 1830–1760 B.C.)*. Cambridge, MA: American Schools of Oriental Research.
Mattingly, Gerald L. 1992. The Cultural-Historical Approach and Moabite Origins. In *Early Edom and Moab: The Beginning of the Iron Age in Southern Jordan*, ed. Piotr Bienkowski, 55–64. Sheffield, UK: J. R. Collis.
———. 1996. Al-Karak Resources Project 1995: A Preliminary Report on the Pilot Season. *Annual of the Department of Antiquities of Jordan* 40:349–368.
Mauss, Marcel. 1925. *The Gift: The Form and Reason for Exchange in Archaic Societies*. New York: W. W. Norton.
Mazar, Amihai. 1990. *Archaeology of the Land of the Bible, 10,000–586 B.C.E*. New York: Doubleday.
Mazar, Benjamin. 1968. The Middle Bronze Age in Palestine. *Israel Exploration Journal* 18(2): 65–97.

McAnany, Patricia A., and Norman Yoffee, eds. 2010. *Questioning Collapse: Human Resilience, Ecological Vulnerability, and the Aftermath of Empire.* Cambridge: Cambridge University Press.

McCarter, P. Kyle. 1980. *I Samuel: A New Translation with Introduction, Notes, and Commentary.* Garden City, NY: Doubleday.

———. 1984. *II Samuel: A New Translation with Introduction, Notes, and Commentary.* Garden City, NY: Doubleday.

———. 2011. The Patriarchal Age: Abraham, Isaac, and Jacob. In *Ancient Israel: From Abraham to the Roman Destruction of the Temple,* ed. Hershel Shanks, 3rd ed., 1–34. Washington, DC: Biblical Archaeology Society.

McCorriston, Joy, and Frank Hole. 1991. The Ecology of Seasonal Stress and the Origins of Agriculture in the Near East. *American Anthropologist* 93(1): 46–69.

McGeough, Kevin. 2007. *Exchange Relationships at Ugarit.* Louvain, BE: Peeters.

McGovern, Patrick E. 1986. *The Late Bronze and Early Iron Ages of Central Transjordan: The Baq'ah Valley Project, 1977–1981.* Philadelphia: University Museum.

———. 1988. Central Transjordan in the Late Bronze and Early Iron Ages: An Alternative Hypothesis of Socio-Economic Transformation and Collapse. In *Studies in the History and Archaeology of Jordan,* ed. Adnan Hadidi, 3:267–273. Amman: Department of Antiquities of Jordan.

McGuire, Randall H., and Dean J. Saitta. 1996. Although They Have Petty Captains, They Obey Them Badly: The Dialectics of Prehispanic Western Pueblo Social Organization. *American Antiquity* 61(2): 197–216.

McIntosh, Roderick J., Joseph A. Tainter, and Susan Keech McIntosh, eds. 2000. *The Way the Wind Blows: Climate, History, and Human Action.* New York: Columbia University Press.

McKenzie, J. L. 1959. The Elders in the Old Testament. *Biblica* 40:522–540.

Mendenhall, George E. 1962. The Hebrew Conquest of Palestine. *Biblical Archaeologist* 25(3): 66–87.

———. 1976. Social Organization in Early Israel. In *Magnalia Dei: The Mighty Acts of God: Essays on the Bible and Archaeology in Memory of G. Ernest Wright,* ed. Frank Moore Cross, Werner E. Lemke, and Patrick D. Miller, 132–151. Garden City: Doubleday.

———. 1983. Ancient Israel's Hyphenated History. In *Palestine in Transition: The Emergence of Ancient Israel,* ed. David Noel Freedman and David Frank Graf, 91–103. Sheffield, UK: Almond Press.

Merling, David, and Lawrence T. Geraty, eds. 1993. *Hesban after 25 years.* Berrien Springs, MI: Andrews University Press.

Metzger, Bruce M., and Roland E. Murphy, eds. 1991. *The New Oxford Annotated Bible with Apocryphal/Deuterocanonical Books.* New York: Oxford University Press.

Meyers, Carol. 1988. *Discovering Eve: Ancient Israelite Women in Context.* Oxford: Oxford University Press.

———. 1997. The Family in Early Israel. In *Families in Ancient Israel,* ed. Leo G. Perdue, Joseph Blenkinsopp, John J. Collins, and Carol Meyers, 1–47. Louisville: Westminster John Knox Press.

Milgrom, Jacob. 1992. Book of Numbers. In *The Anchor Bible Dictionary,* ed. David Noel Freedman, 1146–1155. Garden City, NY: Doubleday.

Miller, J. Maxwell. 1989. The Israelite Journey through (around) Moab and Moabite Toponymy. *Journal of Biblical Literature* 108(4): 577–595.

———, ed. 1991. *Archaeological Survey of the Kerak Plateau*. Atlanta: Scholars Press.

———. 1992. Early Monarchy in Moab? In *Early Edom and Moab: The Beginning of the Iron Age in Southern Jordan*, ed. Piotr Bienkowski, 77–91. Sheffield, UK: J. R. Collis.

Miller, John H., and Scott E. Page. 2007. *Complex Adaptive Systems: An Introduction to Computational Models of Social Life*. Princeton, NJ: Princeton University Press.

Miller, Robert D. 2005. *Chieftains of the Highland Clans: A History of Israel in the Twelfth and Eleventh Centuries B.C.* Grand Rapids, MI: Wm. B. Eerdmans.

Monroe, Christopher. 2009. Seeing the World. *Bulletin of the American Schools of Oriental Research* 356:81–87.

Moorey, P. R. S. 1991. *A Century of Biblical Archaeology*. Louisville: Westminster John Knox Press.

Moormann, Frank. 1959. *The Soils of East Jordan: Report to the Government of Jordan*. Rome: Food and Agricultural Organization of the United Nations.

Moran, William. 1992. *The Amarna Letters*. Baltimore: Johns Hopkins University Press.

Morton, William H. 1989. A Summary of the 1955, 1956, and 1965 Excavations at Dhiban. In *Studies in the Mesha Inscription and Moab*, ed. Andrew Dearman, 239–246. Atlanta: Scholars Press.

Munson, Henry, Jr. 1989. On the Irrelevance of the Segmentary Lineage Model in the Moroccan Rif. *American Anthropologist* 91(2): 386–400.

Murdock, George P., and Suzanne F. Wilson. 1972. Settlement Patterns and Community Organization: Cross-Cultural Codes 3. *Ethnology* 11(3): 254–295.

Najjar, Mohammad. 1991. A New Middle Bronze Age Tomb at the Citadel of Amman. *Annual of the Department of Antiquities of Jordan* 35:105–134.

Nancy, Jean-Luc. 1991. *The Inoperative Community*. Minneapolis: University of Minnesota Press.

Neff, Hector. 2000. Neutron Activation Analysis for Provenance Determination in Archaeology. In *Modern Analytical Methods in Art and Archaeology*, ed. Enrico Ciliberto and Giuseppe Spoto, 81–134. New York: John Wiley & Sons.

Nelson, Ben A. 1994. Approaches to Analyzing Prehistoric Community Dynamics. In *The Ancient Southwestern Community: Models and Methods for the Study of Prehistoric Social Organization*, ed. W. H. Wills and Robert D. Leonard, 3–7. Albuquerque: University of New Mexico Press.

Nelson, Richard D. 1997. *Joshua: A Commentary*. Louisville: Westminster John Knox Press.

Nelson, Sarah. 2003. Feasting the Ancestors in Early China. In *The Archaeology and Politics of Food and Feasting in Early States and Empires*, ed. Tamara Bray, 65–89. New York: Kluwer Academic/Plenum.

Newberry, Percy E., F. Ll. Griffith, and George Willoughby Fraser. 1893. *Beni Hasan*. London: K. Paul, Trench, Trubner.

Niditch, Susan. 2008. *Judges: A Commentary*. Louisville: Westminster John Knox Press.

Nieuwenhuijze, C. A. O. van. 1962. The Near Eastern Village: A Profile. *Middle East Journal* 16(3): 295–308.

Ninow, Friedbert. 2004. First Soundings at Kirbat al-Muʻmmariyya in the Greater Wadi al-Mujib Area. *Annual of the Department of Antiquities of Jordan* 48:257–266.

———. 2006. The 2005 Soundings at Khirbat al-Mu'ammariyya in the Greater Wadi al-Mujib Area. *Annual of the Department of Antiquities of Jordan* 50:147–155.
Noth, Martin. 1968. *Numbers: A Commentary*. Philadelphia: Westminster Press.
———. 1981. *The Deuteronomistic History*. Sheffield, UK: University of Sheffield.
Olàvarri, Emilio. 1965. Sondages à Aro'er sur l'Arnon. *Revue Biblique* 72(1): 77–94.
———. 1969. Fouilles à 'Aro'er sur l'Arnon. *Revue Biblique* 76(2): 230–259.
———. 1977–1978. Sondeo Arqueologico en Khirbet Medeineh junto a Smakieh (Jordania). *Annual of the Department of Antiquities of Jordan* 22:136–149.
———. 1983. La Campagne de Fouilles 1982 à Khirbet Medeinet al-Mu'arradjeh près de Smakieh (Kerak). *Annual of the Department of Antiquities of Jordan* 27: 165–178.
———. 1993. Aroer (in Moab). In *The New Encyclopedia of Archaeological Excavations in the Holy Land*, ed. Ephraim Stern, Ayelet Lewinson-Gilboa, and Joseph Aviram, 92–93. Jerusalem: Israel Exploration Society.
Oleson, John. 2001. Water Supply in Jordan through the Ages. In *The Archaeology of Jordan*, ed. Burton MacDonald, Russel Adams, and Piotr Bienkowski, 603–614. Sheffield, UK: Sheffield Academic Press.
Oren, Eliezer D. 2000. *The Sea Peoples and Their World: A Reassessment*. Philadelphia: University of Pennsylvania Museum.
Palmer, Carol. 1998. "Following the Plough": The Agricultural Environment of Northern Jordan. *Levant* 30:129–165.
Papadopoulos, K. 2011. Illuminating the Burials in the Aegean Bronze Age: Natural and Artificial Light in a Mortuary Context. In *UK Chapter of Computer Applications and Quantitative Methods in Archaeology*, ed. A. Wilson, 67–74. Oxford: Archaeopress.
Parker, S. Thomas, ed. 1987. *The Roman Frontier in Central Jordan: Interim Report on the Limes Arabicus Project, 1980–1985*. Oxford: British Archaeological Reports.
———. 2006. *The Roman Frontier in Central Jordan: Final Report on the Limes Arabicus Project, 1980–1989*. Washington, DC: Dumbarton Oaks Research Library and Collection.
Peregrine, Peter. 1991. Some Political Aspects of Craft Specialization. *World Archaeology* 23(1): 1–11.
Peters, Emrys Lloyd. 1963. Aspects of Rank and Status among Muslims in a Lebanese Village. In *Mediterranean Countrymen: Essays in the Social Anthropology of the Mediterranean*, ed. Julian Pitt-Rivers, 159–200. Paris: Mouton.
———. 1972. Shifts in Power in a Lebanese Village. In *Rural Politics and Social Change in the Middle East*, ed. Richard Antoun and Iliya Harik, 165–197. Bloomington: University of Indiana Press.
Peters, Joris, Nadja Pöllath, and Angela von den Driesch. 2002. Early and Late Bronze Age Transitional Subsistence at Tall al-'Umayri. In *Madaba Plains Project 5: The 1994 Season at Tall al-'Umayri and Subsequent Studies*, ed. Larry Herr, Douglas Clark, Lawrence Geraty, Randall Younker, and Øystein LaBianca, 305–347. Berrien Springs, MI: Andrews University Press.
Piccirillo, Michele. 1978. Una Tomba del Bronzo Medeo ad Amman. *Liber Annuus* 28:73–86.
Platt, Elizabeth E. 2000. The Objects. In *Madaba Plains Project 4: The 1992 Season at Tall al-'Umayri and Subsequent Studies*, ed. Larry G. Herr, Douglas Clark,

Lawrence Geraty, Randall Younker, and Øystein LaBianca, 204–214. Berrien Springs. MI: Andrews University Press.

Platt, Elizabeth, and Larry Herr. 2002. The Objects. In *Madaba Plains Project 5: The 1994 Season at Tall al-'Umayri and Subsequent Studies*, ed. Larry Herr, Douglas Clark, Lawrence Geraty, Randall Younker, and Øystein LaBianca, 156–170. Berrien Springs, MI: Andrews University Press.

Pollock, Susan. 2003. Feasts, Funerals, and Fast Food in Early Mesopotamian States. In *The Archaeology and Politics of Food and Feasting in Early States and Empires*, ed. Tamara Bray, 17–38. New York: Kluwer Academic/Plenum.

Porter, Benjamin. 2004. Authority, Polity, and Tenuous Elites in Iron Age Edom (Jordan). *Oxford Journal of Archaeology* 23:373–395.

———. 2007. The Archaeology of Community in Iron I Central Jordan. PhD diss., University of Pennsylvania.

———. 2010. Testing the Limits of Nonzero: Cooperation, Conflict, and Hierarchy in Ancient Near Eastern Marginal Environments. In *Cooperation in Economy and Society: Research in Economic Anthropology*, ed. R. Marshall, 28:149–171. Lanham, MD: AltaMira Press.

———. 2011. Feeding the Community: Objects, Scarcity, and Commensality in the Early Iron Age Southern Levant. *Journal of Mediterranean Archaeology* 24:27–54.

Porter, Benjamin, and Robert J. Speakman. 2008. Reading Moabite Pigments with Laser Ablation ICP-MS: A New Archaeometric Technique for Near Eastern Archaeology. *Near Eastern Archaeology* 71(4): 238–242.

Porter, Joshua R. 1965. The Legal Aspects of the Concept of "Corporate Personality" in the Old Testament. *Vetus Testamentum* 15(3): 361–380.

Posener, Georges. 1940. *Princes et Pays d'Asie et de Nubie*. Brussels: Queen Elizabeth Egyptological Foundation.

Prewitt, Terry J. 1981. Kinship Structures and the Genesis Genealogies. *Journal of Near Eastern Studies* 40(2): 87–98.

Pritchard, James B. 1975. *Sarepta: A Preliminary Report on the Iron Age*. Philadelphia: University Museum.

Putnam, Robert D. 2000. *Bowling Alone: The Collapse and Revival of American Community*. New York: Simon & Schuster.

Rainey, Anson F. 1994. Remarks on Donald Redford's "Egypt, Canaan, and Israel in Ancient Times." *Bulletin of the American Schools of Oriental Research* 29:81–85.

Rautman, Alison. 1998. Hierarchy and Heterarchy in the American Southwest: A Comment on McGuire and Saitta. *American Antiquity* 63(2): 325–333.

Ray, Paul J., Jr. 2001. *Hesban 6: Tell Hesban and Vicinity in the Iron Age*. Berrien Springs, MI: Andrews University Press.

Redfield, Robert. 1941. *The Folk Culture of Yucatan*. Chicago: University of Chicago Press.

———. 1955. *The Little Community: Viewpoints for the Study of a Human Whole*. Chicago: University of Chicago Press.

Redford, Donald. 1982. Contact between Egypt and Jordan in the New Kingdom: Some Comments on Sources. In *Studies in the History and Archaeology of Jordan*, ed. Adnan Hadidi, 1:115–119. Amman: Department of Antiquities of Jordan.

———. 1992. *Egypt, Canaan, and Israel in Ancient Times*. Princeton, NJ: Princeton University Press.

———. 1996. A Response to Anson Rainey's "Remarks on Donald Redford's Egypt, Canaan, and Israel in Ancient Times." *Bulletin of the American Schools of Oriental Research* 301:77–81.
Redman, Charles L. 2005. Resilience Theory in Archaeology. *American Anthropologist* 107(1): 70–77.
Reviv, Hanoch. 1989. *The Elders in Ancient Israel: A Study of a Biblical Institution*. Jerusalem: Magnes Press.
Rice, Prudence M. 1981. Evolution of Specialized Pottery Production: A Trial Model. *Current Anthropology* 22(3): 219–240.
Robinson, H. Wheeler. 1961. *The One and the Many in the Israelite Conception of God*. Cardiff: University of Wales Press.
———. 1964. *Corporate Personality in Ancient Israel*. Philadelphia: Fortress Press.
Rogerson, John W. 1970. The Hebrew Conception of Corporate Personality: A Re-examination. *Journal of Theological Studies* 21:1–16.
Rosen, Arlene M. 1986. Environmental Change and Settlement at Tel Lachish, Israel. *Bulletin of the American Schools of Oriental Research* 263:55–60.
———. 2007. *Civilizing Climate: Social Responses to Climate Change in the Ancient Near East*. Lanham, MD: AltaMira Press.
Rosen, Lawrence. 1979. Social Identity and Points of Attachment: Approaches to Social Organization. In *Meaning and Order in Moroccan Society: Three Essays in Cultural Analysis*, ed. Clifford Geertz, Hildred Geertz, and Lawrence Rosen, 19–111. Cambridge: Cambridge University Press.
Rosenfeld, Henry. 1972. An Overview and Critique of the Literature on Rural Politics and Social Change. In *Rural Politics and Social Change in the Middle East*, ed. Richard Antoun and Iliya Harik, 45–74. Bloomington: Indiana University Press.
Rothman, Mitchell. 1994. Introduction: Part I, Evolutionary Typologies and Cultural Complexity. In *Chiefdoms and Early States in the Near East: The Organizational Dynamics of Complexity*, ed. Gil Stein and Mitchell S. Rothman, 1–10. Madison, WI: Prehistory Press.
Routledge, Bruce. 2000. Seeing through Walls: Interpreting Iron Age I Architecture at Khirbat al-Mudayna al-'Aliya. *Bulletin of the American Schools of Oriental Research* 319:37–70.
———. 2004. *Moab in the Iron Age: Hegemony, Polity, Archaeology*. Philadelphia: University of Pennsylvania Press.
———. 2008. Thinking "Globally" and Analysing "Locally": South-Central Jordan in Transition. In *Israel in Transition: From Late Bronze II to Iron IIA (c. 1250–850 BCE): 1. The Archaeology*, ed. Lester Grabbe, 144–176. London: T & T Clark.
———. 2009. Average Families?: House Size Variability in the Southern Levantine Iron Age. In *The Family in Life and in Death: The Family in Ancient Israel*, ed. Patricia Dutcher-Walls, 42–60. London: T & T Clark International.
———. 2013. On Water Management in the Mesha Inscription and Moab. *Journal of Near Eastern Studies* 72(1): 51–64.
Routledge, Bruce, Stanley Klassen, and Benjamin Porter. forthcoming. Provenance and Production of Early Iron Age Pottery at Khirbat al-Mudayna al-'Aliya: A Preliminary Analysis. In *Studies in the History and Archaeology of Jordan*, vol. 11. Amman: Department of Antiquities of Jordan.

Routledge, Bruce, and Kevin McGeough. 2009. Just What Collapsed? A Network Perspective on "Palatial" and "Private" Trade at Ugarit. In *Forces of Transformation: The End of the Bronze Age in the Mediterranean*, ed. Christoph Bachhuber and R. Gareth Roberts, 22–29. London: Oxbow Books.

Routledge, Bruce, and Benjamin Porter. 2007. A Place In-between: Khirbat al-Mudayna al-'Aliya in the Early Iron Age. In *Crossing Jordan: North American Contributions to the Archaeology of Jordan*, ed. Thomas Levy, P. Michèle Daviau, Randall Younker, and May Shaer, 323–329. London: Equinox.

Routledge, Bruce, and Carolyn Routledge. 2009. The Balu'a Stela Revisited. In *Studies on Iron Age Moab and Neighbouring Areas in Honour of Michèle Daviau*, ed. Piotr Bienkowski, 71–95. Louvain, BE: Peeters.

Rowlands, Michael. 1987. Centre and Periphery: A Review of a Concept. In *Centre and Periphery in the Ancient World*, ed. Michael Rowlands, Morgens Larsen, and Kristian Kristiansen, 1–11. Cambridge: Cambridge University Press.

Sahlins, Marshall. 1972. *Stone Age Economics*. Chicago: Aldine.

Saitta, Dean J. 1997. Power, Labor, and the Dynamics of Change in Chacoan Political Economy. *American Antiquity* 62(1): 7–26.

Saitta, Dean J., and Randall H. McGuire. 1998. Dialectics, Heterarchy, and Western Pueblo Social Organization. *American Antiquity* 63(2): 334–336.

Saller, Sylvester J. 1965–1966. Iron Age Tombs at Nebo, Jordan. *Liber Annuus* 16:165–298.

Sasson, Jack M. 2004. The King's Table: Food and Fealty in Old Babylonian Mari. In *Food and Identity in the Ancient World*, ed. Cristiano Grottanelli and Lucio Milano, 179–215. Padua: Sargon.

Sauer, James A. 1986. Transjordan in the Bronze and Iron Ages: A Critique of Glueck's Synthesis. *Bulletin of the American Schools of Oriental Research* 263:1–26.

Schloen, J. David. 2001. *The House of the Father as Fact and Symbol: Patrimonialism in Ugarit and the Ancient Near East*. Winona Lake, IN: Eisenbrauns.

Schmandt-Besserat, Denise. 2001. Feasting in the Ancient Near East. In *Feasts: Archaeological and Ethnographic Perspectives on Food, Politics, and Power*, ed. Michael Dietler and Brian Hayden, 391–403. Washington, DC: Smithsonian Institution Press.

Schniedewind, William. 2004. *How the Bible Became a Book: The Textualization of Ancient Israel*. Cambridge: Cambridge University Press.

Schnurrenberger, Douglas, and Jon Cole. 1997. Land Use Management in the Tall al-'Umayri Region. In *Madaba Plains Project 3: The 1989 Season at Tell el-'Umeiri and Vicinity and Subsequent Studies*, ed. Larry Herr, Lawrence Geraty, Øystein LaBianca, Randall Younker, and Douglas Clark, 352–366. Berrien Springs, MI: Andrews University Press.

Schwartz, Glenn M., and Steven E. Falconer. 1994. *Archaeological Views from the Countryside: Village Communities in Early Complex Societies*. Washington: Smithsonian Institution Press.

Scott, James C. 1976. *The Moral Economy of the Peasant: Rebellion and Subsistence in Southeast Asia*. New Haven, CT: Yale University Press.

Segal, Arthur. 1983. *The Byzantine City of Shivta (Esbeita), Negev Desert, Israel*. Oxford: Archaeopress.

Service, Elman. 1975. *Origins of the State and Civilization: The Processes of Cultural Evolution*. New York: W. W. Norton.

Sethe, Kurt. 1926. *Die Ächtung Feindlicher Fürsten, Völker und Dinge auf Altägyptischen Tongefässcherben des Mittleren Reiches*. Berlin: Proceedings of the Prussian Academy of Sciences.

el-Sherbini, A. A., ed. 1979. *Food Security Issues in the Arab Near East: A Report of the United Nations Economic Commission for Western Asia*. Oxford: Pergamon.

Shiloh, Yigal. 1970. The Four-Room House: Its Situation and Function in the Israelite City. *Israel Exploration Journal* 20(3–4): 180–190.

———. 1973. The Four-Room House: The Israelite Type-House? *Eretz-Israel* 11:277–285. (In Hebrew.)

———. 1987. The Casemate Wall, the Four Room House, and Early Planning in the Israelite City. *Bulletin of the American Schools of Oriental Research* 268:3–15.

Simmons, Ellen. 2000. Subsistence in Transition: Analysis of an Archaeobotanical Assemblage from Khirbet al-Mudayna al-'Aliya. MS thesis, University of Sheffield, UK.

Simons, Jan Jozef. 1937. *Handbook for the Study of Egyptian Topographical Lists Relating to Western Asia*. Leiden: Brill.

Smith, Eric Alden, and Jung-Kyoo Choi. 2007. The Emergence of Inequality in Small-Scale Societies: Simple Scenarios and Agent-Based Simulations. In *The Model-Based Archaeology of Socionatural Systems*, ed. Timothy A. Kohler and Sander E. van der Leeuw, 105–119. Santa Fe, NM: School for Advanced Research.

Soggin, J. Alberto. 1981. *Judges: A Commentary*. Philadelphia: Westminster Press.

———. 1989. *Introduction to the Old Testament: From Its Origins to the Closing of the Alexandrian Canon*. Louisville: Westminster John Knox Press.

Spooner, Brian. 1973. *The Cultural Ecology of Pastoral Nomads*. Addison-Wesley Module Publications in Anthropology, no. 45. Reading, MA: Addison-Wesley.

Stager, Lawrence E. 1985. The Archaeology of the Family in Ancient Israel. *Bulletin of the American Schools of Oriental Research* 260:1–35.

———. 1995. The Impact of the Sea Peoples in Canaan (1185–1050 BCE). In *The Archaeology of Society in the Holy Land*, ed. Thomas Levy, 332–348. New York: Facts on File.

van der Steen, Eveline. 2004. *Tribes and Territories in Transition: The Central East Jordan Valley in the Late Bronze and Iron Age: A Study of the Sources*. Louvain, BE: Peeters.

Stern, Ephraim. 2001. *Archaeology of the Land of the Bible: The Assyrian, Babylonian, and Persian Periods (732–332 BCE)*. New York: Doubleday.

Steward, Julian H. (1955) 1963. *Theory of Culture Change: The Methodology of Multilinear Evolution*. Urbana: University of Illinois Press.

Strange, John. 2001. The Late Bronze Age. In *The Archaeology of Jordan*, ed. Burton MacDonald, Russel Adams, and Piotr Bienkowski, 291–321. Sheffield, UK: Sheffield Academic Press.

Swinnen, Ingrid M. 2009. The Iron Age I Settlement and Its Residential Houses at al-Lahun in Moab, Jordan. *Bulletin of the American Schools of Oriental Research* 354:29–53.

Tannous, Afif I. 1944. The Arab Village Community of the Middle East. In *Annual Report of the Board of Regents of the Smithsonian Institution Showing the Operations, Expenditures, and Condition of the Institution for the Year Ended June 30, 1943*, 523–543. Washington, DC: Government Printing Office.

Thompson, Henry O. 1986. An Iron Age Tomb at Madaba. In *The Archaeology of Jordan and Other Studies*, ed. Lawrence Geraty and Larry G. Herr, 331–363. Berrien Springs, MI: Andrews University Press.
Thompson, Thomas L. 1992. *Early History of the Israelite People: From the Written and Archaeological Sources*. Vol. 4 of *Studies in the History of the Ancient Near East*. Leiden: Brill.
Timm, Stefan. 1989. *Moab Zwischen den Mächten: Studien zu historischen Denkmälern und Texten*. Wiesbaden: Harrassowitz.
Tönnies, Ferdinand. 1887. *Gemeinschaft und Gesellschaft*. New York: American Book.
Tosi, Maurizio. 1984. The Notion of Craft Specialization and Its Representation in the Archaeological Record of Early States in the Turanian Basin. In *Marxist Perspectives in Archaeology*, ed. Matthew Spriggs, 22–52. Cambridge: Cambridge University Press.
Tufnell, Olga. 1958. *Lachish IV: The Bronze Age*. London: Oxford University Press.
Tushingham, A. Douglas. 1972. The Excavations at Dibon (Dhiban) in Moab. The Third Campaign, 1952–1953. In *Annual of the American Schools of Oriental Research*, vol. 40. New Haven, CT: American Schools of Oriental Research.
Twiss, Katheryn, ed. 2007. *The Archaeology of Food and Identity*. Carbondale: Center for Archaeological Investigations, Southern Illinois University Press.
Varien, Mark D., and James Potter, eds. 2008. *The Social Construction of Communities: Agency, Structure, and Identity in the Prehispanic Southwest*. Lanham, MD: AltaMira Press.
Vaughn, Kevin, Jelmer Eerkens, and John Kantner, eds. 2010. *The Evolution of Leadership: Transitions in Decision Making from Small-Scale to Middle-Range Societies*. Santa Fe, NM: School for Advanced Research.
Velde, Bruce, and Isabelle C. Druc. 1999. *Archaeological Ceramic Materials: Origin and Utilization*. Berlin: Springer.
Venturi, Fabrizio, ed. 2010. *Societies in Transition: Evolutionary Processes in the Northern Levant between Late Bronze Age II and Early Iron Age*. Bologna: University Bookstore Cooperative Bologna Press.
Walker, Brian, and David Salt. 2006. *Resilience Thinking: Sustaining Ecosystems and People in a Changing World*. Washington, DC: Island Press.
Wallén, C. C. 1967. Aridity Definitions and Their Applicability. *Geografiska Annaler Series A, Physical Geography* 49(2–4): 367–384.
Wallerstein, Immanuel. 1974. *The Modern World-System I: Capitalist Agriculture and the Origins of the European World-Economy in the Sixteenth Century*. New York: Academic Books.
Ward, William A. 1972. The Shasu "Bedouin": Notes on a Recent Publication. *Journal of the Economic and Social History of the Orient* 15:35–60.
Ward, William A., and Martha S. Joukowsky, eds. 1992. *The Crisis Years: The 12th Century B.C. from Beyond the Danube to the Tigris*. Dubuque, IA: Kendall/Hunt.
Ward, William, and Malachi Martin. 1964. The Balu'a Stele: A New Transcription with Paleographical and Historical Notes. *Annual of the Department of Antiquities of Jordan* 8–9:529.
Weber, Max. 1968. *Economy and Society: An Outline of Interpretive Sociology*. New York: Bedminster Press.

Weinstein, James. 1975. Egyptian Relations with Palestine in the Middle Kingdom. *Bulletin of the American Schools of Oriental Research* 217:1–16.

———. 1982. The Egyptian Empire in Palestine: A Reassessment. *Bulletin of the American Schools of Oriental Research* 241:1–28.

Weisman, Ze'ev. 1977. Charismatic Leaders in the Era of the Judges. *Zeitschrift für die Alttestamentliche Wissenschaft* 89(3): 399–411.

West, Colin Thor. 2009. Domestic Transitions, Desiccation, Agricultural Intensification, and Livelihood Diversification among Rural Households on the Central Plateau, Burkina Faso. *American Anthropologist* 111(3): 275–288.

Whitelam, Keith W. 1996. *The Invention of Ancient Israel: The Silencing of Palestinian History*. London: Routledge.

Wiessner, Polly, and Wulf Schiefenhövel, eds. 1996. *Food and the Status Quest: An Interdisciplinary Perspective*. New York: Berghahn Books.

Wilk, Richard R., and Wendy Ashmore. 1988. *Household and Community in the Mesoamerican Past*. Albuquerque: University of New Mexico Press.

Wilkinson, Tony. 2006. From Highland to Desert: The Organization of Landscape and Irrigation in Southern Arabia. In *Agricultural Strategies*, ed. Joyce Marcus and Charles Stanish, 38–68. Los Angeles: Cotsen Institute of Archaeology.

Wilkinson, Tony J., J. H. Christiansen, Jason Ur, Magnus Widell, and Mark Altaweel. 2007. Urbanization within a Dynamic Environment: Modeling Bronze Age Communities in Upper Mesopotamia. *American Anthropologist* 109(1): 52–68.

Willey, Gordon R. 1953. *Prehistoric Settlement Patterns in the Virú Valley, Perú*. Washington, DC: Government Printing Office.

Willey, Gordon R., and Jeremy L. Sabloff. 1993. *A History of American Archaeology*, 3rd ed. San Francisco: W. H. Freeman.

Wimmer, Donald. 1987. Tell Safut Excavations, 1982–1985: Preliminary Report. *Annual of the Department of Antiquities of Jordan* 31:159–174.

Winnett, Fred, and William Reed. 1964. The Excavations at Dibon (Dhiban) in Moab. In *Annual of the American Schools of Oriental Research*, vols. 36–37. New Haven, CT: American Schools of Oriental Research.

Wittfogel, Karl A. 1957. *Oriental Despotism: A Comparative Study of Total Power*. New Haven, CT: Yale University Press.

Wolf, Eric. 1956. Aspects of Group Relations in a Complex Society: Mexico. *American Anthropologist* 58(6): 1065–1078.

———. 1966. *Peasants*. Englewood Cliffs: Prentice Hall.

———. 1982. *Europe and the People without History*. Berkeley: University of California Press.

Wood, Bryant G. 1990. *The Sociology of Pottery in Ancient Palestine: The Ceramic Industry and the Diffusion of Ceramic Style in the Bronze and Iron Ages*. Sheffield, UK: Journal for the Study of the Old Testament Press.

Worschech, Udo. 1985. *Northwest Ard el-Kerak 1983 and 1984: A Preliminary Report*. Munich: Manfred Gorg.

———. 1989. Preliminary Report on the Second Campaign at the Ancient Site of el-Balu' in 1987. *Annual of the Department of Antiquities of Jordan* 33:111–121.

———. 1990. *Die Beziehungen Moabs zu Israel und Ägypten in der Eisenzeit: Siedlungsarchäologische und siedlungshistorische Untersuchungen im Kernland Moabs (Ard el-Kerak)*. Wiesbaden: Harrassowitz.

———. 2003. *A Burial Cave at Umm Dimis North of el-Balu'*. Frankfurt: Peter Lang.

———. 2009. Environments and Settlements in the Ard al-Karak: Remarks on the Socio-Ecological and Socio-Economic Conditions in the Iron Age. In *Studies on Iron Age Moab and Neighbouring Areas in Honour of Michèle Daviau*, ed. Piotr Bienkowski, 47–70. Louvain, BE: Peeters.

Worschech, Udo, and Friedbert Ninow. 1994. Preliminary Report on the Third Campaign at the Ancient Site of el-Balu' in 1991. *Annual of the Department of Antiquities of Jordan* 38:195–203.

———. 1999. Preliminary Report on the Excavation at al-Balu' and a First Sounding at al-Misna in 1997. *Annual of the Department of Antiquities of Jordan* 43:169–173.

Worschech, Udo, Uwe Rosenthal, and Fawzi Zayadine. 1986. The Fourth Survey Season in the North-West Ard el-Kerak, and Soundings at Balu' 1986. *Annual of the Department of Antiquities of Jordan* 30:285–310.

Wright, Jacob L. 2010a. Commensal Politics in Ancient Western Asia: The Background to Nehemiah's Feasting (Pt. 1). *Zeitschrift für die Alttestamentliche Wissenschaft* 122 (2):212–233.

———. 2010b. Commensal Politics in Ancient Western Asia: The Background to Nehemiah's Feasting (Pt. 2). *Zeitschrift für die Alttestamentliche Wissenschaft* 122(3): 333–352.

Yaalon, Dan. 1997. Soils in the Mediterranean Region: What Makes Them Different. *Catena* 28(3–4): 157–169.

Yadin, Yigael, and Shimon Angress. 1960. *Hazor II: An Account of the Second Season of Excavations, 1956*. Jerusalem: Hebrew University.

Yaeger, Jason. 2000. The Social Construction of Communities in the Classic Maya Countryside: Strategies of Affiliation in Western Belize. In *The Archaeology of Communities: A New World Perspective*, ed. Marcello Canuto and Jason Yaeger, 123–142. London: Routledge.

Yaeger, Jason, and Marcello Canuto. 2000. Introducing an Archaeology of Communities. In *The Archaeology of Communities: A New World Perspective*, ed. Marcello Canuto and Jason Yaeger, 1–15. London: Routledge.

Yasur-Landau, Assaf. 2010. *The Philistines and Aegean Migration at the End of the Late Bronze Age*. Cambridge: Cambridge University Press.

Yoffee, Norman. 1993. Too Many Chiefs? (or, Safe Texts for the '90s). In *Archaeological Theory: Who Sets the Agenda?*, ed. Norman Yoffee and Andrew Sherratt, 60–78. Cambridge: Cambridge University Press.

———. 2005. *Myths of the Archaic State: Evolution of the Earliest Cities, States, and Civilizations*. Cambridge: Cambridge University Press.

Younker, Randall. 1989. Present and Past Plant Communities of the Tell el-'Umeiri Region. In *Madaba Plains Project 1: The 1984 Season at Tell el-'Umeiri and Vicinity and Subsequent Studies*, ed. Lawrence Geraty, Larry Herr, Øystein LaBianca, and Randall Younker, 32–40. Berrien Springs, MI: Andrews University Press.

———. 1991. The Judgment Survey. In *Madaba Plains Project 2: The 1987 Season at Tell el-'Umeiri and Vicinity and Subsequent Studies*, ed. Larry G. Herr, Lawrence Geraty, Øystein LaBianca, and Randall Younker, 269–334. Berrien Springs, MI: Andrews University Press.

———. 1997. Moabite Social Structure. *Biblical Archaeologist* 60(4): 237–248.

Zaccagnini, Carlo. 1983. Patterns of Mobility among Ancient Near Eastern Craftsmen. *Journal of Near Eastern Studies* 42(4): 245–264.

Zayadine, Fawzi. 1991. Sculpture in Ancient Jordan. In *Treasures from an Ancient Land: The Art of Jordan*, ed. Piotr Bienkowski, 31–61. Stroud, UK: Alan Sutton.

Zayadine, Fawzi, Mohammad Najjar, and Joseph Greene. 1987. Recent Excavations on the Citadel of Amman (Lower Terrace): A Preliminary Report. *Annual of the Department of Antiquities of Jordan* 31:299–311.

Zertal, Adam. 2004. *The Manasseh Hill Country Survey*, Vols. 1-2. Leiden: Brill.

Zohary, Michael. 1962. *Plant Life of Palestine: Israel and Jordan*. New York: Ronald Press.

Zuckerman, Sharon. 2007. "Slaying Oxen and Killing Sheep, Eating Flesh and Drinking Wine": Feasting in Late Bronze Age Hazor. *Palestine Exploration Quarterly* 139(3): 186–204.

van Zyl, A. H. 1960. *The Moabites*. Leiden: Brill.

Index

Abraham, 70, 114
Abu Kharakha, 156n34
Abu Kharaz, Tall, 59
Abu Shunnar Tomb, 165n12
Abu Snesleh, 58
Achaemenid Empire, 42
adaptive cycle, 27–29, 30–31, 134–139
Adir, 53, 141
agency, 132, 151n5
agricultural cycle, 85–86
agro-pastoralism, 82–90; agricultural cycle in, 85–86; anthropogenic structures and, 161n22; climate and, 82–83, 158n9; crop diversification in, 86–87; domesticated animals in, 88, 89–91; fruit harvesting in, 87; grains in, 86; risks of, 86; soil rejuvenation and, 159n14; soil type and, 83–84, 158–159n10; storage strategies and, 90–96; surplus in, 91; vegetation zones and, 159–160n15; viticulture in, 87; wadi canyon systems and, 83, 84; wild animal species and, 87–88; wild flora and, 87
Ahmose, 40
al-'Aliya. See al-Mudayna al-'Aliya, Khirbat
Alt, Albrecht, 70–71
Amarna correspondence, 40–41

'Amman Airport, 59
'Amman Citadel, 58, 156n34
'Amman Roman Theatre, 156n34
Ammon, 39, 42, 52
Ammonites, 49, 51
'Amr, 58
animals: domesticated, 88, 89–91; wild, 87–88
architecture, 16; anthropogenic, 161n22; defensive system, 78–82; ethnic labels for, 45; gate, 64, 65, 81–82; moat, 64, 65, 80–81; pillared building, 62, 74–78, 116; storage, 91–94; tomb, 111; tower, 64, 65, 79–80, 81, 82
arid-zone settlements, 33–34; communal complexity and, 35–36
Arnon River, 49
'Aro'er, 53, 62, 66, 122, 155n26
Assyrian Empire, 42
authority, 25–26; Balu'a stele and, 109–110; Baq'ah Valley Cave A4 and, 111; charismatic, 11, 106, 108, 110, 111, 131, 132; in chiefdom, 105–106; Hebrew Bible on, 106–109; of judge, 107–108; limits of, 127–131; mortuary practice and, 110–111; patrimonial, 11, 106–107, 108, 109, 111, 131–132; strategies of, 105–112

197

Babylonian Empire, 42
Bahrain, 33
Balak, 51
Baluʻa, 53, 62, 66, 153n12, 155n27; ceramic vessels at, 100, 122; data from, 139; defensive systems at, 78
Baluʻa stele, 109–110
Baqʻah Valley, 61–62
Baqʻah Valley Cave A2 and B3, 59
Baqʻah Valley Cave A4, 111
Barak, 107
Bekaʻa Valley, 9
Bible. *See* Hebrew Bible
biblical archaeology, 38–39, 43–44, 144
Bourdieu, Pierre, 17–18, 24
building activities, 74–82; defensive system, 78–82; pillared building, 74–78; storage facility, 95. *See also* architecture
burial practices, 110–111, 165n12, 165n13
Burkino Faso, 148
Byzantine Empire: agricultural intensification under, 34–35

Canaanite society, 38, 39–40, 143; Egyptian influences on, 40–41; structure of, 40–41
capital, 24–25. *See also* wealth
cattle, 89–90
ceramic vessels, 96–102; bowl, 97, 98, 122, 123; clay for, 100, 101–102, 163n34; in commensal events, 121–127; cooking pot, 97, 98, 100–101, 115; decorated, 122–127, 162–163n31, 166n17, 166n18; in food preparation, 115–116; instrumental neutron activation analysis of, 100–102, 163n32; jar, 97, 98, 100; krater, 97, 98, 115–116, 122; petrographic analysis of, 100; production techniques for, 34, 98–99, 101, 124–125, 130, 162n29, 162n30, 163n34; red pigment for, 122, 123, 125; residence distribution of, 101; in settlement dating, 66, 156n34, 157n37; simulated presentation of, 125, 126, 166–167n22; for storage, 95–96, 98

charismatic authority, 11, 106, 108, 110, 111, 131, 132
Chavez Pass Pueblo, 19–20
chiefdom, 105–106, 135, 164n4, 164n5
city-states: of Middle Bronze Age, 39–40
civilization: collapse of, 27; concept of, 13
climate: agro-pastoralism and, 82–83; changes in, 158n9
collapse discourse, 27, 36–37
collective punishment, 105
commensal practices, 113–115, 120–127; visual representation of, 121
communal complexity, 5–6, 20–26, 134; adaptive cycle and, 28–29, 134–138; practice-based perspective on, 23–25, 134 (*see also* production practices); in preindustrial Middle Eastern marginal zones, 31–36
community: artifact style and, 16–17; boundary-preserving measures of, 16; building design and, 16; concept of, 2–3, 6, 13, 145–146, 150n6; contemporary perspective on, 1, 147–148; corporate groups in, 16–17; definitions of, 14, 15–16; egalitarianism in, 19–20; face-to-face interaction and, 23; factions in, 16–17; habitus and, 17–19; hierarchy in, 19–20; household production practices in, 32; inequality in, 22, 24–25, 30–31; labor projects of, 16; within landscape, 15–16; mobility practices of, 14–15; vs. nomadism, 137, 138; Redfield on, 146; resilience of, 26–31, 137; shared assemblage and, 14; social evolution of, 15; spatial definition of, 15–16, 29–30; typology of, 5, 14–15
complex adaptive systems, 21–22, 134–139, 151n4; conservation phase (K phase) of, 27–28, 135–136; context and, 22–23; growth phase (R phase) of, 27, 135; release phase (Omega phase) of, 28, 137; reorganization phase (Alpha phase) of, 28, 137–138
complexity studies, 21
cooking practices, 115–116, 118–120

core-periphery frameworks, 29–30
corporate groups, 16–17
corporate personality, 105, 163–164n1
corporate responsibility, 163–164n1
covenant ceremonies, 114

David, 43, 47, 106, 114
Deborah, 107
defensive systems, 78–82
desert and sown paradigm, 6–7, 33
Deuteronomistic School, 47–48, 106–107
Dhiban, 53, 122, 139, 156n34
Diamond, Jared, 27
discourse, 18–19, 23–24
Division of Labour in Society, The (Durkheim), 2–3
domesticated animals, 88, 89–91
Dor, 168n7
doxa, 18–19, 23–24
Dubab, 59–60
Durkheim, Émile, 2–3, 19, 164n2

Early Bronze Age: Jawa settlement of, 35
Early Iron Age, 150n7; destabilizing events of, 41, 61–62, 145; settlement number in, 61–62
Early Iron Age societies, 7, 9–12; abandonment of, 11, 36–37, 66–67, 127–129, 130; authority in (*see* authority); conflict among, 128, 130; Egyptian sources on, 42–43; epigraphic sources on, 42; ethnicizing of, 45–46, 48–49, 125; Hebrew Bible on, 43, 47–49; historicizing of, 45–46, 48–49; inequalities in, 10–11, 129 (*see also* inequality); interactions among, 130–131; political organization of, 55–57, 62–67; production strategies of, 10–11 (*see also* production practices); regional diversity of, 44–46; settlement size and, 62–65; social evolutionary paradigms and, 10; social histories of, 46–47; twentieth-century archeology on, 42–43. *See also specific archaeological sites*

economic capital, 24
Economy and Society (Weber), 149n3
Edom, 42
egalitarianism, 5, 104; corporate personality and, 105; pueblo society and, 19–20
Eglon, 51
Egypt: Canaanite relationship with, 40–41; Eighteenth Dynasty of, 40; New Kingdom empire of, 40, 42; southern Levant campaigns of, 40, 60
Ehud, 107
elders (*zaqenim*), 106–107, 109
ethnicizing: of Early Iron Age societies, 45–46, 48–49, 125, 142

face-to-face interaction, 3, 22, 23
factions, 16–17
family, 16; definition of, 157n1
feasting: in Early Iron Age societies, 11, 114, 120–127; in San Lorenzo, 113
Fertile Crescent, 6–7, 33
floodwater farming, 86
fluvial environments: prehistoric, 152n10
food: commensal practices and, 113–115, 120–127; Hebrew Bible on, 114–115; preparation of, 115–116, 118–120; production of (*see* agro-pastoralism); storage facilities for, 11, 90–96, 117, 118; symbolic value of, 114; as wealth, 11, 112–120, 165–166n14
fortifications, 65, 78–82
fruit harvesting, 87
al-Fukhar, Tall, 59
"Functional and Evolutionary Implications of Community Patterning" seminar, 14–15

gates, 64, 65, 81–82
Gemeinschaft, 2
Gesellschaft, 2
Gezer Calendar, 42, 85, 86, 87
Gideon, 107–108
gift exchange, 113
Glueck, Nelson, 52–54, 58–59, 153n12
goats, 88, 89–90

grains, 86; grinding installations for, 118–190; storage of (see storage facilities)
grapes, 87
Grasshopper Pueblo, 19–20
grinding installations, 118–120

habitus, 17–19
al-Hasa, Wadi, 61, 83, 154n22, 155n24
Hazor, 39
Hebrew Bible, 38, 42, 152n1; on agricultural practices, 70, 85; on ancient Israel, 43–44, 47; on authority, 106–109; Book of Joshua, 38, 43, 47; Book of Judges, 38, 43, 47, 51, 106, 107–108, 144, 154n19, 165n8; Book of Numbers, 49, 51–52, 153n11; Book of Samuel, 38, 43, 47, 106, 114, 144; on Early Iron Age, 43, 47–49; on food, 114–115; historical accuracy of, 48; on kingship, 51–52, 53, 54, 106–107, 109; on kinship, 56; research use of, 47–49, 52, 144–145; subsistence categories in, 70–71; on tribe, 55; on west-central Jordon, 49, 51–52, 53'
Hesban: domesticated animal species at, 89, 90, 160–161n18; Early Iron Age settlements at, 61; grains at, 159n11; Late Bronze Age settlements at, 59; Middle Bronze Age settlements at, 58; wild flora at, 87
hierarchy, 104; pueblo society and, 5, 19–20. See also authority; leadership
Hittite Empire, 41
household: as analytic unit, 32; definition of, 157n1

Iktanu: Late Bronze Age settlement at, 59
inequality, 10–11, 22, 36, 112, 116, 131–132; capital distribution and, 24–25; settlement abandonment and, 129, 137
instrumental neutron activation analysis (INAA), 100–102, 163n32, 166n19
'Iraq al-Amir, 156n34
Irbid, 59

Iron Age: later, 47–48, 53–54, 107. See also Early Iron Age
Isaac, 70
'Isal, Wadi, 61
Israel, 39, 42; Egyptian sources on, 43; Hebrew Bible on, 43–44
Israelites/Israelite society, 9, 38, 49; Ammonite encounters with, 49, 51; chiefdoms of, 105–106; corporate personality in, 105, 163–164n1; corporate responsibility in, 163–164n1; elders in, 106–107, 109; judge in, 107–108; of Late Bronze Age, 43, 49, 51; Moabite encounters with, 49, 51, 140, 154n23; segmentary lineage system of, 56; social evolutionary stages of, 105–106, 164–165n5; subsistence practices of, 71
'Izbet Sartah, 157n2
'Izbet Sartah inscription, 42

Jacob, 70
Jalul, 59
jar. See ceramic vessels
Jawa, 35
Jerusalem, 43
Jordan. See west-central Jordan
Judah, 39, 42
judge, 107–108, 165n9

Karak, 141
Karak Plateau, 141; data from, 139; Early Iron Age settlements at, 61; Late Bronze Age settlements at, 59–60; Middle Bronze Age settlements at, 58
kings: Ammonite, 49, 51; Canaanite, 40–41; Israelite, 43, 47; Moabite, 49, 51
kingship, 109, 131; Balu'a stele and, 109–110; Hebrew Bible on, 51–52, 53, 54, 106–107, 109
kinship: tribalism and, 55–57

labor projects, 16. See also agropastoralism; architecture; ceramic vessels

Lahun, 62, 66, 155n28; cooking practices at, 116, 117, 120; data from, 139; defensive systems at, 78; map of, 63; pillared buildings at, 74, 96
landscape: community within, 15–16
laser ablation–inductively coupled plasma–mass spectrometry (LA-ICP-MS), 124, 166n21
Late Bronze Age, 40; destabilizing events of, 41, 61–62, 145; Israelite society of, 43, 49, 51; political organization during, 58–60
leadership, 104–105, 132, 137; capital distribution and, 25–26, 31; in chiefdoms, 105–106; military, 107–108; social knowledge and, 19; *zaqenim*, 106–107. *See also* authority
Levantine society: of central highlands, 9, 44–46, 49, 143, 157n3; of Early Iron Age, 7–9, 150n7 (*see also* Early Iron Age societies); of northern regions, 143–144; regional diversity in, 45; of southern coastal plain, 44–46, 49; of southwest region, 143; thirteenth century BCE destabilization of, 41, 61–62, 145. *See also* west-central Jordan
Levirate marriage, 105
Lévy-Bruhl, Lucien, 164n2
limestone slabs, 119, 120
Little Community: Viewpoints for the Study of a Human Whole, The (Redfield), 146

Madaba, 139
Madaba Tomb A, 165n12
managerial mutualism, 22
marginal societies, 4–6, 29–30; adaptive cycles of, 30–31. *See also* Early Iron Age societies
marginal zones, 6–9, 31–36
Mediterranean diet, 115
Megiddo, 39, 168n7
Merneptah, 43
Mesha Inscription, 140
Micah: house of, 154n19
Middle Bronze Age, 39; political organization during, 57–58

Middle East: community in, 6–12, 31–32; definition of, 150n5; marginal zones of, 6–9, 31–36
military leadership, 107–108
Moab, 39, 42, 52–53, 153n16
Moabites, 38; Israelite encounters with, 49, 51, 140, 154n23
moats, 64, 65, 80–81
mobility practices, 14–15
mortuary practices, 165n12, 165n13; authority genres and, 110–111
al-Muʿammariyya, Khirbat, 62, 66, 156n32, 158n8; defensive systems at, 78, 80, 81; storage facilities at, 91, 92
al-Mudayna al-ʿAliya, Khirbat, 62, 66, 155n29; abandonment of, 129; agriculture at, 86, 87; Building 500 of, 116–120, 129, 131–132; building sizes at, 116; ceramic vessels at, 100–102; data from, 139, 140; decorated vessels at, 122–127; defensive systems at, 78, 79–80, 81, 82; domesticated animal species at, 88, 89–91, 160n17, 160n18; food preparation at, 118–120; map of, 64; pillared buildings at, 74, 75, 76, 77, 95–96; radiocarbon dates at, 156–157n36; storage facilities at, 92–95, 117, 118; wild animal species at, 87–88, 160n17; wild flora at, 87
al-Mudayna al-Muʿarradja, Khirbat, 62, 66, 156n31; data from, 139; defensive systems at, 78, 79, 80, 81–82; map of, 65; pillared buildings at, 74–75
al-Mudayna al-Mujib, Khirbat, 139, 156n34
al-Mujib, Wadi, 58, 66, 83, 101–102

al-Nahas, Khirbat, 168n7
Nancy, Jean-Luc, 1
Near East: definition of, 150n5
New Kingdom Egypt, 40
nomadic pastoralism, 6–7, 52–53, 70–72, 128; vs. sedentary community, 137, 138. *See also* agro-pastoralism

Oman, 33
ovens, 116, 118, 120

panarchy, 152n8
patrimonial authority, 11, 106–107, 108, 109, 111, 131–132
patron-client relationship, 22
peasant society, 157–158n4
Pella, 59
Philistia, 42
Philistines, 38, 41, 49
Phoenicia, 42
pigs, 90
pillared buildings, 62, 74–78; activities in, 75–76; communal construction of, 77–78; design of, 75; labor requirements for, 78; size of, 116; storage facilities in, 95–96, 116
political organization: chiefdom, 105–106, 135, 164n4, 164n5; Early Iron Age, 55–57, 62–67; Hebrew Bible on, 49, 51–52, 54; of Israelite society, 105–106; kingdom, 51–54; Late Bronze Age, 58–60; Middle Bronze Age, 57–58; tribal, 32, 54–56; in west-central Jordan, 51–68
precipitation: agro-pastoralism and, 82–83, 85
Prehistoric Settlement Patterns in the Virú Valley, Perú (Willey), 14
preindustrial communities: analytic approaches to, 14–20; face-to-face interaction in, 3, 22, 23; on the margins, 4–6 (*see also* Early Iron Age societies); organizational dynamics, 20–26; twentieth-century, 3. *See also* community
production practices, 10–11; agro-pastoralism, 82–84; building, 74–82; capital distribution and, 25–26; ceramic vessel, 96–102; community-managed, 25–26, 73–74, 94–95, 133; cottage industry, 72; domestic (household), 32, 72, 73–74, 133; habitus and, 17–19; multivariable frameworks for, 72; at San Lorenzo, 17–19; storage, 90–96; workshop, 72–73
pueblo societies, 5, 19–20, 151n3
pulses, 87

Qasr, 141
Qatar, 33

al-Rabba, 141
Ramses II, 60
Ramses III, 41
Redfield, Robert, 146
resilience, 5–6, 26–31, 69–70, 151n6; adaptive cycle and, 27–28, 137; definition of, 26; vs. system optimization, 26–27. *See also* production practices
riparian zones, 10, 83, 84, 85
Roman Empire: agricultural intensification under, 34–35
Rujm al-'Abd stele, 165n10

al-Safi, Tell, 168n7
Safut, 59, 156n34
Sahab, 58, 59, 62, 66; defensive systems at, 158n7
Sahab Tomb A, 165n12
San Lorenzo community (Belize), 17, 18–19, 113, 150–151n2
Saudi Arabia, 33
Saul, 43, 47, 106, 114
Sea Peoples, 41
sedentary agriculture, 70–72; intensification measures in, 34–35. *See also* agro-pastoralism
segmentary lineage system, 56–57, 154n18
semi-arid zone, 4, 34; definition of, 149n4; settlements in, 34–36
Shasu, 55, 110
Shechem, 39
sheep, 88, 89–90
Shutu, 57–58, 154n20
Sihon, 51
small-scale societies: complexity of (*see* communal complexity); inequality in, 22; vs. large urban societies, 3. *See also* community
social evolutionary framework, 9, 10, 15, 54–57, 105–106
socionatural system, 22–23, 151n6
soils, 10, 83–84, 85, 158–159n10, 159n14
Song of Deborah, 153n8

storage facilities, 11, 90–96; communal, 94–95; residential, 95–96, 117, 118
subsistence categories, 70–72
symbolic capital, 24

al-Thamad, Wadi, 83
Thutmose III, 40, 60
Tönnies, Ferdinand, 2
towers, 64, 65, 79–80, 81, 82
tribe, 32, 54–56, 164n3

Ugarit, 40, 41
al-'Umayri, Tall: abandonment of, 127–128; ceramic vessels at, 66; cooking practices at, 115–116; defensive systems at, 75, 80–81, 158n7; domesticated animal species at, 89–90, 160–161n18; Early Iron Age settlement at, 62, 66, 156n33; Late Bronze Age settlement at, 59, 60; Middle Bronze Age settlement at, 58; pillared buildings at, 75, 78, 95–96; wild animal species at, 87–88
Umm Dimis tomb, 165n12

vegetation zones, 159–160n15
visual culture, 121–127
viticulture, 87

wadi canyon systems, 83, 84, 85
al-Wala, Wadi, 83
wealth, 24–25; building size and, 116; egalitarian/ranked practices and, 20, 36; food as, 112–120, 165–166n14; inequalities in, 22, 24–25, 30–31, 36, 112, 116, 137
Weber, Max, 19, 108, 149n3
west-central Jordan: climate of, 82–83; Early Iron Age societies of (see Early Iron Age societies); geographic definition of, 8, 9, 49, 50; Hebrew Bible on, 49, 51–52, 53; nomadic communities in, 52–53; political organization of, 51–68; social evolutionary categories of, 54–57; soils of, 83–84; twentieth-century research on, 44; vegetation zones of, 159–160n15
Willey, Gordon, 14

Yemen, 33

zaqenim (elders), 106–107, 109
al-Zarqa, Wadi, 83
al-Zarqa Ma'in, Wadi, 83

About the Author

Benjamin W. Porter is an archaeologist whose research focuses on the Bronze and Iron Age societies of the Middle East and Eastern Mediterranean. He is an assistant professor of Near Eastern archaeology at the University of California–Berkeley and a curator of Near Eastern archaeology at the Phoebe A. Hearst Museum of Anthropology. He received his PhD in anthropology from the University of Pennsylvania in 2007. He co-directs the Dhiban Excavation and Development Project, an archaeological field project in Jordan that examines how communities living under the shadow of empires organized themselves in the region's semi-arid environment. He also co-directs the Dilmun Bioarchaeology Project, which investigates skeletal evidence and artifacts from Peter B. Cornwall's 1941 expedition to Bahrain and Saudi Arabia. Porter is completing a co-edited volume of studies that integrates mortuary archaeology and bioarchaeological techniques to investigate ancient Near Eastern burial rituals, soon to be published by the University of Colorado Press. For more information about the author's research, visit http://nes.berkeley.edu/Web_Porter/Welcome.html.